ALSO BY THE AMERICAN HEART ASSOCIATION

American Heart Association Cookbook, 5th Edition

American Heart Association Low-Salt Cookbook

American Heart Association Kids' Cookbook

American Heart Association Family Guide to Stroke

American Heart Association Brand Name Fat and Cholesterol Counter

American Heart Association Quick and Easy Cookbook

Living Well, Staying Well
(coauthored with the American Cancer Society)

THE AMERICAN HEART ASSOCIATION

Low-Fat, Low-Cholesterol Cookbook

Recipes Created and Tested by
Laureen Mody, R.D.
Leni Reed, R.D.
Sherry Ferguson

Recipes Analyzed by
Nutrition Scientific
Pasadena, California

Illustrations by
Regina Scudellari

LOW-FAT, LOW-CHOLESTEROL COOKBOOK

More than 200 delicious, heart-healthful recipes for the whole family

Editors

Scott M. Grundy, M.D., Ph.D.
Director, Center for Human Nutrition
University of Texas Southwestern Medical Center
Dallas, Texas

Mary Winston, Ed.D., R.D.
Senior Science Consultant
American Heart Association National Center
Dallas, Texas

THREE RIVERS PRESS
NEW YORK

LOW

LOW

Published by...
Member of th...

Random House...
www.randomhou...

...and the Three
...om House, Inc.

THREE RIVERS P...
Rivers Press colopho...

This work was original... in hardcover in 1989 and in trade
paperback in 1991 by Ti...es Books.

Printed in the United States of America

Art direction by Naomi Osnos
Book design by MM Design 2000

Library of Congress Cataloging-in-Publication Data
Grundy, Scott M.   Heart Association low-fat, low-cholesterol
   The American Heart Association low-fat, low-cholesterol
cookbook / by Scott M. Grundy and Mary Winston.
      Includes index.
      1. Low-fat diet—Recipes.   2. Low-cholesterol diet—Recipes.
   I. Winston, Mary.   II. American Heart Association.   III. Title.
RM237.7.G78   1989
641.5'635—dc19   88-36665

ISBN 0-8129-2475-4

10 9

Preface

For more than forty years the American Heart Association has been waging a war against heart disease. Our weapons are medical research, professional and public education and community programs. We continue to educate the public about the benefits of adopting a healthful lifestyle—to avoid smoking, control high blood pressure, maintain a low blood cholesterol level and be physically active. Incorporating these habits into your daily life and that of your family can greatly reduce the probability of having a heart attack.

This book is devoted to one of these major risk factors. It will show you how to reduce your blood cholesterol level in an effective, and even enjoyable, way. In the introduction, Dr. Scott Grundy, one of the foremost lipid specialists in this country and one of the AHA's most eminent science volunteers, explains the medical aspects of high blood cholesterol and the reasons why diet modification is the primary treatment for lowering it. Associating your diet with a treatment plan may conjure up thoughts of dull, unappetizing meals, but the two-hundred newly created recipes in this book will quickly dispel that notion. The cooking and shopping tips will help you modify your own favorite recipes so that they will contribute to a healthy heart as well. If you have to lose weight, this cookbook includes several tips for success.

Eating out may be a part of your daily life or something you enjoy only occasionally. Regardless, you need not give it up. Suggestions for various types of restaurant menu selections are also provided.

Finally, Dr. Grundy discusses various drugs and how they work. For some of you they will be a necessary part of your treatment along with diet modification.

As in everything, practice makes perfect, and provided you are willing to make an effort, your cholesterol-lowering diet can gradually become an enjoyable diet for life. The AHA recognizes that change is difficult for all of us, but acquiring a healthful lifestyle will become a reality if you introduce the needed changes slowly.

To the enjoyment of delicious meals, health and happiness!

Rodman D. Starke, M.D.
Senior Vice President
Office of Scientific Affairs
American Heart Association National Center

Acknowledgments

This book is the result of the hard work, dedication and encouragement of many American Heart Association volunteers and staff.

I especially want to thank AHA Executive Vice President Dudley Hafner and Deputy Executive Vice President Cass Wheeler for creating an environment in which this project could be developed and for always finding a solution to apparently unsolvable problems.

I have much gratitude and admiration for my learned colleague and cookbook co-editor Scott Grundy, the director of the Center for Human Nutrition at the University of Texas Southwestern Medical Center at Dallas. His expert knowledge of lipid metabolism and diet and drug therapies for treating high blood cholesterol has made this more than a cookbook—it's a step-by-step blueprint for lowering blood cholesterol.

Besides offering an easy-to-understand eating plan, this book contains two hundred tasty, innovative recipes individually created and tested by nutritionists Laureen Moody and Leni Reed and food stylist Sherry Ferguson. I was in on the taste tests, and believe me, this trio has proven conclusively that meals can be both low in fat and delicious!

Each recipe in this cookbook has been expertly analyzed for protein, carbohydrate, fat, sodium and calories by Nutrition Scientific of Pasadena, California.

Kudos also go to Sam Inman, vice president, Office of Corporate Relations and Development, AHA, for skillfully negotiating the business aspects of the project, and to his assistant, Ann Yanosky, for following through on every detail. David Livingston, corporate counsel for AHA, provided legal expertise. My thanks to Pat Covington and Jane Ruehl for copy editing, to Jean Davis and Carol Boswell for their able secretarial help, always cheerfully given, and last but not least to my son, Rick, whose patience surpassed all understanding during the writing of this manuscript.

The most important thanks of all goes to the American Heart Association's Nutrition Committee for expertise, feedback and continued support and encouragement. It has been a delight to work with this team of professionals.

Mary Winston, Ed.D., R.D.
Senior Science Consultant
Office of Scientific Affairs
American Heart Association National Center

Contents

INTRODUCTION

Heart disease is the number one killer of Americans. Despite recent advances in prevention and treatment, it takes the lives of almost one million of us each year.

Currently, more than five million people in the U.S. are diagnosed as having heart disease. What's more, millions of others are at risk of heart attack or stroke and don't even know it. According to a landmark study completed by the National Heart, Lung and Blood Institute (NHLBI) in 1986, 80 percent of all middle-aged American men are at increased risk of dying prematurely from heart disease.

Now for the good news: The death rate for heart disease in Americans began to fall in 1968—a trend that continues today. Physicians and scientists who have studied the reasons for the decline conclude that reducing the blood cholesterol level is the single largest contributor to improved cardiac health, followed by reducing or quitting cigarette smoking.

In 1985, Oxford University's Richard Peto said, "We know two things about how to prevent death in middle age: smoking and cholesterol. Each of those two things is responsible for about one third of all deaths in middle age." When these two factors are grouped with high blood pressure, the three account for 85 percent of all premature heart attacks.

There is no longer any question about high blood cholesterol's role in heart disease. Medical science has proven a causal relationship between high blood cholesterol and heart attack in a number of large clinical trials. The NHLBI landmark study referred to previously included 3,800 men with high blood cholesterol. Half were given a cholesterol-lowering drug called cholestyramine, and the other half were given an inactive medication or placebo. The men receiving the cholestyramine experienced significantly lower cholesterol levels than the men receiving placebos. The cholestyramine group also had fewer heart attacks. The results, reported in 1984, showed beyond a doubt that lowering blood cholesterol reduces the risk of heart attack. Other clinical trials using cholesterol-lowering drugs have had similar results.

In addition to clinical trials using drugs to lower cholesterol, a number have focused on cholesterol-reducing diets. One, conducted in Oslo, Norway, showed that modifying diet to lower blood cholesterol can indeed prevent heart attacks. Other diet-oriented trials reported from Los Angeles, Minneapolis and Helsinki, Finland, have provided similar results.

By averaging the results of all the clinical trials, it's now possible to estimate the degree to which lowering cholesterol reduces the risk of heart attack. As a general rule, a 1-percent reduction in total cholesterol level causes a 2-percent reduction in heart attack risk. This means that if you lower your blood cholesterol from 250 to 200 milligrams per deciliter (mg/dl), for example, you'll reduce your risk by 40 percent.

This cookbook has been developed to help you reduce your cholesterol level and lower your risk of heart attack by following a low-fat, low-cholesterol diet.

YOUR CHOLESTEROL GOAL

One of the most dangerous aspects of high blood cholesterol is that you don't feel it or see it. In fact, for 40 percent of heart attack victims, the first symptom of high blood cholesterol is death. That's why it's so important for your physician to check your blood cholesterol level as well as other coronary risk factors at least every five years. Be sure to keep a running record of your blood cholesterol (also known as serum cholesterol) so you can track any changes.

Your blood cholesterol level will fit into one of the following classifications. This makes it easy for your doctor to classify you according to risk. However, his or her advice will also take into account other aspects of your physical and medical history.

CHOLESTEROL (mg/dl)	CLASSIFICATION
Less than 200	Desirable
200 to 240	Borderline high
More than 240	High

If your cholesterol level is less than 200, blood cholesterol is not a major risk factor for you at this time. You should have it checked again in five years. Of course, if other major risk factors are present (smoking and high blood pressure), you're still in danger of heart disease and should follow the diet in this book. In fact, even if you have no other risk factors and your cholesterol is below 200, we recommend The American Heart Association Diet. After all, most authorities will tell you that when it comes to blood cholesterol, the lower the better.

If your cholesterol is between 200 and 240, you're in a borderline zone and face twice the risk of heart attack as people whose levels are well below 200. And you're not alone: About 40 percent of American adults fall into this category. It's a situation that shouldn't be ignored, especially if you have other risk factors. In fact, even if you're in the borderline-high range, your doctor will probably advise you to follow a diet to lower your blood cholesterol level and ask you to return to have your cholesterol level checked.

Finally, if your cholesterol is over 240, you could be at high risk of heart attack, and further tests will be needed to determine the best treatment plan for you.

DIET: YOUR FIRST LINE OF DEFENSE

Since most cases of high blood cholesterol are caused by diet, it stands to reason that most cases can be reversed by diet. Most of the time, that logic holds true. However, a few individuals may not be able to reduce their cholesterol level to below 200 without medication. Remember, if you've had a heart attack or have other major risk factors, lowering your cholesterol to below 200 is extremely important. It is also important to reduce your low density lipoprotein (LDL) cholesterol, the kind that is most likely to build up in your arteries, to below 130. (For a complete discussion of lipo-proteins, see page 357.)

If you have no other risk factors and have not had a heart attack, you should aim—at the very least—to reduce your cholesterol level to below 240 and your LDL-cholesterol level to below 160. But again, the lower, the better.

To accomplish this, you'll want to reduce your intake of fat, especially cholesterol and saturated fat, which tends to raise your blood cholesterol level. When you eat fats, stick to polyunsaturated or monounsaturated fats. They will not contribute to increasing your blood cholesterol level. You can reduce your fat consumption by eating more complex carbohydrates like fruits, vegetables, nuts, seeds and whole-grain breads, cereals and pastas.

How much will you have to change your diet to achieve your goals? That depends on a number of factors. For many people, some relatively minor changes can make a signifi-cant difference in cholesterol and LDL-cholesterol levels. For others, more extensive changes are necessary. That's why the American Heart Association has developed the Step-One Diet and the Step-Two Diet, which vary in the levels of saturated fat and dietary cholesterol they suggest.

USING THE STEP-ONE AND STEP-TWO DIETS

The Step-One Diet is similar to the program that the American Heart Association recommends for the general public. It calls for reductions in saturated fat and cholesterol and in total calories for those who are overweight. The components of this diet are outlined in the table below, with details discussed in Appendix C. All recipes in this book may be used for both the Step-One and Step-Two Diets.

STEP-ONE DIET NUTRITIONAL COMPONENTS

NUTRIENT	RECOMMENDED INTAKE
Total fat	30% or less of total calories
Saturated fatty acids	Less than 10% of total calories
Polyunsaturated fatty acids	Up to 10% of total calories
Monounsaturated fatty acids	10% to 15% of total calories
Carbohydrates	50% to 60% of total calories
Protein	10% to 20% of total calories
Cholesterol	Less than 300 milligrams per day
Total calories	To achieve and maintain desirable weight

Before advising you to adopt a Step-One Diet, your doctor will check your blood cholesterol level. Four to six weeks into the diet, he or she will check it again. Don't be discouraged if your cholesterol level has not changed much or even shows an increase. At this stage there can be a variation of plus or minus 10 percent. Have it checked again after three months. By this time your cholesterol level will have stabilized. If you've reached your target level for blood cholesterol, pat yourself on the back and stay with the Step-One Diet.

If the Step-One Diet doesn't lower your cholesterol to

your goal, your doctor may refer you to a Registered Dietitian for additional help. The dietitian can help you review the principles and strengthen your resolve to stay with the Step-One Diet program. Once you've mastered the diet, have your doctor check your cholesterol level again. If you still haven't reached your target, the doctor or dietitian may recommend the Step-Two Diet.

STEP-TWO DIET NUTRITIONAL COMPONENTS

NUTRIENT	RECOMMENDED INTAKE
Total fat	30% or less of total calories
Saturated fatty acids	Less than 7% of total calories
Polyunsaturated fatty acids	Up to 10% of total calories
Monounsaturated fatty acids	10% to 15% of total calories
Carbohydrates	50% to 60% of total calories
Protein	10% to 20% of total calories
Cholesterol	Less than 200 milligrams per day
Total calories	To achieve and maintain desirable weight

As you can see from the table above, the Step-Two Diet is more restrictive in saturated fats and cholesterol and, consequently, will produce a greater reduction in your blood cholesterol. Once you've adjusted to the Step-Two Diet, ask your doctor to check your cholesterol level again. If you still haven't reached your goal, the doctor may decide that you're a candidate for cholesterol-lowering drugs. (See Appendix G for additional information on drug therapy.)

Both the Step-One and Step-Two Diets are based on a nutritious eating plan in which foods containing saturated fat and cholesterol are replaced with similar foods low in saturated fatty acids and cholesterol. The recipes offered are designed to help you include your new diet as part of an overall lifestyle change.

The diets are outlined in detail in Appendix C. Both, however, address the following general concerns.

Total Calories. Obesity contributes to high blood cholesterol, and if severe (greater than 30 percent overweight), is a coronary risk factor in its own right. It's important for those who are carrying excess weight to reduce caloric intake, increase caloric expenditure or both. The fact is, many overweight Americans could lose weight simply by changing their sedentary lifestyles to include more exercise. Exercise alone or exercise combined with cutting calories is healthier than severely restricting caloric intake, which could result in deficiencies of important nutrients. The only successful weight-reducing diet is one that will allow you to lose weight and monitor it. A modest calorie reduction of 500 calories a day is best. As a rule of thumb, a reduction diet for men contains about 1600 to 2000 calories, and for women, not fewer than 1200 to 1600. This should allow you to meet all your nutrient needs, minimize hunger and promote a lifelong healthful eating pattern.

Total Fats. In both the Step-One Diet and Step-Two Diet, total fat intake should account for no more than 30 percent of total calories. The American Heart Association has recommended this amount for years. Some investigators recommend reducing fat intake to 20 or even 10 percent of total calories, believing that the lower the amount of total fat in the diet, the lower the blood cholesterol level. However, recent research indicates that fat restrictions of 10 to 20 percent of total calories are not necessary to produce adequate reductions in blood cholesterol as long as the diet is restricted in saturated fatty acids.

To demonstrate the distinction between *total* fat and *type* of fat, compare the Asian diet, which includes just 10 to 20 percent fat, primarily monounsaturated, to the Mediterranean diet, which includes approximately 40 percent fat, primarily monounsaturated with some polyunsaturated. Both result in similarly low blood cholesterol levels. So, the type of fat—not just amount of fat—seems to be the most important factor in controlling blood cholesterol levels.

For most Americans, a diet that includes 30 percent fat

is considered more palatable than a diet extremely low in fat. Either type of diet, though, can result in an adequate cholesterol reduction.

Dietary Cholesterol. The Step-One Diet calls for less than 300 milligrams of dietary cholesterol each day. The Step-Two Diet calls for no more than 200 milligrams of dietary cholesterol per day.

Saturated Fatty Acids. The Step-One Diet recommends that saturated fatty acids be reduced to no more than 10 percent of total calories. Saturated fatty acids are found in animal products and in some plant products. Some animal sources are cheese, butter, cream, whole milk, ice cream, fatty beef, pork, lamb and poultry skin. Coconut oil, palm kernel oil and palm oil are plant sources of saturated fatty acids. In the typical American diet, 14 to 16 percent of total calories are provided by saturated fatty acids. That means most Americans should reduce their saturated fat intake by about one third to achieve the recommended levels. The Step-Two Diet calls for further reduction in saturated fatty acids, to less than 7 percent of total calories. Remember that this reduction applies to *saturated fats,* not all fats. So if you advance to the Step-Two Diet, you will not be required to reduce your total fat intake below 30 percent, although you are free to do so if you wish.

Polyunsaturated Fatty Acids. As you decrease your intake of saturated fats, you may substitute polyunsaturated fatty acids, up to a point. Substitute polyunsaturated margarines and oil for butter and lard. Use vegetable oils such as corn, safflower and sunflower and margarines that have one of these oils listed as its primary ingredient. These are high in polyunsaturates. However, polyunsaturated fatty acids should not account for more than 10 percent of your daily caloric intake, because no large population has ever eaten a greater proportion of polyunsaturated fat with proven safety. Without further knowledge, it is prudent to advise a limited intake.

Monounsaturated Fatty Acids. For the visible fats in

your diet such as salad dressings, spreads and cooking oils, choose products composed of polyunsaturated and monounsaturated fatty acids. In fact, monounsaturates should account for between 10 and 15 percent of your total caloric intake. Olive oil and rapeseed (canola) oil are two major sources of monounsaturates.

Carbohydrates. Approximately 55 to 60 percent of your calories should come from carbohydrates; most should be complex carbohydrates (starches and fibers) as opposed to simple sugars. Complex carbohydrates (provided by fruits, vegetables and whole grains) are rich in vitamins, minerals and fiber.

Protein. The recommended protein intake in both plans is just 15 percent of total calories. Protein should be obtained from a variety of foods—such as dried peas, navy beans, tofu, meat, fish and poultry. Both plant and animal proteins provide a wide range of vitamins, minerals, fiber and other nutrients.

WHAT TO EAT

Dairy Products

To lower your blood cholesterol through diet, substitute margarine for butter and skim milk products for cheese, cream and ice cream. It's important to reduce your intake of products containing butter fat substantially, including whole milk, butter, cheese, cream and ice cream. Butter fat raises the blood cholesterol level more than most fats because it contains large quantities of both saturated fatty acids and cholesterol. Since dairy products traditionally play an important role in the typical American diet, we'll look into each more closely.

Whole, Lowfat and Skim Milk. Whole milk gets 49 percent of its calories from fat, and skim milk gets about .04 percent. Whole milk also contains a significant level of cholesterol. These are two persuasive reasons to virtually eliminate whole milk from your diet. While 2-percent lowfat milk is preferable to whole milk, it still gets an unacceptable 35 percent of its total calories from fat. And, again, that fat is highly saturated. That's why we recommend you choose 1-percent or skim milk. Both are rich in protein, calcium and other nutrients without having too much fat. Review the Dairy Products section of the Food Table in Appendix D, and the importance of choosing skim milk over whole milk will become obvious.

Butter, Cream and Ice Cream. These dairy products contain even more fat than whole milk and should, therefore, be avoided. Unfortunately, butter and cream are often "hidden" in foods, especially in baked goods and desserts. It's important to make sure you know what's in the food you buy by checking the ingredients lists.

Cheese. Cheese is mistakenly considered an acceptable high-protein substitute for meat. However, most cheeses are also high in highly saturated fat. In fact, 60 to 70 percent of the calories in cheese come from butter fat, about the same percentage as that in ice cream. For these reasons, select lowfat or part-skim milk cheeses.

Eggs

One large egg yolk contains almost the entire daily allowance for cholesterol, approximately 250 to 275 milligrams. It's a good idea to limit your egg yolk consumption to three per week on the Step-One Diet and to one per week on the Step-Two Diet. Egg whites, on the other hand, contain no cholesterol and are a good source of protein. Feel free to eat as many egg whites as you wish and to substitute them for whole eggs in most recipes (see page 31).

Meat Products

A total of six ounces of poultry, fish or lean meat per day (in one or two portions) is quite adequate. If the meat is reasonably lean, six ounces will usually contain between 500 and 600 calories, which is about one third of total required calories, depending on the caloric intake established for your diet.

Beef, Lamb, Pork and Veal. If you thought a cholesterol-lowering diet meant giving up red meat, you'll be pleased to know it's an unnecessary sacrifice. A three-ounce portion of red meat contains about 70 to 75 milligrams of cholesterol and an acceptable level of saturated fats, provided you take certain precautions. First, look for lean cuts of meat—those that contain a minimum of visible fat. Second, trim all outside fat from the meat before cooking.

Processed Meats. Processed meats, including sausage, bologna, salami and hot dogs, are rich in fat and calories, with about 70 to 80 percent of the total calories provided by fat. Processed meats should be used sparingly. Today, some processed meats are available with "reduced fat." Read the nutrition label and select those varieties with no more than 10 percent fat (by weight) or three grams fat per ounce.

Organ Meats. These include liver, sweetbreads, kidney, brain and heart. All, except heart, which is really more like a red meat, are extremely high in cholesterol and should be eaten sparingly, if at all.

Poultry. Often touted as a preferable substitute for red meat, poultry is in demand by the health-conscious. It is a good substitute only if the red meat is particularly fatty and the poultry is a lean variety, eaten without skin. Remember that chicken and turkey are leaner than goose or duck. Since the skin has the highest concentration of fat, it's a good idea to remove it before cooking.

Fish

While not free of cholesterol, fish generally contains less than red meat. For a cholesterol-lowering diet, this gives fish a slight edge over lean red meat and a definite edge over fatty red meat. For this reason, many authorities recommend that fish be eaten about two or three times a week. Fish can be either fatty or lean. Omega-3 fatty acids, found in some varieties of fatty fish, are currently being investigated for potential cholesterol-lowering benefits. Some fish high in Omega-3 fatty acids are Atlantic and coho salmon, albacore tuna, club mackerel, carp, lake whitefish, sweet smelt and lake and brook trout.

Shellfish

Shrimp, lobster, crab, crayfish and most other shellfish are very low in fat, although ounce for ounce some varieties contain more cholesterol than do poultry, meat or other fish. Even these, however, can be eaten occasionally within the recommended guidelines of less than 300 milligrams of cholesterol per day.

Fruits, Vegetables, Grains and Legumes

Foods in these categories have no cholesterol, tend to be low in fat and, in many cases, are high in fiber and vitamins. There are, however, a few exceptions. For example, coconut meat is high in saturated fatty acids. Olives and avocados are also high in fat, but since the fat is largely unsaturated, they need to be limited only because of their high calorie counts. Also, be careful to check the ingredient labels of processed foods made from vegetables, grains or legumes for fats or cholesterol added during processing. (Breads and pasta made with egg yolks, for instance, should be eaten sparingly.) Be aware that many processed and preserved vegetables contain excessive amounts of sodium. If your doctor has advised you to restrict your sodium intake, read the ingredient labels and buy only the many frozen foods (and some canned) without added sodium. Fresh produce is always a good choice. Generally, there is no reason to restrict your intake of fruits, vegetables, grains and legumes except to avoid excessive calories.

Nuts and Seeds

These tasty snacks tend to contain high concentrations of fat, and their caloric value is often greater than people realize. Nuts and seeds, though, do not contain cholesterol, and most of their fat is unsaturated. They are also good sources of incomplete proteins and can replace other high-protein foods to some degree. Incomplete proteins need other carbohydrate sources of protein to make them as nutritious a protein source as meat.

Bakery Goods

Foods in this category—cakes, pies, doughnuts, cookies and candy—offer few benefits to a cholesterol-lowering diet. They're typically high in calories and low in vital nutrients. Baked goods made with egg yolks and saturated fats not only lack nutritional benefits but are harmful to your diet. Commercially produced baked goods are usually the worst offenders. Homebaked goods prepared with unsaturated oils and egg whites instead of whole eggs are preferable. Still, baked goods of all kinds should be limited because of their high caloric content.

Fats and Oils

Saturated, Monounsaturated and Polyunsaturated Fatty Acids. These can come from either plant or animal sources. Fats and oils high in saturated fatty acids tend to become hard at room temperature: butter, lard and tallow from animals and coconut, palm and palm kernel oils from plants are common examples. These saturated fats raise blood cholesterol and should be avoided. Oils that stay liquid at room temperature are high in unsaturated fats. They include corn, safflower, sunflower, olive and rapeseed (canola) oils. All are low in saturated fatty acids and can be used to help lower blood cholesterol. Peanut oil has a somewhat higher level of saturated fatty acids, but can be used in cooking for flavoring.

Hydrogenated Oils. These oils would ordinarily be found in liquid form at room temperature but have been artificially hardened to produce margarines and shortenings. Their effect on blood cholesterol depends on how much they are hydrogenated. It's best to look for margarines that have the hydrogenated oil listed as the second ingredient.

Beverages

Very high consumption of coffee and possibly tea—that is, ten or more cups per day—is suspected of raising cholesterol levels. A modest amount of these beverages (one or two cups) seems to be okay. Alcohol has been erroneously credited with preventing heart disease. In moderation, alcohol does not appear to be harmful. But when excess alcohol is consumed, the ill effects are well established. Alcohol intake should, on the average, be limited to one ounce per day.

SHOPPING FOR LOW-FAT, LOW-CHOLESTEROL FOOD

Before you can effectively make healthy changes in the way you eat, you may need to make some changes in what you buy. The tips that follow can help you put the right foods into your cart and, ultimately, into your body.

BE A LABEL READER

When you see the words "No cholesterol" on a label, it means that the product does not contain any cholesterol, but be aware it may still contain saturated fat, which raises blood cholesterol. Basically, any product that does not contain ingredients from an animal source is naturally cholesterol-free. But coconut, palm and palm kernel oil are three plant sources that contain saturated fat.

A few product labels will give you the percent of calories from fat. Peanut butter and margarine labels often give this information, alerting you to the fact that these products contain primarily fat.

The words "low calorie" mean the product contains no more than 40 calories per serving. "Reduced calorie" means the product has at least one third fewer calories than the product for which this food is substituted. For example, reduced-calorie salad dressing is readily available.

When you shop, compare labels. Some premixed, frozen or prepared foods have a lower saturated fatty acid or cholesterol content than others. Now that many products list their fat and cholesterol content, shopping for low-saturated-fatty-acid, low-cholesterol foods is easier. With a little guidance, you can learn how to use these labels when you shop. First, look at the ingredients.

All food labels list the product's ingredients in order by

weight. The ingredient in the greatest amount is listed first. The ingredient in the least amount is listed last. To avoid too much total fat or saturated fatty acids, limit your use of products that list a fat or oil first, or that list many fat and oil ingredients. The checklist below helps you identify the names of common saturated fatty acid and cholesterol sources in foods.

SOURCES OF SATURATED FATTY ACIDS AND CHOLESTEROL

Animal Fat	Cream	Palm Kernel Oil*
Bacon Fat	Egg and Egg Yolk Solids	Palm Oil*
Beef Fat	Ham Fat	Pork Fat
Butter	Hardened Fat or Oil	Turkey Fat
Chicken Fat	Hydrogenated Vegetable Oil*	Vegetable Oil**
Cocoa Butter*	Lamb Fat	Vegetable Shortening*
Coconut*	Lard	Whole-Milk Solids
Coconut Oil*		

* Sources of saturated fat only   ** Could be coconut, palm or palm kernel oil

READ THE NUTRITION INFORMATION

Look on the label for the amount of total fat, polyunsaturated and saturated fatty acids, and cholesterol. The amount of monounsaturated fatty acids are not listed on labels. The following samples show you how to compare and identify products lower in saturated fatty acids and cholesterol. The labels give the amount of fat in grams (gm) and cholesterol in milligrams (mg) per serving. You can see that skim milk has less fat and cholesterol than whole milk. Tub and some stick margarines have less saturated fat and cholesterol than butter.

COMPARING LABEL INFORMATION

Nutrition Information per Serving	Whole Milk	Skim Milk
Serving Size	1 cup	1 cup
Calories	150 kcal	86 kcal
Protein	8 gm	8 gm
Carbohydrates	11 gm	12 gm
Fat	8 gm	less than 1 gm
Polyunsaturates	less than 1 gm	0 gm
Saturates	5 gm	less than 1 gm
Cholesterol	33 mg	4 mg

Nutrition Information per Serving	Butter, Stick	Margarine, Tub
Serving Size	1 tbsp.	1 tbsp.
Calories	101 kcal	101 kcal
Protein	0.1 gm	0.1 gm
Carbohydrates	0.1 gm	0.1 gm
Fat	11.4 gm	11.4 gm
Polyunsaturates	0.4 gm	3.9 gm
Saturates	7.1 gm	1.8 gm
Cholesterol	31 mg	0 mg

Note: The amount of monounsaturated fat is unlisted but can be approximately calculated by subtracting polyunsaturates and saturates from total fat.

The nutrition label also tells you what types of nutrients the product provides, the proportions of those nutrients and their contributions to the U.S. Recommended Daily Allowances for protein, vitamins and minerals.

SHOPPING TIPS

With a little practice, shopping with these things in mind will become second nature.

• Plan your menus (if time is at a premium, confine this to the entrees) for the week and make a list *before* you go shopping to help avoid impulse buying of items that may not fit into your diet plan.

- Never go shopping on an empty stomach. Hunger may tempt you to reach for the wrong foods.
- Buy specials or sale items only if they fit into your food plan for the week and into your overall dietary program. Otherwise, they may go to waste. Or to waist.
- If you want to cut costs by trying store brands in place of your usual brand products, be sure to compare the ingredients lists and nutritional labeling to make sure you're getting what you expect.
- Check ingredients lists for salt and other high-sodium additives. Be alert to any food label that has the word "sodium" on it.
  - —When you see the words "sodium-free" on a label it means the item has less than 5 milligrams of sodium per serving. "Very low-sodium" means less than 35 milligrams of sodium per serving.
  - —"Low-sodium" means 140 milligrams or less per serving. "Reduced sodium" means the product was processed to reduce the usual sodium level by 75 percent.
  - —"Unsalted," "no salt added" or "without added salt" means made without the salt that is normally used, but the product still contains the sodium that is the natural part of the food.

Meat, Fish and Poultry

When you shop, choose USDA select or choice grades of lean beef such as round steak, sirloin tip, tenderloin and extra lean ground beef. Even the leanest ground beef has more fat than allowed in the Step-Two Diet Plan. Other things to remember are listed below.

- "Prime" grades are heavily marbled, making them high in saturated fatty acids.

- Liver, brains, kidney and sweetbreads are high in cholesterol and should be limited or omitted.
- Select lean pork such as tenderloin, loin chops, center-cut ham (fresh and cured) and Canadian bacon.
- All cuts of veal are lean except veal cutlets (ground or cubed) and breast. Examples of lean veal are chops and roast.
- The lean cuts of lamb are leg, arm and loin.
- Some wild game, such as venison, rabbit, squirrel and pheasant, are very lean; duck and goose are not.
- Processed meats should be eaten only if they contain no more than 10 percent fat or 3 grams fat per ounce. Many processed meats (luncheon meats, wieners) and sausage are high in saturated fatty acids.
- Because most fish is lower in saturated fatty acids and cholesterol than meats and poultry, it makes a better entree choice.
- All fresh and frozen fish are good selections, as is tuna, canned in water or rinsed. Uncreamed or smoked herring and sardines, canned in tomato sauce or rinsed, are good choices.
- Shellfish contains less fat than does meat or poultry. Although shrimp and crayfish are relatively high in cholesterol, they can be eaten occasionally in the Step-One Diet. However, since the cholesterol is further limited in the Step-Two Diet plan, these shellfish should be limited on that plan.
- Since much of the fat in poultry is in the skin, removing it greatly reduces the fat content. Select chicken, cornish hens and turkey for your entree. Avoid goose, duck and processed poultry products, which are high in saturated fatty acids.
- You will often see the words "lean," "lite" and similar terms used to designate beef, lamb and pork that have less trimmable fat (fat surrounding the meat) and sometimes, less marbling. These labels are also seen on processed meats and other foods. While the terms "light,"

"lite," "leaner" and "lower fat" generally refer to foods containing less fat, they can be confusing. Light may also mean light color, as in vegetable oil, or fewer calories, as in drinks. Such products are not necessarily low in fat.

Dairy Products

You don't have to give up all dairy products to lower your cholesterol—just follow these recommendations and choose carefully.

• Buy lowfat or skim dairy products such as skim milk, lowfat yogurt, nonfat dry milk and lowfat cottage cheese. And don't forget buttermilk! Despite its name and rich taste, buttermilk is very low in fat, since it's made from cultured skim milk.

• Look for lowfat or part-skim cheeses, lowfat or dry curd cottage cheese, farmer cheese, part-skim mozzarella or ricotta, or dry, grated cheese such as Parmesan or Sap Sago. Because they are made with skim milk, lowfat or imitation cheeses that have between two and five grams of fat per ounce are good choices. Creamy cheeses such as brie or processed cheese spreads are high in saturated fats and should be selected infrequently.

Individuals on the Step-Two Diet should select only skim, nonfat dairy products and cheese with two grams of fat or less per ounce. For desserts, choose frozen lowfat yogurt, ices, ice milk and sherbet.

• Cream substitutes—nondairy coffee creamers, sour cream substitutes and whipped toppings—often contain coconut, palm or palm kernel oil and are therefore high in saturated fatty acids. Read labels carefully and avoid those products high in saturated fatty acids.

Fats and Oils

Selecting acceptable fats and oils will be easy if you keep these things in mind.

- Buy margarine in place of butter and always look for a margarine that lists liquid oil as the first ingredient or a diet margarine that lists liquid oil as the second ingredient (water is the first ingredient in diet margarines). Next on the list of ingredients should be one or more partially hydrogenated vegetable oils.
- Because diet margarine contains water, it is often difficult to use for cooking. However, it is still useful as a spread.
- Check the label of your vegetable oil and select safflower, corn, sunflower, soybean, olive or canola. Use peanut oil for a flavor change only.
- Buy nonstick vegetable sprays to use in place of butter or oil on pans and baking sheets.
- Because of their high fat content, some nuts, except coconut, and any variety of seeds, olives, peanut butter and avocado are listed in the category of fats. Because they are so high-calorie, select them only occasionally.
- Chocolate, coconut, coconut oil, palm kernel oil and palm oil contain more saturated than unsaturated fat. When selecting commercial food items containing these ingredients, look for fatty acid information on the label. The foods you buy should contain more polyunsaturated than saturated fatty acids. Currently, information about monounsaturated fatty acids is not listed on the nutrition label, but they can be calculated approximately by subtracting polyunsaturates and saturates from total fat.

Breads, Cereal, Pasta and Starchy Vegetables

Most breads are low in fat. Some commercially baked products contain large amounts of saturated fatty acids, e.g., croissants, muffins, biscuits, butter rolls and doughnuts. The whole-grain types contain more fiber than others.

- Check the labels on baked foods. Many are made with whole milk and dried egg yolks, and should be only selected occasionally.
- Check the labels on crackers for fats and oils. Scandina-

vian-style rye crackers and other whole-grain crackers are often made without fats or oils and with little or no salt.

- Try buying brown rice, bulgur wheat, millet and other whole grains to cook in seasoned broth for a side dish. They're high in fiber, relatively low in calories and economical.
- Buy dried beans, peas and lentils to substitute for meats in casseroles, stews and soups. They're excellent protein sources and very economical.
- Check the ingredients lists on packaged cereals. Most of these are low in saturated fatty acids, but many contain large quantities of sugar, some contain salt, and a few even contain fat. Be particularly cautious of so-called natural cereals and granolas, which may contain all three. They often contain coconut or coconut oil.
- Look for reduced-salt versions of canned soups and canned vegetables. They may be found either in the diet section or on the shelves with their "regular" counterparts.
- Canned or dehydrated varieties of soup should have no more than two grams of fat per cup.

Vegetables and Fruits

Fresh vegetables and fruits have little or no fat, except avocados and olives. When shopping for processed foods, there are a few things to keep in mind.

- Vegetables prepared with butter, cream or cheese can be high in fat.
- Fried vegetables have several times more fat and calories than vegetables prepared without fat.
- Fruits that are fresh or canned in water are lower in calories than fruits canned in juice or in syrup. Drain fruits canned in syrup.

Optional Foods

Before reaching for a snack, consider how it fits into your diet plan.

- A few types of commercially prepared cookies are low in fat, such as Newton-type cookies and gingersnaps. Plain angel food cake has no fat. If uncertain, choose only those labeled two grams of fat or less per portion.
- Desserts (cakes, pies, cookies and puddings) may be made at home with allowed margarine or oil, skim or 1-percent milk, allowed eggs, egg substitute or egg whites.
- Many snack products, such as chips and rich crackers, are high in saturated fatty acids. However, some chips are cooked in unsaturated oil. Choose only those labeled as having more polyunsaturated than saturated fatty acids.

Free Foods

These foods and drinks contain fewer than 20 calories and no fat per portion.

DRINKS

Bouillon or broth without fat *
Carbonated drinks, sugar-free **
Carbonated water
Club soda *
Cocoa powder, unsweetened
Coffee or tea
Drink mixes, sugar-free **
Tonic water, sugar-free **

FRUITS

Cranberries, unsweetened
Rhubarb, unsweetened

CONDIMENTS

Try flavored peppers, herb blends, spice blends, vinegars and other seasonings in place of salt.

SWEET SUBSTITUTES **

Candy, hard, sugar-free
Gelatin, sugar-free
Gum, sugar-free
Jam or jelly, sugar-free
Sugar substitutes (saccharin or aspartame)

* High in sodium. Look for seltzers or soda with no salt added.
** Sweet substitutes are listed for the benefit of those following a diabetic diet.

COOKING TIPS

Heart-healthy cooking is more than a matter of what foods you prepare. It's also a function of how you prepare them. The fact is, some cooking methods are better than others for cutting cholesterol, fat and calories while enhancing the nutritional value of your diet. As a rule of thumb, avoid all cooking methods that add fat or allow food to cook in its own fat. (Deep-fat frying or pan frying are two common offenders.) Instead, try some of the following heart-healthy cooking techniques.

Roasting. Always place a rack in the bottom of the roasting pan, so the meat or poultry doesn't sit in its own fat drippings. And be sure to roast at a low temperature, about 350°, to avoid searing the meat or poultry and sealing in the fat. For basting, use fat-free liquids such as wine, tomato juice or lemon juice.

Baking. Poultry, fish and meat can be baked in covered cookware with a little additional liquid. The moisture that the liquid adds makes this method particularly good for fish or chicken breasts, which tend to be a little dry.

Braising or Stewing. This method uses a little more liquid than baking does. It can be done in a covered container on top of the stove or in the oven. If you're braising or stewing meat or poultry, begin a day ahead of time and refrigerate the dish overnight. The next day, when the chilled fat has congealed, you can remove it easily before reheating. Braising is also an excellent way to cook vegetables.

Poaching. To poach chicken or fish, immerse it in a pan of simmering liquid on top of the stove. This method works especially well when you serve the food with a sauce made of pureed vegetables and herbs.

Grilling or Broiling. Placing food on a rack and cooking with these methods lets the fat drip away from meat or poultry. It's also a tasty way to cook fish steaks or whole fish. For extra flavor, try marinating food before putting it over the coals or under the broiler. Skewered vegetables also taste great browned over an open flame.

Sautéing. Fish, poultry and vegetable dishes can be sautéed in an open skillet with little or no fat; the high temperature and motion keep food from sticking. Try sautéing with a tiny bit of polyunsaturated oil rubbed onto the pan with a paper towel. Better still, use nonstick vegetable spray or sauté in a small amount of broth or wine.

Stir-Frying. Done in a Chinese wok, this method relies on the same principle as sautéing. The high temperature and the constant movement of the food keep it from sticking and burning. Try stir-frying vegetables and diced poultry or seafood with a tiny bit of cottonseed or peanut oil.

Microwave Cooking. This is a fast, easy cooking method that requires no added fat. You don't have to add fat to keep the food from sticking to the pan because foods don't tend to stick in the moist heat of microwaving. In fact, you can drain food of fat as it cooks by placing it in the microwave between two paper towels.

If you want to adapt a recipe for microwaving, try cutting the cooking time to one fourth to one third of the conventional time. If the food needs more cooking, increase it a little at a time. You might also look for a microwave recipe similar to the one you're trying to adapt. Keep the following hints in mind when microwave cooking.

- Choose foods that cook well in moist heat: chicken, fish, ground meat, vegetables, sauces and soups.
- Pieces that are about equal in size and shape will cook more uniformly.
- You can reduce the liquid used in cooking beverages, soups, vegetables, fruits and main dishes by about one third because less evaporates in microwave cooking.
- Choose a microwave-safe container slightly larger than the

dish required for cooking the recipe in a conventional oven.

- Use a high setting (100 percent power) for soups, beverages, fruits, vegetables, fish, ground meat and poultry. Use a medium-high setting (70 percent power) for simmering stews and a medium setting (50 percent power) for baking breads, cakes and muffins, and cooking less tender cuts of meat.
- To create a crusty look on baked items, grease pans with an acceptable vegetable oil and add ground nuts or crumbs.
- Add lowfat cheese and other toppings near the end of cooking to keep the top from becoming tough or soggy.
- Stay away from coating meat with flour if you will be adding liquid for cooking. The coatings become soggy.
- Use quick-cooking instead of long-grain rice.

Steaming. Cooking food in a basket over simmering water leaves the natural flavor, color and nutritional value of vegetables intact. Try adding herbs to the steaming water or using broth instead to add even more flavor to the finished dish.

Additional Tips

There are many variables in making your food heart-healthy. There are lots of little ways to trim cholesterol, fat, salt and calories without trimming taste. There are also ways to enhance the flavors of your selected foods—and some special ways to handle food. The following tips may come in handy.

- Trim all visible fat from meat before cooking.
- After you roast meat or poultry, chill the drippings in the refrigerator. Once cooled, the fat will rise to the top and harden; you can remove it easily and save the stock to use in stews, sauces and soups.

- Buy only the leanest ground beef, pork and turkey (no more than 15 percent fat). After browning, put ground meat into a strainer or colander lined with paper towels. Allow fat to drain out. "Ground" meat is generally higher in fat than nonground meat. Even the leanest ground beef contains more fat than is recommended for those on the Step-Two Diet. Instead of buying prepackaged ground beef, have your butcher grind a sirloin steak for you. Be sure to have him remove all visible fat and clean the grinder to remove any fat from previous grindings.
- When figuring serving sizes, remember that meat loses about 25 percent of its weight during cooking. (For example, 4 ounces of raw meat will be about 3 ounces cooked.)
- To make gravy without fat, blend a tablespoon of cornstarch with a cup of room-temperature broth by shaking the two together in a tightly lidded jar. Then heat the rest of the broth in a saucepan and add the blended liquid. Simmer until thickened.
- Make a habit of skinning chickens before cooking and removing all visible fat below the skin. The skin will be easier to remove if you use paper towels or a clean cloth to take hold of it. Be certain to scrub the cutting surface and utensils well with hot sudsy water after preparing poultry for cooking.
- Fresh fish should be cooked for ten minutes per inch of thickness. Add five minutes if it's wrapped in foil. Frozen fish requires twenty minutes per inch of thickness, plus ten minutes if it's wrapped in foil. Cooking time may vary, depending on the cooking method used, but fish is done when the flesh is opaque and it flakes easily.
- Prepare scrambled eggs or omelettes so that only one egg yolk per portion is used. Add a few extra egg whites to the mixing bowl to make more generous servings.
- To remove oils or salty liquids, drain canned salmon, tuna or sardines. Then add water to the can and drain again to rinse.

- Seal natural juices into foods by wrapping them in foil before cooking. Or try wrapping foods in edible pouches made of steamed lettuce or cabbage leaves.
- Cook vegetables just long enough to make them tender-crisp. Overcooked vegetables lose both flavor and important nutrients.
- Clean mushrooms as you use them by wiping them with a damp cloth. A quick rinse in cold water is fine, but never soak them or they'll get soggy.
- Be sure to wear rubber gloves when handling hot peppers or wash hands thoroughly after handling. Skin, especially around the eyes, is very sensitive to the oil from peppers.
- Cut down on cholesterol by using more vegetables and less poultry or meats in soups, stews and casseroles. Finely chopped vegetables are great for stretching ground poultry or meat, too.
- Cut down on fat in creamy salad dressing by mixing it with plain lowfat yogurt.
- Sweeten plain lowfat or nonfat yogurt with pureed fruit or applesauce instead of buying prepared fruit yogurt.

Recipe Substitutions

You probably have quite a few favorite recipes you hate to give up as you start your heart-healthy diet program. The happy fact is, you can salvage many of them simply by making a few simple adaptations and substitutions.

WHEN YOUR OWN RECIPE CALLS FOR:	USE:
Sour cream	Mock Sour Cream (see recipe page 32); lowfat cottage cheese plus lowfat yogurt for flavor; ricotta cheese made from partially skimmed milk (thinned with yogurt or buttermilk, if desired); one can of chilled evaporated skim milk whipped with one teaspoon of lemon juice; or lowfat buttermilk or lowfat yogurt.
Whipped Cream	Creamy Dessert Topping or Mock Whipped Cream (see recipes pages 262 and 319).
Unsweetened Baking Chocolate	Unsweetened cocoa powder or carob powder blended with unsaturated oil or margarine (one 1-ounce square of chocolate = 3 tablespoons of cocoa or carob plus 1 tablespoon polyunsaturated oil or margarine). Because carob is sweeter than cocoa reduce the sugar in the recipe by one fourth.
Butter	Unsaturated margarine or oil. (One tablespoon butter = 1 tablespoon margarine or ¾ tablespoon oil.) If you wish to substitute margarine for oil, use 1¼ cups margarine for 1 cup of oil. Use 1¼ tablespoons of margarine for 1 tablespoon of oil.
Eggs	Use commercially produced, cholesterol-free egg substitutes according to package directions. Or use one egg white plus 2 teaspoons of unsaturated oil for each egg. For each two whole eggs in baking recipes, substitute three egg whites. For one whole large egg, substitute two egg whites. The table on how eggs add up on pages 368–369 will show you the approximate whole egg content of various prepared foods.
Whole Milk	Use 1 cup of skim or nonfat milk plus 1 tablespoon of unsaturated oil as a substitute for 1 cup of whole milk.
Cream Cheese	Blend 4 tablespoons of margarine with 1 cup dry lowfat cottage cheese. Add a small amount of skim milk if needed in blending mixture. Vegetables such as chopped chives or pimiento and herbs and seasonings may be added for variety.

MOCK SOUR CREAM

**MAKES ABOUT 1¼ CUPS,
CONTAINING ABOUT
200 CALORIES**

2 tablespoons skim milk
1 tablespoon lemon juice
1 cup lowfat cottage cheese

P lace all ingredients in a blender and combine on medium-high speed until smooth and creamy.

Some Additional Substitution Ideas

- Use evaporated skim milk for cream when making whipped topping. (Be aware that the evaporated milk won't whip unless it's well chilled first.)
- Substitute plain lowfat or nonfat yogurt for sour cream in baking recipes.
- Substitute plain lowfat or nonfat yogurt for sour cream in sauces. Mix 1 tablespoon of cornstarch with 1 tablespoon of yogurt and mix into the yogurt. It will prevent the yogurt from separating.
- Try plain lowfat or nonfat yogurt or buttermilk in place of sour cream or mayonnaise in salad dressing recipes.
- Substitute lowfat or skim milk for cream or whole milk in baking recipes.
- Thicken soups, stews or sauces with cornstarch or flour dissolved in cold liquid or with pureed vegetables.
- Substitute chopped vegetables for some of the bread when you make poultry stuffing.
- Since most recipes include more sugar than necessary, you can usually reduce the amount of sugar by one fourth to one third.
- Reduce salt in nonyeast baking recipes.

- Substitute herbs and seasonings for salt as you cook. See below for herb seasoning recipes.
- Substitute onion or garlic flakes or powder for onion salt and garlic salt.
- Add a drop of lemon juice to the water you cook pasta in and eliminate the salt.
- Substitute brown rice for white rice to add whole-grain roughage.
- Use a blend of whole-wheat flour and all-purpose flour in recipes that call for regular flour.
- Use wheat germ, bran and whole-wheat bread crumbs in place of buttered crumbs to top casseroles.
- Using vegetable oil for shortening in cakes that require creaming will affect the texture. Use margarine instead; use vegetable oil in recipes calling for melted butter.

HERB SEASONING

Use this in casseroles, stews or fresh vegetable dishes. It makes a great substitute for salt.

MAKES APPROXIMATELY ⅓ CUP

½ teaspoon cayenne pepper
1 tablespoon garlic powder
1 teaspoon dried basil
1 teaspoon dried marjoram
1 teaspoon dried thyme
1 teaspoon dried parsley
1 teaspoon dried savory
1 teaspoon mace
1 teaspoon onion powder
1 teaspoon freshly ground black pepper
1 teaspoon powdered sage

Combine all ingredients in medium bowl. Toss gently with spoon until well blended. Store in an airtight container in a cool, dry, dark place for up to six months.

LEMON HERB SEASONING

MAKES APPROXIMATELY I CUP

The flavors of the blended spices of this mix mingle well with the flavors of fish, chicken or turkey. For extra lemony flavor, add seasoning mix to meat and then sprinkle with fresh lemon juice.

4^1/$_2$ tablespoons dried basil
3^3/$_4$ tablespoons dried oregano
1^1/$_2$ tablespoons powdered black pepper
1^1/$_2$ tablespoons granulated onion
1^1/$_2$ tablespoons whole celery seed
1^1/$_4$ tablespoons powdered basil
^{1}/$_2$ teaspoon granulated garlic
^{1}/$_2$ teaspoon lemon rind, grated (optional)

Combine all ingredients in medium bowl. Toss gently with spoon until well blended. Store in an airtight container in a cool, dry, dark place for up to six months.

SALAD HERB BLEND

For a salad bursting with flavor,
sprinkle this on before adding
dressing.

MAKES APPROXIMATELY 1 CUP

¼ cup dried parsley
¼ cup dried marjoram
2½ tablespoons dried basil
1½ tablespoons sesame seeds
1½ tablespoons chili pepper flakes
1½ tablespoons powdered rosemary
1¼ tablespoons powdered celery seed
2½ teaspoons dried savory
2½ teaspoons powdered sage
2¼ teaspoons dried thyme
2 teaspoons granulated onion
2 teaspoons dried dillweed
1¼ teaspoons powdered black pepper
¾ teaspoon granulated garlic

Combine all ingredients in medium bowl. Toss gently with spoon until well blended. Store in an airtight container in a cool, dry, dark place for up to six months.

HOW TO USE THESE RECIPES

The recipes in this book have been analyzed by computer. Each analysis is based on a single serving, except where indicated otherwise. The number of calories and the amount of protein, carbohydrates, total fat, saturated fatty acids, polyunsaturated fatty acids, monounsaturated fatty acids, cholesterol and sodium per serving has been calculated. The values for saturated, monounsaturated and polyunsaturated fatty acids will not add up precisely to the total fat in the recipe because the total fat includes not only fatty acids, but other fatty substances and glycerol. The values are as accurate as possible.

The caloric values are for physiological energy values. They represent the energy values remaining after the losses in digestion and metabolism have been deducted from the gross energy. Caloric values are based on the Atwater system for determining energy values.

In the recipes calling for vegetable oil, choose corn, safflower or sunflower oil because they contain polyunsaturated fat. Canola or olive oil are acceptable monounsaturated oils. You may also use peanut oil occasionally for variety.

The nutritional information for a serving of a particular recipe includes such additions as salad dressings and garnishes. However, nutritional information is provided for each salad dressing.

The calories in alcohol evaporate when heated, and this reduction is reflected in the calculations.

When a marinade is used, the total amount of the marinade is calculated.

Salt is not used in most of these recipes, and where it is used, the amount is very small. The analyses therefore also include salt where applicable, although salt is often marked as optional.

All serving sizes and figures for total amount made are approximate.

Specific ingredients listed were used in the analysis. However, use your own judgment when selecting ingredients. For example, when the recipe calls for fresh lemon juice and you have only reconstituted lemon juice, use it. Other ingredients can also be substituted if necessary. For example, yellow onions and red wine vinegar can be replaced with white onions and apple cider vinegar. Several recipes give optional ingredients. Let your individual taste be your guide—and enjoy the heart-healthy food you create!

RECIPES

APPETIZERS AND SPREADS

Zucchini Spread
Hummus (Chickpea Dip)
Apple-Almond Butter
Rice Cake and Cheese Snack
Stuffed Mushrooms
Baked Garlic
Potato Skins
Chicken Triangles
Scallop and Ham Roll-ups
Melon Balls with Turkey and Ham

ZUCCHINI SPREAD

SERVES 8
¼ CUP PER SERVING

A food processor makes preparation simple! Serve with crackers, vegetable sticks or rounds of crusty French bread. Or, use as a sandwich spread. For example, line a pita half with zucchini spread and stuff with vegetables.

3½ cups unpeeled, shredded zucchini, about 3 small zucchini
1 tablespoon olive oil
2 tablespoons red wine vinegar
¼ cup finely chopped fresh parsley or cilantro
1 clove garlic, minced
¼ teaspoon salt (optional)
Freshly ground black pepper to taste
2 tablespoons finely chopped walnuts or pecans

NUTRIENT ANALYSIS*

Calories	38.14 kcal
Protein	1.05 g
Carbohydrate	2.65 g
Total Fat	2.95 g
Saturated	0.36 g
Polyunsaturated	0.93 g
Monounsaturated	1.43 g
Cholesterol	0.00 mg
Sodium	66.99 mg

* For entire recipe.

Squeeze zucchini to remove excess water. In a blender or the workbowl of a food processor fitted with a metal blade, combine zucchini, oil, vinegar, parsley or cilantro, garlic, salt and pepper. Process until smooth, scraping down sides as needed. Spoon mixture into serving container and fold in nuts. Cover and chill before serving.

HUMMUS (CHICKPEA DIP)

SERVES 8
¼ CUP PER SERVING

Hummus is a Middle-Eastern specialty traditionally served with flat Syrian bread, warm pita or as a dip for raw vegetables. It is an excellent source of protein, and this recipe is lower in fat than the usual version.

Tahini, a sesame seed paste, is found in health-food stores and some supermarkets. If unavailable, it can be made by blending together ½ cup sesame seeds, 1 tablespoon water, 1 tablespoon lemon juice and a few drops of vegetable oil.

1 19-ounce can chickpeas, rinsed and drained
½ cup fresh lemon juice
¼ cup tahini
2 cloves garlic, minced
1 teaspoon acceptable vegetable oil
½ teaspoon ground cumin, or to taste
⅛ teaspoon cayenne pepper (optional)
Freshly ground black pepper to taste
¼ teaspoon salt (optional)
¼ cup water
½ cup finely chopped fresh parsley

In a blender or a food processor fitted with a metal blade, combine chickpeas, lemon juice, tahini, garlic, oil, cumin, cayenne, pepper, salt and water. Blend, scraping sides occasionally. If mixture is too thick, add more water, a few drops at a time. The mixture should be a smooth paste. Stir in parsley.

Hummus tastes best when refrigerated for 24 hours before serving, allowing the flavors to blend.

NUTRIENT ANALYSIS

Calories	176.57 kcal
Protein	8.74 g
Carbohydrate	22.31 g
Total Fat	6.79 g
Saturated	0.86 g
Polyunsaturated	3.01 g
Monounsaturated	2.24 g
Cholesterol	0.00 mg
Sodium	82.43 mg

APPLE-ALMOND BUTTER

Apple butter is available in supermarkets and health food stores. Apple-Almond Butter tastes great on whole-wheat toast or English muffins.

SERVES 20
I TABLESPOON PER SERVING

1 cup whole almonds, with skins
1 cup sweetened apple butter

P reheat oven to 375° F.

Toast almonds in a single layer on a baking pan for 5 to 10 minutes, or until golden, turning once. Put into work-bowl of a food processor fitted with metal blade and process continuously, scraping sides as needed, until almonds become a thick paste. (At first almonds become powdery, like almond meal; then if you keep processing, you will get almond butter, a thick paste.) Add apple butter and continue to process, scraping sides as needed, until mixture is smooth. Refrigerate.

NUTRIENT ANALYSIS

Calories	70.99 kcal
Protein	1.37 g
Carbohydrate	8.58 g
Total Fat	3.92 g
Saturated	0.31 g
Polyunsaturated	0.74 g
Monounsaturated	2.63 g
Cholesterol	0.00 mg
Sodium	0.62 mg

RICE CAKE AND CHEESE SNACK

Try this for an easy-to-fix snack. It's
a great after-school treat for kids—
and an anytime treat for adults.

SERVES 2
I RICE CAKE PER SERVING

2 rice cakes, unsalted
1 teaspoon prepared yellow mustard
¼ cup grated Defatted Cheddar Cheese (see pages 349–350) or
   commercial lowfat cheddar cheese

P reheat oven to 350° F.
   Place rice cakes on baking sheet or aluminum foil and
bake 3 to 4 minutes, or until crisp. Remove from oven,
spread with mustard and top with cheese. Return to oven
and bake 3 to 4 minutes, or just until cheese melts. Serve
immediately.

NUTRIENT ANALYSIS

Calories	29.18 kcal
Protein	1.22 g
Carbohydrate	6.13 g
Total Fat	0.20 g
Saturated	0.02 g
Polyunsaturated	0.07 g
Monounsaturated	0.02 g
Cholesterol	2.58 mg
Sodium	31.60 mg

STUFFED MUSHROOMS

This hot appetizer is an ideal party food. Prepare it an hour in advance and put it in the oven as guests arrive. The aroma is mouth-watering!

SERVES 6
3 MUSHROOMS PER SERVING

18 large mushrooms
1 tablespoon olive oil
¼ cup minced onion
1 clove garlic, minced
¼ cup finely chopped walnuts
1 shredded wheat biscuit, crushed
1 tablespoon grated Parmesan cheese
½ teaspoon Herb Seasoning (see pages 33–34)
Freshly ground black pepper to taste
½ teaspoon paprika (optional)

NUTRIENT ANALYSIS

Calories	86.08 kcal
Protein	2.76 g
Carbohydrate	6.65 g
Total Fat	5.98 g
Saturated	0.88 g
Polyunsaturated	2.39 g
Monounsaturated	2.26 g
Cholesterol	0.82 mg
Sodium	26.15 mg

Preheat oven to 350° F.

Clean mushrooms with a vegetable brush or wipe with a damp cloth. Remove and finely chop stems. Heat oil in a nonstick skillet over medium-high heat. Sauté chopped mushroom stems, onions, garlic and walnuts until onion is tender, 4 to 5 minutes. Remove from heat. Stir in shredded wheat, Parmesan cheese, herb seasoning and pepper. Stuff mushroom caps, packing mixture firmly. Arrange mushrooms in a shallow baking dish. Sprinkle tops lightly with paprika. Bake 20 to 25 minutes, or until mushrooms are tender.

BAKED GARLIC

This dish has a surprisingly mild taste. For a delicious appetizer, spread the garlic over thin slices of French bread or Melba toast.

SERVES 6
⅓ GARLIC HEAD PER SERVING

2 large heads garlic
1 teaspoon olive oil

Preheat oven to 350° F.

Do not remove the paper skin from the garlic. Cut each head of garlic in half horizontally. Drizzle ¼ teaspoon oil on cut side of each half of garlic. Place halves together and wrap securely in foil. Bake 1 hour, or until soft.

Remove from oven and allow to cool slightly. When cool enough to touch, squeeze the garlic from the skin onto a small plate.

NUTRIENT ANALYSIS

Calories	27.23 kcal
Protein	0.93 g
Carbohydrate	4.63 g
Total Fat	0.78 g
Saturated	0.11 g
Polyunsaturated	0.08 g
Monounsaturated	0.55 g
Cholesterol	0.00 mg
Sodium	2.86 mg

POTATO SKINS

These are perfect for entertaining
or just for snacking.

SERVES 12
4 PER SERVING

4 teaspoons nonfat "butter" granules
6 medium baking potatoes, scrubbed and baked
1/2 teaspoon garlic powder
Freshly ground black pepper to taste

P reheat oven to 450° F.

Reconstitute the "butter" granules according to the directions on the package.

Cut each potato in half. Scoop out the center, leaving about 1/4 inch of potato on the inside of each skin. (Use leftover potato to make Shepherd's Pie, see pages 177–178.) Cut skins into quarters. Dab liquid butter substitute onto the white side of each potato skin. Sprinkle with garlic powder and pepper, if desired.

Place prepared skins, skin-side down, on a baking sheet. Bake 15 minutes, or until lightly browned. Turn skins over and bake another 5 minutes, or until crisp. Serve immediately.

NUTRIENT ANALYSIS

Calories	27.93 kcal
Protein	0.74 g
Carbohydrate	6.32 g
Total Fat	0.06 g
Saturated	0.00 g
Polyunsaturated	0.03 g
Monounsaturated	0.00 g
Cholesterol	0.01 mg
Sodium	29.40 mg

CHICKEN TRIANGLES

SERVES 12
2 PER SERVING

These are neat little phyllo triangles of "garlicky" chicken. They're great as nibbles, hors d'oeuvres or a side dish.

Phyllo is a paper-thin dough, available frozen in 1-pound packages of about 24 sheets in most large supermarkets and specialty stores. Phyllo should be defrosted in the refrigerator. Unopened, the defrosted dough will keep for a month, if refrigerated. Refreezing can make the dough crumbly. When working with the dough, keep it covered with a damp cloth to prevent drying.

1 pound boneless chicken breasts, skinned, all visible fat
 removed
½ tablespoon olive oil
2 tablespoons lemon juice
2 cloves garlic, minced
1 tablespoon minced fresh parsley
1 tablespoon fresh or ½ teaspoon dried tarragon, oregano or
 basil
¼ teaspoon salt (optional)
10 sheets phyllo pastry
3 tablespoons acceptable margarine, melted

Finely chop chicken. Combine oil, lemon juice, garlic, parsley, tarragon and salt in a small bowl. Add chicken and toss to coat. Cover and refrigerate for at least 1 hour.

Preheat oven to 400° F.

Lightly brush a sheet of phyllo with melted margarine. Stack a second sheet on top. Cut the two-layer sheet into five short strips, crosswise, with scissors or a sharp knife.

Place a teaspoon of chicken filling on a two-layer strip, 1 inch away from the bottom. Fold a corner across the filling and continue folding, corner to corner (the way a flag is folded). The filling expands during cooking, so do not fold the dough too tightly. Tuck the excess dough under the triangle, then place on a baking sheet. Repeat with the remaining eight sheets of phyllo and chicken. Lightly brush the prepared triangles with melted margarine. Bake 15 to 20 minutes, or until golden brown.

To freeze for later use, place unbaked triangles on baking sheets and freeze. Store frozen triangles in freezer in plastic freezer bags. To bake, place on baking sheets in a preheated 400° F. oven, 20 to 25 minutes.

NUTRIENT ANALYSIS

Calories	95.92 kcal
Protein	8.76 g
Carbohydrate	5.83 g
Total Fat	4.05 g
Saturated	0.72 g
Polyunsaturated	1.13 g
Monounsaturated	1.87 g
Cholesterol	19.19 mg
Sodium	94.56 mg

SCALLOP AND HAM ROLL-UPS

Soaking toothpicks before using
helps prevent charring the wood
when broiling.

SERVES 12
2 PER SERVING

24 sea scallops, about ¾ pound
6 ounces thinly sliced lean ham, visible fat removed
24 pineapple chunks, canned in their own juice, about ½ of a
    20-ounce can
24 toothpicks soaked in water for at least 30 minutes

Preheat broiler.
  If the muscle is still attached to the scallop, remove it.
Cut ham into approximately 6- × 1¼-inch strips. Wrap one
strip around each scallop and skewer with a toothpick. Add
one pineapple chunk to each toothpick. Place prepared
toothpicks on a baking pan with sides.
  Broil five inches from heat for 4 minutes. Turn scallops
and broil another 3 minutes. Serve hot.

NUTRIENT ANALYSIS

Calories	50.64 kcal
Protein	7.48 g
Carbohydrate	1.85 g
Total Fat	1.35 g
Saturated	0.42 g
Polyunsaturated	0.21 g
Monounsaturated	0.49 g
Cholesterol	19.58 mg
Sodium	140.27 mg

MELON BALLS WITH TURKEY AND HAM

This is an easy-to-fix appetizer that combines fresh melons with ham, chicken and a tangy-sweet, minted mustard dip.

SERVES 15
3 BALLS PER SERVING

1 medium honeydew melon, cut in half and seeded
1 medium cantaloupe melon, cut in half and seeded
4 ounces thinly sliced lean ham, visible fat removed
4 ounces thinly sliced turkey

Dipping Sauce
1/4 cup spicy brown mustard
2 tablespoons honey
12 fresh mint leaves, chopped

NUTRIENT ANALYSIS

Calories	89.07 kcal
Protein	5.46 g
Carbohydrate	13.94 g
Total Fat	1.93 g
Saturated	0.51 g
Polyunsaturated	0.27 g
Monounsaturated	0.67 g
Cholesterol	13.33 mg
Sodium	144.30 mg

Using the large side of a melon-baller, make balls from the melons; set aside. Cut the ham and turkey into 4 × 1-inch strips. Wrap each melon ball in either a strip of ham or turkey and skewer with a toothpick.

In a small bowl, combine sauce ingredients. Serve with wrapped melon balls.

SOUPS

Country-Style Vegetable Soup
Light and Lemony Chicken and Spinach Soup
Lentil-Spinach Soup
Mock Condensed Cream of Chicken Soup
Mock Condensed Cream of Mushroom Soup
Mock Condensed Cream of Celery Soup
Cream of Corn Soup
Split Pea Soup
Tomato Soup
Tomato, Orange and Tarragon Soup
Fresh Melon and Mango Soup
Yogurt Gazpacho

COUNTRY-STYLE VEGETABLE SOUP

A great anytime dish, this hearty
soup is an excellent way to take
advantage of an abundant supply of
fresh vegetables. It can be served as
an appetizer or a main lunch
course.

SERVES 10
APPROXIMATELY 1 CUP
PER SERVING

1 medium onion, chopped
4 large carrots, chopped
1 pound potatoes, scrubbed and chopped, about 3 medium
    potatoes
3 stalks celery, chopped
2 medium zucchini, chopped
¼ teaspoon salt (optional)
Freshly ground black pepper to taste
2 bay leaves
¼ cup finely chopped fresh parsley
6 cups homemade Chicken Stock (see page 352)
6 ounces (¾ cup) crumbled Defatted Cheddar Cheese (see
    pages 349–350) or commercial lowfat cheddar cheese

In a large heavy saucepan or Dutch oven, combine onion,
carrots, potatoes, celery, zucchini, salt, pepper, bay leaves
and parsley. Cover with stock, bring to a boil and simmer,

covered, 45 to 60 minutes, or until vegetables are very tender. Remove bay leaves.

Serve hot, topped with cheese.

NUTRIENT ANALYSIS

Calories	120.41 kcal
Protein	9.08 g
Carbohydrate	17.20 g
Total Fat	6.00 g
Saturated	1.27 g
Polyunsaturated	0.15 g
Monounsaturated	0.40 g
Cholesterol	7.58 mg
Sodium	147.36 mg

LIGHT AND LEMONY CHICKEN AND SPINACH SOUP

The unusual flavor combination makes this a wonderful winter soup.

SERVES 2
APPROXIMATELY 1 CUP PER SERVING

2 cups homemade Chicken Stock (see page 352)
2 teaspoons fresh lemon juice
1/4 teaspoon dried thyme, crushed
1/8 teaspoon salt (optional)
4 leaves spinach or other greens such as escarole, rinsed and
    torn
Top of 1 green onion, thinly sliced

In a 1-quart saucepan, bring stock, lemon juice, thyme and salt to a boil. Put torn leaves of fresh spinach into individual soup bowls and pour hot soup over them. Top with green onions. Serve immediately.

NUTRIENT ANALYSIS

Calories	56.36 kcal
Protein	5.76 g
Carbohydrate	8.12 g
Total Fat	0.88 g
Saturated	0.18 g
Polyunsaturated	0.30 g
Monounsaturated	0.17 g
Cholesterol	6.80 mg
Sodium	208.78 mg

LENTIL-SPINACH SOUP

The cheese or yogurt completes the protein in the lentils, making this delicious soup a nourishing, high-protein main dish. This is a good recipe to double and freeze. Omit the cheese or yogurt when freezing.

SERVES 8
APPROXIMATELY 1½ CUPS PER SERVING

2 tablespoons olive oil
1 large onion, chopped
1 pound lentils, rinsed and drained
4 cups homemade Chicken Stock (see page 352)
4 cups water
1 pound fresh spinach, washed, stemmed and torn into bite-size pieces, or 1 10-ounce package frozen, chopped spinach, defrosted and squeezed dry
½ teaspoon freshly ground black pepper, or to taste
⅛ teaspoon ground allspice
4 ounces shredded part-skim mozzarella cheese or 4 ounces lightly beaten, plain, nonfat yogurt

In large stock pot or Dutch oven, heat oil over medium-high heat. Add onion and sauté until golden brown, 3 to 4 minutes. Stir in lentils, stock and water. Bring to a boil, reduce heat and cover. Simmer 45 to 60 minutes, or until lentils are tender, stirring occasionally.

Stir in spinach, pepper and allspice. Simmer, covered, 15 minutes longer. Thin the soup with additional chicken stock or water, if desired.

Serve hot, topped with either shredded cheese or whipped yogurt.

NUTRIENT ANALYSIS*

Calories	135.43 kcal
Protein	8.24 g
Carbohydrate	18.04 g
Total Fat	4.49 g
Saturated	0.65 g
Polyunsaturated	0.72 g
Monounsaturated	2.68 g
Cholesterol	3.65 mg
Sodium	54.87 mg

* Made with yogurt.

MOCK CONDENSED CREAM OF CHICKEN SOUP

MAKES ABOUT 1½ CUPS

Here is a recipe for a healthful condensed cream of chicken soup. It is excellent for use in other recipes—just use this when the recipe calls for the canned counterpart.

1 cup homemade Chicken Stock (see page 352)
1 bay leaf
¼ pound boneless chicken breast, skinned, all visible fat removed
1 tablespoon acceptable vegetable oil
3 tablespoons all-purpose flour
⅓ cup skim milk
1 tablespoon nonfat "butter" granules
Freshly ground black pepper to taste
⅛ teaspoon garlic powder
⅛ teaspoon salt (optional)

In a small saucepan, heat stock and bay leaf, uncovered, over medium-high setting until liquid simmers. Add chicken. When stock begins to simmer again, reduce heat, cover and simmer about 5 minutes, or until chicken is no longer pink inside. Remove from heat. Remove chicken from stock and set aside.

In a small saucepan, heat oil over medium heat. Add flour, stirring constantly for 1 minute. Gradually add the stock (with bay leaf), milk, "butter" granules and pepper, stirring constantly until mixture thickens, about 2 to 3 minutes. Remove from heat. Remove and discard bay leaf.

Pour into a blender or the workbowl of a food processor fitted with the metal blade and blend until smooth. Add cooked chicken, garlic powder and salt. Blend until puréed.

NUTRIENT ANALYSIS*

Calories	407.00 kcal
Protein	32.66 g
Carbohydrate	29.84 g
Total Fat	17.10 g
Saturated	2.66 g
Polyunsaturated	8.79 g
Monounsaturated	4.25 g
Cholesterol	68.44 mg
Sodium	643.19 mg

* For entire recipe.

MOCK CONDENSED CREAM OF MUSHROOM SOUP

This soup tastes incredibly similar to the store-bought version, yet it's lower in fat and sodium. Use this when a recipe calls for condensed cream of mushroom soup.

MAKES ABOUT 1⅓ CUPS

1 6-ounce can or jar sliced mushrooms
1 tablespoon acceptable vegetable oil
3 tablespoons all-purpose flour
1 bay leaf
⅓ cup skim milk
1 tablespoon nonfat "butter" granules
Freshly ground black pepper to taste
⅛ teaspoon garlic powder

NUTRIENT ANALYSIS*	
Calories	274.44 kcal
Protein	7.90 g
Carbohydrate	29.33 g
Total Fat	14.44 g
Saturated	1.91 g
Polyunsaturated	8.22 g
Monounsaturated	3.37 g
Cholesterol	1.68 mg
Sodium	851.96 mg

* For entire recipe.

Drain the liquid from the mushrooms into a measuring cup and add water, if needed, to bring the total liquid to ½ cup. Set aside.

In a small saucepan, heat oil over medium heat. Add flour and bay leaf, stirring constantly for 1 minute. Gradually add mushroom liquid, milk, "butter" granules and pepper, stirring constantly until mixture thickens, about 2 to 3 minutes. Remove pan from heat. Remove and discard bay leaf.

Pour into a blender or the workbowl of a food processor fitted with a metal blade and blend until smooth. Add mushrooms and garlic powder. Blend until puréed.

MOCK CONDENSED CREAM OF CELERY SOUP

When a recipe calls for canned
cream of celery soup, use this
instead.

¾ *cup homemade Chicken Stock (see page 352)*
1 bay leaf
1 cup thinly sliced celery
1 tablespoon acceptable vegetable oil
3 tablespoons all-purpose flour
⅓ cup skim milk
1 tablespoon nonfat "butter" granules
Freshly ground black pepper to taste
⅛ teaspoon garlic powder
⅛ teaspoon salt (optional)

In a small saucepan, heat stock, bay leaf and celery, uncovered, over medium-high setting until liquid simmers. Reduce heat, cover and cook at a low simmer 10 minutes, or until celery is tender. Remove from heat. Remove celery from stock and set aside.

In a small saucepan, heat oil over medium heat. Add flour, stirring constantly for 1 minute. Gradually add the stock (with bay leaf), milk, "butter" granules and pepper, stirring constantly until mixture thickens, about 2 to 3 minutes. Remove from heat. Remove and discard bay leaf.

Pour into a blender or the workbowl of a food processor fitted with a metal blade and blend until smooth. Add celery, garlic powder and salt. Blend until celery is puréed.

NUTRIENT ANALYSIS*

Calories	323.88 kcal
Protein	11.36 g
Carbohydrate	37.57 g
Total Fat	14.99 g
Saturated	2.10 g
Polyunsaturated	8.24 g
Monounsaturated	3.51 g
Cholesterol	8.42 mg
Sodium	782.82 mg

* For entire recipe.

CREAM OF CORN SOUP

Try this recipe when fresh corn is plentiful. This flavorful and economical soup is a real family-pleaser—and easy to halve or double if you need to.

SERVES 6
APPROXIMATELY I CUP
PER SERVING

2 cups fresh or frozen corn
   kernels
1 cup water
1 cup skim milk
¼ teaspoon freshly ground
   black pepper, or to taste
2 teaspoons low-sodium soy
   sauce
1 tablespoon cold water
1½ teaspoons cornstarch
3 egg whites from large eggs,
   lightly beaten
Hot pepper sauce to taste

NUTRIENT ANALYSIS

Calories	70.22 kcal
Protein	4.92 g
Carbohydrate	13.44 g
Total Fat	0.36 g
Saturated	0.08 g
Polyunsaturated	0.15 g
Monounsaturated	0.08 g
Cholesterol	0.82 mg
Sodium	121.40 mg

In a blender or the workbowl of a food processor fitted with the metal blade, blend corn and water until creamy. Add milk and pepper.

In a 3-quart saucepan, heat mixture over medium-high heat to boiling. Reduce heat and simmer, covered, 5 minutes. In a small bowl, mix soy sauce and 1 tablespoon cold water; add cornstarch and stir to dissolve. Add cornstarch mixture to soup and stir to thicken.

Remove from heat and add egg whites, slowly, while stirring with a fork.

Serve hot. Season with hot sauce at the table.

SPLIT PEA SOUP

SERVES 10
APPROXIMATELY 1 CUP
PER SERVING

Traditional recipes for split pea soup call for salt pork. This recipe breaks with tradition and uses ham instead: you get the taste without the fat. To cut back on sodium, use low-sodium soy sauce, generally available in the Asian or diet food section of your supermarket.

1 pound dried split green peas, rinsed and drained
8 cups water
2 carrots, scrubbed but not peeled, cut into eighths
2 medium yellow onions, cut into eighths
3 cloves garlic, quartered
2 stalks celery with leaves, cut into eighths
4 ounces lean ham, visible fat removed, cut into bite-size pieces
3 tablespoons low-sodium soy sauce
1 teaspoon chopped fresh oregano or ½ teaspoon dried oregano
½ teaspoon grated fresh ginger or ⅛ teaspoon dried ginger
3 dashes hot pepper sauce, or to taste
Freshly ground black pepper to taste

In a large saucepan or Dutch oven, bring peas, water, carrots, onions, garlic, celery and ham to a rapid boil over medium-high heat. Reduce heat and cook, covered, at a gently rolling boil, 1 to 1½ hours or until peas are soft.

Add soy sauce, oregano, ginger, hot pepper sauce and pepper. Simmer 10 minutes to blend flavors. In a blender or the workbowl of a food processor fitted with a metal blade, process two to three cups at a time, until puréed. Return to saucepan and reheat, if necessary. Serve hot.

This soup freezes well.

NUTRIENT ANALYSIS

Calories	203.73 kcal
Protein	14.68 g
Carbohydrate	34.50 g
Total Fat	2.57 g
Saturated	0.51 g
Polyunsaturated	0.85 g
Monounsaturated	0.64 g
Cholesterol	7.30 mg
Sodium	310.93 mg

TOMATO SOUP

Fresh-picked tomatoes and fresh
dill are perfect for this soup.

SERVES 6
APPROXIMATELY 1 CUP
PER SERVING

1 tablespoon olive oil
1 small onion, chopped
4 green onions, including tops, chopped
1 clove garlic, minced
2 tablespoons all-purpose flour
4 cups homemade Chicken Stock (see page 352)
3 medium ripe tomatoes (about 1 pound), chopped
½ teaspoon salt (optional)
Freshly ground black pepper to taste
½ teaspoon sugar
2 tablespoons chopped fresh dill or 1 teaspoon dried dill weed

Garnish
½ cup plain nonfat yogurt, lightly beaten
2 tablespoons chopped fresh dill (optional)

In a large saucepan, heat oil over medium-high heat. Add
onions and sauté for 2 to 3 minutes or until translucent.
Add garlic and flour; cook 1 minute, stirring constantly.
Pour in stock and heat to boiling, stirring well to combine
flour and liquid. Add tomatoes, salt, pepper, sugar and dill.
Reduce heat and simmer, covered, 30 to 40 minutes, or
until tomatoes are reduced to a pulp. Allow to cool for a
few minutes, then purée in small batches in a blender or
food processor. Reheat soup.

Serve hot. Drizzle about 1 tablespoon yogurt over each
serving and sprinkle with dill.

NUTRIENT ANALYSIS

Calories	109.21 kcal
Protein	5.35 g
Carbohydrate	15.54 g
Total Fat	3.03 g
Saturated	0.43 g
Polyunsaturated	0.29 g
Monounsaturated	1.77 g
Cholesterol	4.85 mg
Sodium	219.88 mg

TOMATO, ORANGE AND TARRAGON SOUP

Establish your culinary reputation
with this! A refreshing soup that can
be served hot or cold is a sure
winner.

SERVES 6
1½ CUPS PER SERVING

1 tablespoon acceptable vegetable oil
1 medium yellow or white onion, sliced
3 small potatoes, diced
3 large tomatoes, about 3½ pounds, chopped
2 tablespoons chopped fresh tarragon or 1 teaspoon dried
    tarragon
1 clove garlic, crushed
2 cups homemade Chicken Stock (see page 352)
¼ teaspoon salt (optional)
Freshly ground black pepper to taste
1 cup freshly squeezed orange juice
1 teaspoon freshly grated orange rind

Garnish
Few sprigs of parsley or tarragon

In a heavy saucepan, heat oil over medium-high heat. Sauté
onions and potatoes 2 to 3 minutes, or until onions are
translucent. Add tomatoes, tarragon, garlic, stock, salt and
pepper. Bring to a boil, reduce heat and simmer, covered,
20 to 25 minutes, or until vegetables are tender.

In a blender or the workbowl of a food processor fitted
with a metal blade, process in small batches until liquefied.
Pass through a sieve to remove coarse skins. Discard the
pulp that remains in the sieve.

Mix strained liquid with orange juice and rind. Reheat or
serve chilled. Garnish with fresh tarragon or parsley.

NUTRIENT ANALYSIS

Calories	106.67 kcal
Protein	3.46 g
Carbohydrate	17.68 g
Total Fat	2.76 g
Saturated	0.35 g
Polyunsaturated	1.41 g
Monounsaturated	0.60 g
Cholesterol	2.26 mg
Sodium	105.83 mg

FRESH MELON AND MANGO SOUP

Soup made with melons? You bet! With the wine and liqueur, not only is this soup beautiful, but it has a delightful taste that will surprise you.

SERVES 14
APPROXIMATELY ½ CUP PER SERVING

2 medium peaches, peeled, pitted and cubed
2 large ripe mangos, peeled, pitted and cubed
1 small ripe cantaloupe, peeled, seeded and cubed
3 cups frozen unsweetened strawberries
⅓ cup frozen orange juice concentrate
½ cup plain, nonfat yogurt
Juice of ½ lime
⅓ cup port wine
2 tablespoons orange liqueur
1½ teaspoons raspberry vinegar (see pages 111– 112)

Garnish
½ cup plain nonfat yogurt

NUTRIENT ANALYSIS

Calories	72.46 kcal
Protein	1.27 g
Carbohydrate	14.91 g
Total Fat	0.35 g
Saturated	0.03 g
Polyunsaturated	0.02 g
Monounsaturated	0.04 g
Cholesterol	0.14 mg
Sodium	9.80 mg

In the workbowl of food processor fitted with a metal blade, process all ingredients until thick and creamy. Pour into a serving bowl and freeze for about 20 minutes. Spoon into individual bowls and garnish each serving with a heaping teaspoon of yogurt. Serve immediately.

YOGURT GAZPACHO

You don't have to like yogurt to enjoy Yogurt Gazpacho. It's a sure hit when served as an appetizer before Chicken Fajitas (see pages 154–155).

SERVES 11
½ CUP PER SERVING

4 cups plain nonfat yogurt
¼ cup picante sauce
2 medium ripe tomatoes, quartered
3 green onions, including tops, quartered
⅛ teaspoon garlic powder
Fresh cilantro to taste

In a blender, process all ingredients. Pour into chilled stemware glasses and serve.

NUTRIENT ANALYSIS

Calories	56.21 kcal
Protein	5.16 g
Carbohydrate	8.46 g
Total Fat	0.21 g
Saturated	0.09 g
Polyunsaturated	0.00 g
Monounsaturated	0.03 g
Cholesterol	1.45 mg
Sodium	119.83 mg

SALADS

Salad with Creamy Mustard Vinaigrette
Spinach Salad
Boston Lettuce with Grapefruit and Pecans
Crispy Tortilla Salad
Orange Blossom Salad
Warm Mushroom Salad
Potato Salad
Tabouli Salad
Marinated Vegetable Salad
Carrot and Cabbage Stuffed Peppers
Guacamole
Deviled Eggs
Cucumbers in "Sour Cream"
Cucumber-Melon Salad with Raspberry Vinaigrette
Fresh Fruit Salad
Fresh Fruit Salad with Poppy Seed and Yogurt Dressing
Herbed Chicken Salad
Ham and Rice Salad
Salmon and Pasta Salad
Seafood Pasta Salad

SALAD WITH CREAMY MUSTARD VINAIGRETTE

This recipe makes a double batch of dressing (approximately 10 tablespoons). Use half for this recipe and save the rest for another salad.

SERVES 8

Dressing

½ cup Oil and Vinegar
    Dressing (see page 109)
½ cup tofu, 4 ounces, drained
2 tablespoons water
½ teaspoon honey
½ teaspoon Dijon mustard

Salad

1 head leaf lettuce or a
    mixture of lettuce greens,
    about ½ pound, rinsed
    and dried

Garnish

3 dried apricots, slivered
2 teaspoons sunflower seeds, toasted

NUTRIENT ANALYSIS	
Calories	140.87 kcal
Protein	3.45 g
Carbohydrate	5.69 g
Total Fat	12.41 g
Saturated	1.63 g
Polyunsaturated	1.44 g
Monounsaturated	7.92 g
Cholesterol	0.00 mg
Sodium	15.93 mg

Preheat oven to 300° F. Place sunflower seeds in baking pan and bake 12 minutes, or until very lightly browned. Remove from pan and let cool.

In a blender, process dressing ingredients until creamy.

Toss salad greens with 5 tablespoons of dressing and garnish with apricots and sunflower seeds. Refrigerate remainder of dressing for later use.

SPINACH SALAD

This colorful salad makes a wonderful light lunch or a welcome accompaniment to dinner. The dressing is best made several hours ahead and refrigerated to allow the flavors to blend.

Oil and Vinegar Dressing
3 tablespoons olive oil
3 tablespoons cider or wine vinegar
2 tablespoons water
1 to 2 teaspoons stone-ground mustard
1 tablespoon finely chopped fresh or ½ teaspoon dried herbs
   (parsley, basil, oregano, chives or tarragon)

Salad
1½ pounds fresh spinach
2 hard-cooked eggs, whites only, chopped
12 cherry tomatoes, quartered
1 small red onion, cut into thin rings
Freshly ground black pepper to taste

Combine ingredients for dressing, mix well and refrigerate.
   Thoroughly rinse spinach in cold water. Drain well. Remove and discard stems and bruised or tough leaves. Tear spinach into bite-size pieces, place in a large salad bowl and top with remaining salad ingredients.
   Pour dressing over salad and serve immediately.

NUTRIENT ANALYSIS

Calories	90.19 kcal
Protein	3.17 g
Carbohydrate	4.43 g
Total Fat	7.14 g
Saturated	0.93 g
Polyunsaturated	0.70 g
Monounsaturated	5.00 g
Cholesterol	0.00 mg
Sodium	51.23 mg

BOSTON LETTUCE WITH GRAPEFRUIT AND PECANS

SERVES 6

1 large head Boston, butter or bibb lettuce, rinsed and dried
2 grapefruit
1 tablespoon fresh lemon juice
1/3 cup pecan pieces, toasted

Tear leaves for salad. Peel and section grapefruit, collecting the juice in a bowl. Mix in the lemon juice and pour over lettuce. Toss to coat evenly.

Place lettuce on individual plates, and garnish each portion with several grapefruit sections and a sprinkling of pecan pieces.

NUTRIENT ANALYSIS

Calories	88.56 kcal
Protein	1.80 g
Carbohydrate	10.80 g
Total Fat	4.87 g
Saturated	0.41 g
Polyunsaturated	1.20 g
Monounsaturated	2.81 g
Cholesterol	0.00 mg
Sodium	4.67 mg

CRISPY TORTILLA SALAD

This crispy, light Mexican-style salad
is a favorite among chalupa lovers.
Prepare the ingredients in advance
and assemble them just before
serving.

SERVES 6

6 corn tortillas, 6-inch
   diameter
1 head iceberg lettuce,
   shredded, about 6 cups
4 ounces part-skim
   mozzarella cheese,
   shredded
2 ounces Defatted Cheddar
   Cheese (see pages 349–
   350) or commercial lowfat
   cheddar cheese, grated
1 19-ounce can kidney beans,
   rinsed and drained
3 medium tomatoes, chopped
1 cup bottled or homemade
   Salsa (see page 260)

NUTRIENT ANALYSIS

Calories	276.35 kcal
Protein	16.78 g
Carbohydrate	36.94 g
Total Fat	8.45 g
Saturated	4.27 g
Polyunsaturated	1.20 g
Monounsaturated	2.07 g
Cholesterol	20.93 mg
Sodium	624.55 mg

Preheat oven to 350° F. Bake tortillas in a single layer on a
baking sheet for 10 to 15 minutes, or until crisp and lightly
browned.

Top each tortilla with layers of shredded lettuce, cheeses,
kidney beans, tomatoes and salsa. Serve with additional
salsa on the side.

ORANGE BLOSSOM SALAD

This recipe features orange-flower water, which is available at most Middle-Eastern markets and some liquor stores, pharmacies and supermarkets. This salad goes especially well with Marinated Steak or Poached Fish in Oriental Broth (see pages 173–174 and 119–120).

3 navel oranges
4 large leaves of Boston, butter or bibb lettuce, rinsed and dried
Orange-flower water or orange liqueur (optional)
¼ cup slivered almonds, toasted

Remove the peel and pith from the oranges. Cut into ¼-inch slices. Place a lettuce leaf on each salad plate. Arrange orange slices on top. Put a few drops of orange-flower water or orange liqueur on each slice. Top with toasted almonds. Serve immediately.

NUTRIENT ANALYSIS

Calories	125.94 kcal
Protein	2.83 g
Carbohydrate	20.22 g
Total Fat	4.11 g
Saturated	0.34 g
Polyunsaturated	0.77 g
Monounsaturated	2.69 g
Cholesterol	0.00 mg
Sodium	1.56 mg

WARM MUSHROOM SALAD

SERVES 4
¼ CUP PER SERVING

2½ tablespoons balsamic or rice vinegar
1½ tablespoons water
3 tablespoons port wine (or any sweet red wine)
2 cloves garlic, finely minced
8 ounces fresh mushrooms, sliced into ¼-inch slices
1 teaspoon margarine
⅛ teaspoon freshly ground black pepper, or to taste
4 leaves of Boston lettuce, rinsed and dried
1 teaspoon chopped fresh parsley

In a nonstick skillet, heat vinegar, water, wine and garlic over medium-high heat until small bubbles begin to form. Add mushrooms and stir frequently 8 to 10 minutes, or until all liquid evaporates. Add margarine and pepper; stir to coat evenly.

Arrange mushrooms on lettuce leaves and sprinkle with chopped parsley. Serve warm.

NUTRIENT ANALYSIS

Calories	30.89 kcal
Protein	1.84 g
Carbohydrate	3.98 g
Total Fat	1.17 g
Saturated	0.18 g
Polyunsaturated	0.38 g
Monounsaturated	0.43 g
Cholesterol	0.00 mg
Sodium	23.40 mg

POTATO SALAD

A must for summer picnics and
parties, this salad is best made at
least a few hours in advance to
allow the flavors to blend. The
yogurt dressing is a low-fat version
of an all-mayonnaise dressing.

SERVES 8
I CUP PER SERVING

2 pounds potatoes, about 6 medium
2 green onions with tops, chopped
1 small red or green bell pepper, chopped
4 to 5 small radishes, minced
2 stalks celery, finely chopped
¼ cup finely chopped fresh parsley

Dressing
¼ cup reduced-calorie mayonnaise
½ cup plain nonfat yogurt
2 tablespoons cider or wine vinegar
½ teaspoon salt (optional)
1 teaspoon Dijon mustard, or to taste
½ teaspoon celery seeds
1 tablespoon fresh dill weed or 1 teaspoon dried dill weed
Freshly ground black pepper to taste

Garnish
2 tablespoons finely chopped fresh parsley
½ teaspoon paprika

B oil potatoes until tender. When cool enough to handle, peel and cut into ½-inch cubes. In a large bowl, combine potatoes with onions, bell pepper, radishes, celery and parsley. Mix together dressing ingredients and add to potato mixture. Toss gently.

Sprinkle parsley and paprika over the top. Cover and chill for at least 2 hours before serving.

NUTRIENT ANALYSIS

Calories	113.25 kcal
Protein	3.45 g
Carbohydrate	19.35 g
Total Fat	2.79 g
Saturated	0.54 g
Polyunsaturated	1.13 g
Monounsaturated	1.04 g
Cholesterol	5.25 mg
Sodium	237.87 mg

TABOULI SALAD

SERVES 6
½ CUP PER SERVING

Make this dish well in advance—the flavors improve with age. Bulgar, a finely cracked wheat, is available at health-food stores and most supermarkets. To serve, place a scoop of the salad on a leaf of lettuce, or use it to stuff tomatoes, zucchini, or peppers.

1 cup bulgar
4 cups boiling water
2 tablespoons olive oil
¼ cup fresh lemon juice
3 green onions with tops, finely chopped
2 medium tomatoes, finely chopped
¼ cup finely chopped fresh mint or 1 tablespoon dried mint
¼ cup finely chopped fresh parsley
Freshly ground black pepper to taste

NUTRIENT ANALYSIS	
Calories	149.66 kcal
Protein	3.64 g
Carbohydrate	23.39 g
Total Fat	5.06 g
Saturated	0.67 g
Polyunsaturated	0.57 g
Monounsaturated	3.37 g
Cholesterol	0.00 mg
Sodium	6.02 mg

In a large heatproof bowl, combine bulgar and boiling water. Cover and allow to stand for 1 hour, or until most of the water is absorbed. Drain bulgar, using cheesecloth to help extract most of the moisture.

Combine oil and lemon juice. Add to bulgar along with onions, tomatoes, mint, parsley and pepper. Gently toss mixture with a fork and refrigerate at least 1 hour to allow flavors to blend. Serve chilled or at room temperature.

MARINATED VEGETABLE SALAD

This salad is bright and beautiful. For a delicious sandwich, drain any leftovers and use the vegetables to stuff a pita. Garnish with a little low-fat cheddar cheese and lettuce.

SERVES 8
½ CUP PER SERVING

1 16-ounce bag frozen mixed vegetables, defrosted
1 15-ounce can chickpeas, rinsed and drained
⅓ cup low-calorie Italian salad dressing
¼ cup frozen apple juice concentrate, defrosted
1 tablespoon acceptable vegetable oil
1 tablespoon rice or white wine vinegar
2 tablespoons fresh lemon juice
2 cloves garlic, finely minced, or ¼ teaspoon garlic powder
⅛ teaspoon freshly ground black pepper, or to taste
8 leaves lettuce, rinsed and dried

NUTRIENT ANALYSIS

Calories	60.01 kcal
Protein	0.92 g
Carbohydrate	8.61 g
Total Fat	2.85 g
Saturated	0.36 g
Polyunsaturated	1.65 g
Monounsaturated	0.63 g
Cholesterol	0.60 mg
Sodium	85.32 mg

Combine frozen vegetables and chickpeas in a bowl.

In a jar with a tight-fitting lid, shake the salad dressing, juice concentrate, oil, vinegar, lemon juice, garlic and pepper to mix well. Pour over vegetable-bean mixture and mix well. Let marinate for a few hours in refrigerator. Arrange salad over lettuce leaves. Serve chilled.

CARROT AND CABBAGE STUFFED PEPPERS

Stuff pepper halves with cool, crunchy carrots and cabbage for a refreshing salad. Serve with hamburgers, baked chicken or any barbecue dish.

SERVES 6
½ PEPPER PER SERVING

3 cups finely shredded
    cabbage, about ½ pound
3 medium carrots, finely
    shredded
1 small onion, finely chopped
1 teaspoon poppy seeds
2 tablespoons olive oil
2 tablespoons cider or wine
    vinegar
1 teaspoon sugar
½ teaspoon Herb Seasoning
    (see pages 33–34)
3 green, red or yellow bell
    peppers, split in half and
    seeded

NUTRIENT ANALYSIS

Calories	99.99 kcal
Protein	2.42 g
Carbohydrate	12.82 g
Total Fat	5.11 g
Saturated	0.68 g
Polyunsaturated	0.63 g
Monounsaturated	3.37 g
Cholesterol	0.00 mg
Sodium	41.02 mg

Combine cabbage, carrots, onion and poppy seeds in a bowl. Toss lightly.

In a jar with a tight-fitting lid, shake the oil, vinegar, sugar and seasoning to blend. Pour over the cabbage-carrot mixture and mix well. Spoon mixture evenly into each pepper half. Wrap each pepper with plastic wrap and refrigerate. Serve chilled or at room temperature.

GUACAMOLE

SERVES 8
1½ TABLESPOONS
PER SERVING

A tomatillo is a small green tomato enclosed in a thin, papery husk. It is available in Latin-American markets and also may be found in some supermarkets. Guacamole can be served with Corn Crisps (see page 288) as an appetizer. It is also a great accompaniment to Mexican foods. Place a small scoop next to a serving of Mexican Beef and Cornbread Pie (see pages 185–186) or use it to garnish Chicken Fajitas (see pages 154–155).

1 medium ripe avocado,
    peeled, seeded and mashed
1 tablespoon fresh lime juice,
    about ½ of a large lime
¼ teaspoon ground cumin
1½ tablespoons Salsa (see
    page 260) or mild or
    medium picante sauce
1 medium ripe tomato or 8
    cherry tomatoes, chopped,
    about 1 cup
2 tablespoons finely chopped
    onion
1 tomatillo, husk removed, finely chopped (optional)
2 tablespoons chopped fresh cilantro, lightly packed
1 clove garlic, finely minced
Freshly ground black pepper to taste

NUTRIENT ANALYSIS

Calories	48.00 kcal
Protein	0.76 g
Carbohydrate	3.18 g
Total Fat	3.88 g
Saturated	0.61 g
Polyunsaturated	0.50 g
Monounsaturated	2.40 g
Cholesterol	0.00 mg
Sodium	32.91 mg

In a bowl, mix together all ingredients. Serve chilled or at room temperature.

DEVILED EGGS

SERVES 12
2 HALVES PER SERVING

To avoid the fat and cholesterol of regular deviled eggs, this recipe uses tofu instead of egg yolks. Flavorless itself, tofu takes on the flavors of the food mixed with it. Deviled Eggs are a great accompaniment to a picnic lunch and can also be served as appetizers.

1 dozen eggs, hard-cooked
10 ounces tofu, drained
3 tablespoons spicy brown mustard
1 tablespoon reduced-calorie mayonnaise
Paprika if desired

Remove shells from eggs. Slice eggs in half lengthwise; remove yolks and discard. Place tofu in a large bowl. Using a fork, mash tofu into small bits. Add mustard and mayonnaise and mix well. Stuff into egg whites. Top with paprika if desired. Serve chilled.

NUTRIENT ANALYSIS

Calories	40.18 kcal
Protein	5.34 g
Carbohydrate	1.31 g
Total Fat	1.58 g
Saturated	0.24 g
Polyunsaturated	0.78 g
Monounsaturated	0.42 g
Cholesterol	0.83 mg
Sodium	108.35 mg

CUCUMBERS IN "SOUR CREAM"

This is a simple way to make a
sour-cream-like sauce from cottage
cheese, yogurt and a few other
flavorful ingredients. Use the sauce
on baked potatoes or anywhere
you would use sour cream.

SERVES 6
¾ CUP PER SERVING

1 cup lowfat cottage cheese
1 small onion, finely chopped
¼ cup plain nonfat yogurt
1 tablespoon fresh lemon juice
1 tablespoon reduced-calorie mayonnaise
1 teaspoon sugar
3 medium cucumbers, peeled and thinly sliced

In a blender, process the cottage cheese, onion, yogurt,
lemon juice, mayonnaise and sugar until smooth and
creamy. Pour over cucumbers and mix well. Serve chilled.

NUTRIENT ANALYSIS

Calories	60.32 kcal
Protein	5.79 g
Carbohydrate	5.77 g
Total Fat	1.65 g
Saturated	0.65 g
Polyunsaturated	0.39 g
Monounsaturated	0.54 g
Cholesterol	4.67 mg
Sodium	178.87 mg

CUCUMBER-MELON SALAD WITH RASPBERRY VINAIGRETTE

Serve this refreshingly different dish as a salad or a relish. To make a relish, simply chop the ingredients finely.

SERVES 4
¾ CUP PER SERVING

1 cucumber, scrubbed and partially peeled to leave some dark
   green for color
½ large cantaloupe, seeded
1 bunch radishes, scrubbed
¼ cup raspberry vinegar (see pages 111–112)
Freshly ground black pepper (optional)
4 leaves leaf lettuce, rinsed and dried

Cut cucumber into bite-size pieces. Cut cantaloupe into cubes or small melon balls. Thinly slice the radishes. In a medium bowl, combine cucumber, cantaloupe and radishes. Toss with vinegar and sprinkle with pepper. Serve chilled on individual plates lined with leaf lettuce.

NUTRIENT ANALYSIS

Calories	39.06 kcal
Protein	1.36 g
Carbohydrate	9.15 g
Total Fat	0.33 g
Saturated	0.01 g
Polyunsaturated	0.02 g
Monounsaturated	0.00 g
Cholesterol	0.00 mg
Sodium	15.89 mg

FRESH FRUIT SALAD

Choose seasonal fruit such as
peaches, oranges, pineapples,
seedless grapes or fresh or frozen
berries for this refreshing dish.
Purchase raspberry vinegar in
gourmet stores or make at home.

SERVES 4
I CUP PER SERVING

4 cups assorted fresh fruit, sliced
1 to 2 tablespoons raspberry vinegar (see pages 111–112)

S lice fruit and arrange on a serving plate. Sprinkle with
raspberry vinegar, cover and chill.

NUTRIENT ANALYSIS*

Calories	87.26 kcal
Protein	1.28 g
Carbohydrate	22.19 g
Total Fat	0.49 g
Saturated	0.06 g
Polyunsaturated	0.11 g
Monounsaturated	0.04 g
Cholesterol	0.00 mg
Sodium	1.21 mg

* Based on a salad made up of peaches, oranges,
pineapples, seedless grapes and unsweetened
strawberries.

FRESH FRUIT SALAD WITH POPPY SEED AND YOGURT DRESSING

Let your imagination run wild: use dramatically different combinations of fresh fruit. The dressing will only enhance the flavor—guaranteed!

SERVES 6
½ CUP PER SERVING

3 cups assorted fresh fruit, cut into bite-size pieces
1 cup lowfat lemon yogurt
¼ teaspoon poppy seeds

P lace fruit in individual serving bowls. In a small bowl, mix yogurt and poppy seeds with a whisk, then pour over fruit, using 2 to 3 tablespoons per serving.

NUTRIENT ANALYSIS

Calories	92.15 kcal
Protein	2.52 g
Carbohydrate	20.47 g
Total Fat	0.73 g
Saturated	0.35 g
Polyunsaturated	0.09 g
Monounsaturated	0.14 g
Cholesterol	1.60 mg
Sodium	27.62 mg

HERBED CHICKEN SALAD

This salad is excellent used as
stuffing for tomatoes, peppers or
zucchini. It is also good in pita
pockets, in sandwiches or on whole
wheat crackers.

SERVES 6
½ CUP PER SERVING

2 cups cooked chicken, cut
   into bite-size pieces
¼ cup plain nonfat yogurt
¼ cup reduced-calorie
   mayonnaise
2 green onions with tops,
   thinly sliced
1 small carrot, grated
2 radishes, grated
3 tablespoons chopped celery
2 tablespoons chopped green
   pepper
2 tablespoons chopped fresh parsley
1 teaspoon Worcestershire sauce
1 teaspoon Herb Seasoning (see pages 33–34)
¼ teaspoon freshly ground black pepper, or to taste
1½ tablespoons tarragon vinegar

NUTRIENT ANALYSIS

Calories	145.94 kcal
Protein	14.70 g
Carbohydrate	11.70 g
Total Fat	4.59 g
Saturated	1.10 g
Polyunsaturated	1.68 g
Monounsaturated	1.26 g
Cholesterol	40.24 mg
Sodium	111.80 mg

Garnish
Lettuce leaves, rinsed and dried
1 8-ounce can mandarin oranges packed in fruit juice, drained,
   or 3 small tomatoes, sliced

Combine all salad ingredients except garnish. Mix well,
cover and refrigerate at least 1 hour. To serve, place a scoop
of salad on a lettuce leaf and garnish with orange segments
or tomato slices.

HAM AND RICE SALAD

This makes a terrific one-dish entree. Team it with fresh fruit salad and crusty bread.

SERVES 8
1¼ CUPS PER SERVING

1 cup long-grain or brown rice
2 to 2½ cups homemade Chicken Stock (see page 352)
8 ounces lean ham, visible fat removed, cut into ¼-inch cubes
1 cup fresh or frozen corn kernels, defrosted
1 cup frozen green peas, defrosted
4 green onions with tops, thinly sliced
1 medium red, yellow or green bell pepper, finely chopped
4 to 5 radishes, finely chopped
¼ cup minced fresh parsley
1 tablespoon fresh dill weed or 1 teaspoon dried dill weed

Dressing

3 tablespoons acceptable vegetable oil
¼ cup herbed or wine vinegar
½ teaspoon Dijon mustard
¼ teaspoon salt (optional)
Freshly ground black pepper to taste

Garnish

1 small head lettuce, preferably red leaf, rinsed and dried
Few sprigs fresh mint or parsley

Cook rice according to package instructions, substituting stock for liquid and omitting salt. Allow to cool.

In a large bowl, combine rice, ham, corn, peas, green onions, pepper, radishes, parsley and dill weed. In a small bowl, mix together oil, vinegar, mustard, salt and pepper to make the dressing.

Combine dressing and rice mixture, tossing lightly. Store

refrigerated. Serve at room temperature or chilled. Place a scoop on a bed of lettuce and garnish with mint or parsley sprigs.

NUTRIENT ANALYSIS

Calories	221.02 kcal
Protein	10.96 g
Carbohydrate	27.04 g
Total Fat	8.23 g
Saturated	1.62 g
Polyunsaturated	3.54 g
Monounsaturated	2.43 g
Cholesterol	21.69 mg
Sodium	290.16 mg

SALMON AND PASTA SALAD

This easy-to-fix main dish or appetizer salad is great for hot summer days. Mash the bones of the salmon to get full benefit of the calcium they contain. To get all the fiber from the bell pepper, leave in the pith (white inner ribs).

1 cup uncooked elbow macaroni, 4 ounces
2 teaspoons acceptable vegetable oil
1 7⅔-ounce can salmon, drained, skin removed
1 tablespoon Worcestershire sauce
½ medium white onion, minced
1 10-ounce package frozen green peas, slightly defrosted
1 large red bell pepper, diced

Dressing
1 cup lowfat cottage cheese
2 tablespoons fresh lemon juice
2 to 3 dashes hot pepper sauce
1 to 2 tablespoons chopped fresh dill weed or 1 to 2 teaspoons
   dried dill weed

Cook macaroni according to package directions, omitting salt. Drain and rinse under cold running water until noodles are cool. Drain, place in bowl and add oil; mix to coat evenly. Set aside.

In a bowl, mash salmon, including bones. Add Worcestershire, onion, peas, bell pepper and cooked macaroni. Mix well.

In a blender, process cottage cheese, lemon juice and hot pepper sauce until creamy. Mix in dill. Pour over the salmon-noodle mixture and stir. Refrigerate. Serve chilled.

NUTRIENT ANALYSIS

Calories	164.68 kcal
Protein	13.40 g
Carbohydrate	18.31 g
Total Fat	4.27 g
Saturated	1.12 g
Polyunsaturated	1.37 g
Monounsaturated	1.34 g
Cholesterol	11.78 mg
Sodium	314.81 mg

SEAFOOD PASTA SALAD

SERVES 6
1½ CUPS PER SERVING

This versatile, one-dish meal is quick to prepare and elegant to serve. For an interesting look, select pasta shapes such as shells, corkscrews or twists. Prepare a few hours before serving to heighten flavors.

1 10-ounce package dry pasta
2 cups cooked seafood, skin and bones removed (see recipe for Poached Fish and Fish Stock, pages 115–116)
1 small red onion, finely chopped
1 medium red, green or yellow bell pepper, chopped
4 to 5 radishes, finely chopped
1 cup frozen green peas, defrosted
¼ cup minced fresh basil or 2 tablespoons dried basil
¼ cup minced fresh parsley

Dressing
3 tablespoons olive oil
¼ cup herbed wine or white vinegar
½ teaspoon Dijon mustard
¼ teaspoon salt (optional)
Freshly ground black pepper to taste

Garnish
1 small head romaine lettuce, rinsed and dried
2 small tomatoes, cut into wedges

Cook pasta according to package directions, omitting salt. Drain and rinse under cold running water until pasta is cool.

In a large bowl, combine pasta, seafood, onion, pepper,

radishes, peas, basil and parsley. In a small bowl, mix to-gether oil, vinegar, mustard, salt and pepper. Add to the pasta mixture; toss lightly to combine. Store refrigerated. Serve at room temperature or chilled.

For an attractive presentation, line a serving bowl or a platter with lettuce, fill with pasta and top with tomato wedges.

NUTRIENT ANALYSIS

Calories	303.60 kcal
Protein	12.54 g
Carbohydrate	46.27 g
Total Fat	7.89 g
Saturated	1.08 g
Polyunsaturated	0.94 g
Monounsaturated	5.08 g
Cholesterol	11.23 mg
Sodium	144.31 mg

SALAD DRESSINGS

Creamy Vinaigrette
Creamy Herb Dressing
Oil and Vinegar Dressing
Low-Calorie Dressing
Herbed or Fruit Vinegar

CREAMY VINAIGRETTE

Pureeing the artichoke hearts makes this a wonderfully smooth dressing. After making the dressing, you will still have half a can of artichoke hearts left. Just toss them in with your salad!

SERVES 12
1 TABLESPOON PER SERVING

2 cloves garlic, minced
1/2 cup olive oil
2 tablespoons fresh lemon juice
1/2 teaspoon Dijon mustard
1/4 teaspoon freshly ground black pepper
1/2 14-ounce can artichoke hearts, drained

In a blender or the workbowl of a food processor fitted with a metal blade, process all ingredients until silky smooth. Chill and serve over salad greens.

NUTRIENT ANALYSIS

Calories	83.98 kcal
Protein	0.38 g
Carbohydrate	1.49 g
Total Fat	9.04 g
Saturated	1.22 g
Polyunsaturated	0.76 g
Monounsaturated	6.63 g
Cholesterol	0.00 mg
Sodium	6.68 mg

CREAMY HERB DRESSING

Serve this dressing hot or cold! It
can be used as a dip or a dressing
for salads, poultry, baked potatoes
or cold seafood.

SERVES 20
1 TABLESPOON PER SERVING

½ cup nonfat yogurt
½ cup lowfat sour cream
2 tablespoons minced fresh parsley or cilantro
½ teaspoon Lemon Herb Seasoning (see page 34)
1 green onion with top, minced
½ teaspoon honey or sugar
¼ teaspoon Italian seasoning (optional)

U sing a hand beater, whip together yogurt and sour cream.
Stir in remaining ingredients. Keeps well when refrigerated.

To serve hot, gently warm over medium heat, stirring
until heated throughout. Do not boil.

NUTRIENT ANALYSIS

Calories	25.00 kcal
Protein	1.54 g
Carbohydrate	2.97 g
Total Fat	0.83 g
Saturated	0.52 g
Polyunsaturated	0.03 g
Monounsaturated	0.24 g
Cholesterol	3.04 mg
Sodium	22.00 mg

OIL AND VINEGAR DRESSING

Make this dressing several hours
ahead and refrigerate to allow the
flavors to blend.

SERVES 6
1½ TABLESPOONS
PER SERVING

3 tablespoons olive oil
3 tablespoons cider or wine vinegar
2 tablespoons water
1 to 2 teaspoons stone-ground mustard
1 tablespoon finely chopped fresh or ½ teaspoon dried parsley,
    sweet basil, oregano, chives or tarragon

In a jar with a tight-fitting lid, combine ingredients. Shake
well to blend.

NUTRIENT ANALYSIS

Calories	62.62 kcal
Protein	0.17 g
Carbohydrate	0.15 g
Total Fat	6.94 g
Saturated	0.92 g
Polyunsaturated	0.61 g
Monounsaturated	4.99 g
Cholesterol	0.00 mg
Sodium	0.12 mg

LOW-CALORIE DRESSING

Substituting other herbs such as mint, oregano, tarragon or herb seasoning for the parsley will give a range of flavored salad dressings.

SERVES 6
2 TABLESPOONS PER SERVING

1 6-ounce can vegetable or tomato juice
1 tablespoon very finely chopped onion
1 tablespoon very finely chopped celery
1 tablespoon very finely chopped bell pepper
1 tablespoon grated carrot
1 teaspoon fresh lemon juice
1/2 teaspoon sugar
1 tablespoon finely chopped fresh parsley or cilantro or
    1/2 teaspoon dried parsley or cilantro
1/4 teaspoon hot pepper sauce (optional) or 1/2 teaspoon
    Worcestershire sauce (optional)
Freshly ground black pepper to taste

In a jar with a tight-fitting lid, combine all ingredients. Shake well and refrigerate for at least 2 hours, allowing flavors to blend.

NUTRIENT ANALYSIS

Calories	10.95 kcal
Protein	0.39 g
Carbohydrate	2.54 g
Total Fat	0.05 g
Saturated	0.00 g
Polyunsaturated	0.00 g
Monounsaturated	0.00 g
Cholesterol	0.00 mg
Sodium	114.36 mg

HERBED OR FRUIT VINEGAR

**MAKES APPROXIMATELY
1½ QUARTS**

Herbed vinegars are simple to make. They are delicious substitutes for salt
and for high-fat salad dressings: They taste wonderful on salads and
vegetables. Use them as marinades or as a base for mayonnaise. Invent
your own flavors and make several bottles! Here are some ideas to get you
started.

1 quart red or white vinegar
2 tablespoons black, white or green peppercorns, crushed
2 cups fresh herbs such as oregano, rosemary, tarragon, thyme,
    sage or chopped shallots; or berries such as blueberries,
    blackberries or raspberries
2 to 4 cloves garlic (optional)
2 tablespoons juniper berries (optional)

In a nonaluminum saucepan, bring vinegar and pepper
to a boil, remove from heat and allow to cool to 120° to
125° F., or until still very warm.

Wash and dry two quart-size bottles or several smaller
jars. Use inexpensive corked bottles, which are available in
most cookware stores, or use your own clean wine bottles
and corks.

Divide the fresh herbs or berries among the bottles and
add garlic and juniper berries. Pour in vinegar to about 2
inches from the top, allowing room for the flavors to mel-
low. Cork the bottles and allow to mature for at least 2
weeks before using.

Some other good ingredient combinations include:
• White wine vinegar or white distilled vinegar, black pepper, tarragon and
  shallots

- Red wine vinegar, white pepper, rosemary and blueberries
- Red wine vinegar, black pepper, thyme and juniper berries
- Cider vinegar, black pepper, tarragon and garlic
- Balsamic vinegar, sage and blackberries

NUTRIENT ANALYSIS*

Calories	46.15 kcal
Protein	2.15 g
Carbohydrate	10.12 g
Total Fat	0.70 g
Saturated	0.06 g
Polyunsaturated	0.07 g
Monounsaturated	0.06 g
Cholesterol	0.00 mg
Sodium	7.13 mg

* For entire recipe.

FISH

Poached Fish and Fish Stock
Stuffed Fillet of Fish
Poached Fish in Oriental Broth
Broiled Fish Steaks
Halibut Kabobs
Fish in a Package
Fish with Mustard Sauce over Steamed Spinach
Crispy Fish with Fennel Seeds
Fish Stew
Seafood Cioppino
Baked Crabmeat
Tuna-Noodle Casserole
Creamed Tuna and Peas over English Muffins
Tuna Salad Pita Sandwiches

POACHED FISH AND FISH STOCK

SERVES 3
APPROXIMATELY 4 OUNCES
PER SERVING

Poaching is an excellent way to prepare fish. It's easy and requires little cleanup. Try poached fish with the Caper Sauce for Fish (page 255) or the sauce used in the Chilled Stuffed Artichoke recipe (pages 210–211).

To judge the cooking time, measure the fish at its thickest point and allow 10 minutes poaching time for each inch of thickness.

1 small carrot, coarsely chopped
1 stalk celery, coarsely chopped
1 small onion, coarsely chopped
2 tablespoons white wine vinegar or rice vinegar
8 whole black peppercorns
1 bay leaf
1 pound fish fillets, fresh or frozen and defrosted

In a large skillet, place vegetables, vinegar, peppercorns and bay leaf. Lay fish on top and add cool tap water just to cover. Heat, uncovered, over medium heat until water begins to simmer; make sure the water does not boil. Simmer for about 10 minutes per inch of thickness at the thickest point, until flesh is firm and no longer translucent.

Remove fish to a serving platter by carefully lifting with two large, slotted spatulas. Let sit for a few minutes, then drain off any excess liquid. To serve cold, allow fish that has been refrigerated to stand at room temperature for 10 to 15 minutes; this enhances its flavor.

Strain the poaching liquid to make fish stock for use in soups, sauces or for poaching other fish.

The poaching liquid may be stored in the refrigerator for up to 2 days or frozen for up to 3 months.

NUTRIENT ANALYSIS

Calories	120.05 kcal
Protein	21.86 g
Carbohydrate	6.06 g
Total Fat	1.15 g
Saturated	0.19 g
Polyunsaturated	0.39 g
Monounsaturated	0.11 g
Cholesterol	67.36 mg
Sodium	149.53 mg

STUFFED FILLET OF FISH

This dish can be prepared ahead: **SERVES 6**
Fillets can be stuffed, covered with
plastic wrap and refrigerated for
several hours before baking.

Vegetable oil spray
6 fish fillets, such as sole or flounder, about 5 ounces each
½ teaspoon white pepper
½ teaspoon paprika
1 tablespoon acceptable vegetable oil
6 ounces fresh mushrooms, finely chopped
4 green onions with tops, finely chopped
¼ cup chopped almonds
¼ cup unseasoned bread crumbs
¼ cup minced fresh parsley
½ tablespoon acceptable vegetable oil

Garnish
2 tablespoons minced fresh parsley

Preheat oven to 375° F. Lightly grease six ovenproof 6-ounce custard cups or one muffin pan with six 2½ × 1¼-inch cups with vegetable oil spray. Curl each fillet inside a custard or muffin cup. Sprinkle with pepper and paprika.

In a nonstick skillet, heat 1 tablespoon oil over medium-high heat. Add mushrooms and onions and sauté until tender, about 2 minutes. Remove skillet from heat. Stir in almonds, bread crumbs and parsley. Spoon mixture equally into center of each fillet.

Brush tops with remaining oil. Bake 15 minutes, or until fish is no longer translucent. Carefully remove each stuffed fillet from cup, spoon juice over top and garnish with parsley.

NUTRIENT ANALYSIS

Calories	177.26 kcal
Protein	22.25 g
Carbohydrate	6.49 g
Total Fat	7.31 g
Saturated	0.88 g
Polyunsaturated	2.95 g
Monounsaturated	2.77 g
Cholesterol	63.98 mg
Sodium	143.69 mg

POACHED FISH
IN ORIENTAL BROTH

Packed with spices and seasonings,
this broth gives the fish a delicate
flavor. Carrot as the final touch
makes the dish pretty enough for
company.

SERVES 4
APPROXIMATELY 4 OUNCES
PER SERVING

2 tablespoons dry sherry
3 cups homemade Chicken Stock (see page 352)
2 tablespoons low-sodium soy sauce
2 slices fresh lemon
3 thin slices fresh ginger
⅛ teaspoon cayenne pepper
1¼ pounds orange roughy or other thick, mild fish fillets
5 to 6 green onions, tops only, cut into 1-inch pieces
1 medium red bell pepper, cut into ¼ × 1-inch pieces
1 stalk celery, cut into ¼ × 1-inch pieces
½ teaspoon sesame oil
1 carrot, grated
Freshly ground black pepper to taste

In a nonaluminum fish poacher, a wok or a large skillet
bring sherry, chicken stock, soy sauce, lemon, ginger and
cayenne pepper to a boil. Reduce heat and add fish and a
little water, if needed, to just cover fish. Simmer in stock for
10 minutes per inch of thickness at the thickest point, or
just until fish is no longer translucent. Do not overcook.

Remove fish with slotted spatulas and place equal portions in four soup bowls. Return liquid to a boil. Add green
onions, bell pepper and celery. Cook 2 to 3 minutes, or
until tender-crisp. Remove and discard ginger and lemon.
Using a slotted spoon, remove vegetables and place over

fish. Stir sesame oil into poaching liquid. Evenly pour liquid over fish and vegetables in bowls.

Scatter grated carrot and grind fresh pepper over each serving. Serve immediately.

NUTRIENT ANALYSIS

Calories	159.86 kcal
Protein	24.10 g
Carbohydrate	12.05 g
Total Fat	2.21 g
Saturated	0.39 g
Polyunsaturated	0.76 g
Monounsaturated	0.45 g
Cholesterol	68.89 mg
Sodium	496.22 mg

BROILED FISH STEAKS

This elegant entree, accompanied by wild rice and sautéed mixed vegetables or a tossed salad, is quick and easy to prepare. Salmon steaks are particularly delicious prepared this way.

SERVES 6
APPROXIMATELY 4 OUNCES
PER SERVING

6 fish steaks, approximately
 ¹/₂ inch thick, about 5
 ounces each
2 tablespoons reduced-calorie
 mayonnaise
1 tablespoon Lemon Herb
 Seasoning (see page 34)
Paprika to taste

Garnish
1 lemon, sliced thin
6 sprigs fresh parsley

NUTRIENT ANALYSIS

Calories	229.38 kcal
Protein	21.81 g
Carbohydrate	2.79 g
Total Fat	14.93 g
Saturated	3.62 g
Polyunsaturated	4.06 g
Monounsaturated	5.55 g
Cholesterol	86.34 mg
Sodium	142.67 mg

P reheat broiler.

Rinse fish and pat dry. Lightly coat both sides of each fish piece with mayonnaise. Place in a shallow baking dish. Sprinkle with half of the lemon herb seasoning and paprika. Broil 3 to 4 minutes. Turn fish and sprinkle with remaining seasonings. Broil for another 3 to 4 minutes, or until fish flakes when tested with a fork or is no longer translucent. Garnish with lemon slices and a sprig of fresh parsley. Serve immediately.

HALIBUT KABOBS

SERVES 4
I KABOB PER SERVING

This skewered main dish is elegant and easy to prepare. It looks especially pretty when served on a bed of Spaghetti Squash (see page 242). If you use wooden skewers, soak them in water for at least 30 minutes to keep the wood from charring while broiling.

1 pound halibut steak, 1 inch thick
¼ cup fresh lemon juice, juice of 1 lemon
¼ cup olive oil
3 shallots, thinly sliced
1 teaspoon Italian herb seasoning
½ teaspoon dried thyme, crushed
½ large red onion, cut lengthwise into thirds

Garnish
1 lemon, cut into wedges

P reheat broiler.

Cut fish into 1-inch cubes and set aside. In a bowl, mix lemon juice, oil, shallots, herb seasoning and thyme. Add fish and toss to coat. Marinate in refrigerator for at least 5 minutes, but no more than 1 hour.

Pry onion apart into single layers. Thread each skewer, alternating onion and fish, using four pieces of fish and five pieces of onion.

Place skewers on a broiler pan and broil four inches from heat 2 to 2½ minutes on each side, or until fish is no longer translucent. Garnish with lemon wedges.

NUTRIENT ANALYSIS

Calories	149.36 kcal
Protein	16.45 g
Carbohydrate	5.03 g
Total Fat	7.65 g
Saturated	1.06 g
Polyunsaturated	0.89 g
Monounsaturated	5.06 g
Cholesterol	51.03 mg
Sodium	91.08 mg

FISH IN A PACKAGE

SERVES 10
APPROXIMATELY 5 OUNCES
PER SERVING

The fish used in this recipe can be bass, red snapper, large mackerel, bluefish or haddock. To make the preparation easy, use fish fillets. Presenting the fish in foil makes quite a dramatic entree. Serve it with a crisp green salad, wild rice, carrots and a fresh fruit dessert.

1 6- to-7-pound fish, scaled, cleaned and head removed, if
*   desired, or 10 fish fillets, 5 ounces each*

Stuffing
1 tablespoon acceptable vegetable oil
1 small onion, chopped
½ pound fresh mushrooms, sliced
¼ cup minced fresh parsley
2 tablespoons fresh dill weed or 2 teaspoons dried dill weed
½ cup unseasoned bread crumbs
½ teaspoon salt (optional)
Freshly ground black pepper to taste
½ fresh lemon
½ cup white wine or homemade Chicken Stock (see page 352)

Garnish
1 lemon, sliced
Fresh parsley sprigs

P reheat oven to 350° F.

Rinse fish and pat dry. Slit fish along the belly to make a cavity for the stuffing. If using fish fillets, place the stuffing between two fillets, skin-side out.

To prepare the stuffing, heat oil in a heavy, nonstick

skillet over medium-high heat. Sauté onion lightly 2 to 3 minutes, or until translucent. Add mushrooms and continue to sauté for another 5 minutes. Remove from heat. Stir in parsley, dill weed, bread crumbs, salt and pepper. Squeeze lemon juice over stuffing and set aside to cool and to allow bread crumbs to absorb the lemon juice.

Line a baking sheet with a sheet of heavy-duty foil long enough to wrap and seal the foil package around the fish. Place fish in center of foil and spoon stuffing into cavity just before baking. Use toothpicks to secure fish. Drizzle with wine or stock. Wrap foil over fish and seal tightly to prevent steam and flavor from escaping. Bake whole fish 1 to 1¼ hours. If using fillets, bake about 45 minutes, or until fish flakes very easily with fork.

Use caution when opening foil package, to prevent steam burn. Fish is done when no longer translucent. Carefully slide fish onto serving platter and garnish with lemon slices and parsley.

NUTRIENT ANALYSIS

Calories	178.91 kcal
Protein	31.34 g
Carbohydrate	6.70 g
Total Fat	3.18 g
Saturated	0.51 g
Polyunsaturated	1.45 g
Monounsaturated	0.56 g
Cholesterol	95.94 mg
Sodium	309.89 mg

FISH WITH MUSTARD SAUCE OVER STEAMED SPINACH

The golden mustard sauce, white fish and dark green spinach make for a picture-perfect plate.

**SERVES 4
APPROXIMATELY 4 OUNCES
PER SERVING**

4 fish fillets, sole or flounder, about 5 ounces each
1/4 cup prepared reduced-calorie ranch dressing
1 1/2 tablespoons prepared yellow mustard
3 tablespoons plain nonfat yogurt
1/2 pound fresh spinach

NUTRIENT ANALYSIS

Calories	128.71 kcal
Protein	22.53 g
Carbohydrate	6.15 g
Total Fat	2.09 g
Saturated	0.31 g
Polyunsaturated	0.92 g
Monounsaturated	0.31 g
Cholesterol	63.98 mg
Sodium	353.09 mg

Preheat oven to 400° F.

Rinse fish and pat dry. Arrange in ovenproof glass baking dish.

Mix the dressing, mustard and yogurt. Spoon evenly over fish. Bake until done or until fish is no longer translucent, about 10 minutes per inch of thickness at the thickest point.

While fish is baking, remove tough stems from spinach and rinse. Heat a nonstick skillet over medium-high heat. When skillet is hot, add spinach and stir-fry just to wilt the leaves, about 30 seconds. Arrange spinach in single layer on serving plates. Top with baked fish. Serve immediately.

CRISPY FISH WITH FENNEL SEEDS

Here is a low-cholesterol recipe for
people who like their fish breaded
and fried. For a different taste, try
your favorite herb seasoning
instead of fennel seeds.

SERVES 4
APPROXIMATELY 4 OUNCES
PER SERVING

1 cup all-purpose flour
2 large egg whites, lightly beaten
1¼ cups whole-grain wheat and barley nugget cereal
1 tablespoon fennel seeds or 2 tablespoons Lemon Herb
    Seasoning (see page 34)
4 fish fillets, orange roughy or any other white fish, about 5
    ounces each, about ½-inch thick

Garnish
1 lemon, cut into wedges

Preheat oven to 400° F.

Select three pie plates or similar dishes with shallow
sides. In the first dish, place flour. In the second, place egg
whites. In the third, place cereal mixed with fennel seeds or
herb seasoning.

Rinse fish and pat dry. Dredge a fillet in flour, turning to
coat both sides. Shake off excess. Then place it in the egg
whites, again coating both sides. Finally, put it in the cereal-
seasoning mixture, turning to coat both sides. Repeat for
each fillet.

Lay fillets on ungreased baking sheet. Bake until fish is

no longer translucent, allowing about 10 minutes per inch thickness at the thickest point. Serve with lemon wedges.

NUTRIENT ANALYSIS

Calories	308.27 kcal
Protein	27.85 g
Carbohydrate	47.49 g
Total Fat	2.69 g
Saturated	0.22 g
Polyunsaturated	0.51 g
Monounsaturated	0.27 g
Cholesterol	63.97 mg
Sodium	271.11 mg

FISH STEW

SERVES 6
I CUP PER SERVING

A delicacy from the West Indies, this fragrant stew is not only simple to make, it also tastes wonderful and is a refreshing change from the usual baked fish. Serve it with a loaf of crusty bread or on a bed of hot rice.

¼ cup fresh lemon juice
1½ pounds fish fillets, at least ¾-inch thick, skinned, boned and
    cut into 2-inch squares
8 green onions with tops, thinly sliced
1 cup chopped tomatoes
3 cloves garlic, minced
½ tablespoon minced fresh ginger or ½ teaspoon ground ginger
1½ cups water
¼ cup ketchup
½ cup chopped fresh parsley

Sprinkle lemon juice over fish, mix well and set aside.
    In a 2½- to 3-quart saucepan over medium-high heat, cook green onions 1 minute, or until wilted. Add tomatoes and cook an additional 2 to 3 minutes, or until tomatoes are almost reduced to a pulp. Add garlic, ginger, water, ketchup and parsley. Reduce heat, cover pan and allow to simmer 10 minutes.
    Add fish and continue to simmer, covered, another 10 to 15 mintues, or until fish is almost cooked. Remove cover

and simmer another 4 to 5 minutes to thicken sauce. Serve hot.

NUTRIENT ANALYSIS

Calories	102.50 kcal
Protein	16.77 g
Carbohydrate	7.29 g
Total Fat	0.96 g
Saturated	0.15 g
Polyunsaturated	0.31 g
Monounsaturated	0.08 g
Cholesterol	50.83 mg
Sodium	208.45 mg

SEAFOOD CIOPPINO

SERVES 5
2 CUPS PER SERVING

Cioppino, a meal in a bowl, is great for entertaining because there is no last-minute cooking to worry about. Serve with crusty bread, salad and fresh fruit for dessert. This dish freezes well, though afterward the fish will be darker than when fresh; the flavor, however will be just as good or even better.

1 tablespoon acceptable vegetable oil
½ cup coarsely chopped celery
1 large carrot, thinly sliced
1 medium green pepper, coarsely chopped
½ large yellow onion, coarsely chopped
1 6-ounce can no-salt-added tomato puree
3 8-ounce bottles clam juice
1½ cups dry white wine
1 bay leaf
1 8-ounce can baby clams
1 pound halibut or shark steaks, skin removed, cut into 1-inch
  pieces
1 tablespoon chopped fresh basil or 1 teaspoon dried basil
1 teaspoon chopped fresh oregano or ¼ teaspoon dried oregano
1 teaspoon chopped fresh thyme or ¼ teaspoon dried thyme
¼ cup finely chopped fresh parsley
5 crab claws

In a large nonstick skillet over medium-high heat, heat oil. Add celery, carrots, pepper and onion and sauté until tender, about 5 to 7 minutes. Set aside.

In a 4-quart saucepan, bring tomato puree, clam juice, white wine and bay leaf to a boil, covered. Add clams (including juice), shark or halibut, basil, oregano, thyme and parsley. Return mixture to a boil, reduce heat and allow to simmer 15 minutes, partially covered. Add crab and heat for 2 minutes more. Remove bay leaf and serve immediately.

NUTRIENT ANALYSIS

Calories	245.56 kcal
Protein	31.94 g
Carbohydrate	17.20 g
Total Fat	5.52 g
Saturated	0.82 g
Polyunsaturated	2.41 g
Monounsaturated	1.10 g
Cholesterol	111.96 mg
Sodium	256.59 mg

BAKED CRABMEAT

This dish is a real treat—light, festive and healthful.

**SERVES 6 AS AN ENTREE
2 OUNCES PER SERVING
SERVES 12 AS AN APPETIZER
1 OUNCE PER SERVING**

Vegetable oil spray
1 tablespoon acceptable
   margarine
¼ cup finely chopped onion
1 pound crabmeat, all
   cartilage removed
2 tablespoons Dijon mustard
1 teaspoon Worcestershire
   sauce
4 large egg whites, stiffly
   beaten
2 tablespoons Parmesan
   cheese

NUTRIENT ANALYSIS*

Calories	121.45 kcal
Protein	16.70 g
Carbohydrate	2.29 g
Total Fat	4.01 g
Saturated	0.97 g
Polyunsaturated	1.17 g
Monounsaturated	1.37 g
Cholesterol	77.42 mg
Sodium	333.27 mg

* Based on entree-size serving.

Preheat oven to 350° F. Spray a 9 × 9-inch ovenproof casserole dish with vegetable oil spray.

In a small pan over medium-high heat, melt margarine. Add onions and sauté 2 to 3 minutes, or until soft. In a medium bowl, combine onion, crabmeat, mustard and Worcestershire sauce. Gently fold in beaten egg whites. Pour mixture into casserole dish and sprinkle with cheese.

Bake 25 minutes, or until puffed and lightly browned. Remove from oven and cut into squares. Serve immediately.

TUNA-NOODLE CASSEROLE

This lowfat version of an old
standby will please everyone in
your family. Be prepared in case
they ask for seconds!

SERVES 6
1 3 × 5-INCH PORTION
PER SERVING

1 8-ounce package linguine, vermicelli, spaghetti or other thin
    noodles
1 teaspoon acceptable vegetable oil
1 small onion, chopped
1 clove garlic, minced
2 6½-ounce cans tuna, in spring water, drained and rinsed
⅓ cup finely chopped green bell pepper
½ cup finely chopped carrots
¼ cup finely chopped fresh parsley
¼ teaspoon paprika, or to taste
½ cup lowfat sour cream
1 cup lowfat cottage cheese
½ cup plain nonfat yogurt
½ cup bread crumbs, toasted
¼ cup grated Parmesan cheese

Cook noodles according to directions on package, omitting
salt. Rinse and drain.

Preheat oven to 350° F.

In nonstick skillet, heat oil over medium-high heat; sauté
onion and garlic until onion is transparent, 2 to 3 minutes,
stirring frequently.

In a large bowl, combine sautéed onion and garlic with
tuna, green pepper, carrots, parsley and paprika; set aside.

In a small bowl, blend together sour cream, cottage
cheese and yogurt; add to tuna mixture along with noodles.
Pour into a 9 × 11 × 2-inch casserole. Combine bread
crumbs and Parmesan cheese and sprinkle over top of casserole. Bake 30 to 45 minutes, or until top is lightly browned.

NUTRIENT ANALYSIS

Calories	342.36 kcal
Protein	30.25 g
Carbohydrate	40.17 g
Total Fat	5.58 g
Saturated	2.53 g
Polyunsaturated	1.06 g
Monounsaturated	1.43 g
Cholesterol	50.21 mg
Sodium	479.39 mg

CREAMED TUNA AND PEAS OVER ENGLISH MUFFINS

This is one of those homey foods that we seem never to grow tired of. The sherry gives it a flavorful twist.

SERVES 4
¾ CUP SAUCE OVER 2 MUFFIN HALVES PER SERVING

2 tablespoons acceptable
  vegetable oil
3 tablespoons all-purpose
  flour
⅛ teaspoon salt, optional
White pepper to taste
1 bay leaf
2 cups skim milk
1 teaspoon dry sherry,
  optional
1 10-ounce package frozen
  green peas
1 12½-ounce can tuna,
  packed in water, drained and rinsed
4 whole-grain English muffins, split and lightly toasted

NUTRIENT ANALYSIS

Calories	410.05 kcal
Protein	35.33 g
Carbohydrate	43.01 g
Total Fat	11.33 g
Saturated	1.82 g
Polyunsaturated	5.61 g
Monounsaturated	3.16 g
Cholesterol	58.42 mg
Sodium	357.93 mg

In a small saucepan, heat oil over medium heat. Add flour, salt, pepper and bay leaf, stirring constantly, 1 minute. Gradually add milk and sherry, stirring constantly, until mixture thickens, 2 to 3 minutes. Remove from heat and discard bay leaf.

Meanwhile, cook peas half as long as stated on the package; drain. Flake tuna with a fork. Add peas and tuna to sauce and mix well. Heat thoroughly. Place ¾ cup mixture over each split English muffin and serve immediately.

TUNA SALAD PITA SANDWICHES

Here is an old favorite served in a
new-fangled way.

SERVES 6
½ PITA SANDWICH
PER SERVING

1 6½-ounce can tuna in spring water, drained and rinsed
3 green onions with tops, finely chopped
2 tablespoons finely chopped celery
2 tablespoons finely chopped fresh parsley
1 medium carrot, shredded
1 small tomato, finely chopped
2 tablespoons finely chopped green pepper
3 tablespoons reduced-calorie mayonnaise
2 tablespoons Salsa (see page 260) or picante sauce
Freshly ground black pepper to taste
3 whole-wheat pitas, approximately 7 inches in diameter

Accompaniments
6 lettuce leaves, rinsed and dried
1 medium tomato, sliced
6 fresh mushrooms, sliced
½ cup alfalfa or bean sprouts (optional)
6 sprigs parsley

Combine all ingredients except pitas and the accompaniments. Mix well. Refrigerate for at least 1 hour.
    Cut each pita in half. Line each half with a leaf of lettuce,

a slice of tomato, mushroom slices and sprouts. Add tuna salad and garnish with a sprig of parsley.

NUTRIENT ANALYSIS

Calories	178.12 kcal
Protein	12.56 g
Carbohydrate	26.80 g
Total Fat	2.36 g
Saturated	0.39 g
Polyunsaturated	1.10 g
Monounsaturated	0.42 g
Cholesterol	19.58 mg
Sodium	325.80 mg

POULTRY

Cheese/Herb Chicken Medallions
Garlic Chicken Fillets in Balsamic Vinegar
Chinese Chicken Vegetable Stir-Fry
Chicken with Mustard and Herbs
Oriental Grilled Chicken
Chicken Ragout
Chicken in White Sauce
Chicken Fajitas
Chickenwich
Crispy Oven-Fried Chicken
Hearty Chicken Stew
Brunswick Stew
Tandoori Cornish Hens
Roast Cornish Hens
Roast Turkey
Turkey Tetrazzini

CHEESE/HERB CHICKEN MEDALLIONS

Top this family favorite with dabs of zesty Pesto Sauce and carrot curls. Although any fresh vegetable can be used for garnish, carrots add a wonderful splash of color. The medallions can be served hot or at room temperature.

Chilling the mozzarella beforehand keeps it from oozing when baking.

**SERVES 6 AS AN ENTREE
APPROXIMATELY 4 OUNCES
PER SERVING
SERVES 12 AS AN APPETIZER
APPROXIMATELY 2 OUNCES
PER SERVING**

6 boneless chicken breasts, about 5 ounces each, all visible fat
   removed
1 tablespoon finely chopped fresh chives, or 1 teaspoon dried
   chives
1 tablespoon finely chopped fresh basil, or 1 teaspoon dried
   basil
Freshly ground black pepper to taste
¼ teaspoon paprika
3 ounces part-skim mozzarella cheese, shredded

Garnish
2 carrots
2 tablespoons Pesto (see page 259)

Preheat oven to 400° F.

Place chicken breasts on a flat surface; pat dry. Evenly sprinkle each breast with herbs, pepper and paprika.

Form cheese into six loose balls and place one in the center of each breast. Roll chicken around cheese and tie with string to keep together, making sure that the ends are tucked in and tied to prevent the cheese from oozing out.

Place in an ungreased baking dish. Bake 15 to 20 minutes, or until meat has turned white throughout.

While chicken is baking, prepare carrot curls for garnish. Using a potato parer, pare carrots lengthwise into long, fine strips and soak in ice water for at least 10 minutes. Drain and pat dry. Allow chicken to cool for about 10 minutes. To serve, cut each breast into ½-inch medallions and arrange on a bed of carrot curls. Top each medallion with a little Pesto Sauce.

NUTRIENT ANALYSIS*

Calories	217.25 kcal
Protein	34.39 g
Carbohydrate	3.55 g
Total Fat	6.43 g
Saturated	2.41 g
Polyunsaturated	0.91 g
Monounsaturated	2.41 g
Cholesterol	83.21 mg
Sodium	142.26 mg

* Based on entree-size serving.

GARLIC CHICKEN FILLETS IN BALSAMIC VINEGAR

**SERVES 6
5 OUNCES PER SERVING**

This flavorful, tender chicken dish is quick and easy to prepare. The balsamic vinegar, available in some supermarkets and most gourmet shops, makes the sauce smooth and balanced. This entree can be the center of an elegant meal that you can throw together for unexpected company. Team it with Golden Rice or Savory Brown Rice (see pages 240, 241), add a steamed vegetable or a tossed salad and sit back and feast on the raves.

*2 pounds boneless chicken breasts, skinned, all visible fat
    removed
½ cup all-purpose flour
2 tablespoons olive oil
6 to 8 cloves garlic, minced
1 cup homemade Chicken Stock (see page 352)
⅓ cup balsamic vinegar
Freshly ground black pepper to taste
1 tablespoon cornstarch
2 tablespoons water*

Split chicken breasts in half lengthwise and dredge in flour; remove excess.

In a large, heavy nonstick skillet, heat oil over medium-high heat. Cook chicken breasts on one side about 2 to 3 minutes, or until golden. Add garlic. Turn chicken and continue cooking about 2 to 3 minutes, or until golden. Add stock, balsamic vinegar and pepper. Reduce heat to medium-low, cover skillet and cook 5 to 10 minutes, or until chicken is tender. (The timing depends on the thickness of the chicken breasts.) Remove chicken from skillet. Keep warm.

In a small bowl, dissolve cornstarch in water, stirring until smooth. Add to skillet and cook 1 to 2 minutes, or until thick and smooth. Pour sauce over chicken and serve immediately.

NUTRIENT ANALYSIS

Calories	255.04 kcal
Protein	34.17 g
Carbohydrate	10.35 g
Total Fat	7.66 g
Saturated	1.48 g
Polyunsaturated	1.16 g
Monounsaturated	4.31 g
Cholesterol	80.76 mg
Sodium	67.40 mg

CHINESE CHICKEN VEGETABLE STIR-FRY

Serve this dish on a bed of hot rice
or noodles.

SERVES 6
I CUP PER SERVING

1 pound boneless chicken breasts, skinned, all visible fat
    removed and cut into 1-inch cubes
1½ tablespoons low-sodium soy sauce
1 tablespoon grated fresh ginger or 1 teaspoon ground ginger
2 tablespoons acceptable vegetable oil
2 medium green, red or yellow bell peppers, cut into 1-inch
    strips
4 ounces fresh mushrooms, thinly sliced
4 green onions with tops, cut into 1-inch strips
¾ cup pineapple chunks, fresh or canned in juice
1½ tablespoons cornstarch
⅔ cup homemade Chicken Stock (see page 352)
¼ cup pineapple juice, or reserved juice from canned
    pineapple

Garnish
1 tablespoon sesame seeds, toasted

Marinate chicken in soy sauce and ginger 30 to 45 minutes, stirring occasionally. In nonstick wok or skillet, heat
oil over high heat. Add marinated chicken and stir-fry for 2
minutes. Using a slotted spoon, remove chicken, leaving
juices in the pan. Add peppers, mushrooms and onions and
stir-fry for 1 minute. Add pineapple and chicken and stir-
fry another 2 to 3 minutes. Vegetables should be tender-
crisp.

    Blend cornstarch with stock and pineapple juice. Stir

into the chicken mixture and cook about 1 minute, or until thickened. Remove from heat and garnish with sesame seeds.

NUTRIENT ANALYSIS

Calories	182.86 kcal
Protein	18.80 g
Carbohydrate	11.42 g
Total Fat	7.09 g
Saturated	0.94 g
Polyunsaturated	1.59 g
Monounsaturated	3.96 g
Cholesterol	40.57 mg
Sodium	207.05 mg

CHICKEN WITH MUSTARD AND HERBS

This recipe makes an elegant entree for dinner. Cold, it also can be used for special chicken sandwiches. Herb seasonings are handy for adding a dash of flavor. Try them in your cooking and at the table, too.

SERVES 4
APPROXIMATELY 3 OUNCES PER SERVING

4 boneless chicken breasts, about 4 ounces each, skinned, all visible fat removed
1 tablespoon Herb Seasoning for salads (see pages 33–34)
1 teaspoon lemon pepper seasoning
1 tablespoon acceptable vegetable oil
¼ cup spicy brown mustard

NUTRIENT ANALYSIS

Calories	173.64 kcal
Protein	25.39 g
Carbohydrate	2.53 g
Total Fat	6.53 g
Saturated	1.14 g
Polyunsaturated	2.70 g
Monounsaturated	1.72 g
Cholesterol	59.96 mg
Sodium	234.58 mg

Preheat oven to 350° F.

Place chicken breasts in a baking pan. Mix remaining ingredients together to make a paste. Thickly and evenly spread it over top of each chicken breast. Bake 20 minutes, or just until meat has turned white throughout.

ORIENTAL GRILLED CHICKEN

The marinade makes this chicken
delicious. Grilling gives it a slight
barbecue taste. The optional
method of broiling works well also.

SERVES 6
2 PIECES CHICKEN
PER SERVING

Marinade

2 tablespoons acceptable vegetable oil
¼ cup honey
3 tablespoons red wine vinegar
¼ cup low-sodium soy sauce
1 clove garlic, minced
2 tablespoons finely chopped fresh parsley
2 teaspoons grated fresh ginger or 1 teaspoon ginger powder
½ teaspoon freshly ground black pepper

12 pieces chicken, about 3½ to 4 pounds, skinned, all visible fat
   removed

In a bowl, combine all marinade ingredients and mix well.
Add chicken and turn to coat all pieces. Cover and refrigerate for at least 2 hours, turning occasionally.

Grilling Method: Grill chicken pieces 6 inches away from
white-hot coals. Grill 30 to 45 minutes, brushing pieces
with marinade and turning pieces frequently, until chicken
is tender but not dry.

Broiler Method: Preheat broiler. Arrange chicken pieces
on baking sheet and place 5 inches away from the heat.
Broil 25 to 30 minutes, brushing pieces with marinade and
turning frequently, until chicken is tender but not dry.

NUTRIENT ANALYSIS

Calories	286.15 kcal
Protein	33.27 g
Carbohydrate	13.04 g
Total Fat	10.82 g
Saturated	2.42 g
Polyunsaturated	4.25 g
Monounsaturated	3.05 g
Cholesterol	90.24 mg
Sodium	507.26 mg

CHICKEN RAGOUT

This easy French stew is delicately flavored with thyme and tarragon. Using fresh instead of dried herbs will make it extra special. Served in your prettiest casserole, it will be a favorite with guests. Have plenty of crusty French bread on hand to sop up the juices!

1/3 cup plus 2 tablespoons all-purpose flour
1/2 teaspoon freshly ground black pepper, or to taste
12 pieces chicken, about 3 1/2 pounds, skinned, all visible fat removed
Vegetable oil spray
1 teaspoon olive oil
1 medium yellow or white onion, sliced
1 pound fresh mushrooms, sliced
2 cloves garlic, minced
1/4 cup fresh thyme or 1 tablespoon dried thyme
1/4 cup fresh tarragon or 1 tablespoon dried tarragon
1/4 cup finely chopped fresh parsley
1/4 teaspoon salt (optional)
1 cup homemade Chicken Stock (see page 352)
1 cup dry white wine or 1 cup additional homemade Chicken Stock
1/4 cup cold water
2 cups green peas, fresh or frozen

P reheat oven to 400° F.

Combine 1/3 cup flour, pepper and chicken pieces in a plastic bag. Shake well to coat pieces.

Spray a nonstick skillet with vegetable oil spray. Heat skillet over medium-high heat, add chicken pieces a few at a time, and brown on all sides. Remove pieces to an oven-proof casserole or Dutch oven. Repeat process with remaining chicken. In skillet, heat oil, add onions and cook 2 to 3 minutes, or until onions are translucent. Add mushrooms, garlic, thyme, tarragon, parsley, salt, stock and wine; mix together. Pour over chicken pieces. Cover chicken and bake 45 minutes.

In a small bowl, blend 2 tablespoons flour and water. Gradually add to the liquid in the casserole, while stirring lightly. Add peas. Cover and continue to bake another 15 to 20 minutes, or until chicken and peas are tender and sauce thickened.

NUTRIENT ANALYSIS

Calories	291.54 kcal
Protein	34.89 g
Carbohydrate	21.80 g
Total Fat	6.89 g
Saturated	1.85 g
Polyunsaturated	1.63 g
Monounsaturated	2.34 g
Cholesterol	80.09 mg
Sodium	205.66 mg

CHICKEN IN WHITE SAUCE

This is a great dish for entertaining.
You can even make it a day ahead
of time.

SERVES 6
2 PIECES CHICKEN
PER SERVING

Vegetable oil spray
*12 pieces chicken, about 3½ pounds, skinned, all visible fat
    removed*
*¼ cup Madeira or port wine or homemade Chicken Stock (see
    page 352)*
2 tablespoons minced fresh sage or 1 teaspoon dried sage
2 tablespoons minced fresh thyme or 1 teaspoon dried thyme
3 green onions with tops, thinly sliced
¼ cup finely chopped fresh parsley
¼ teaspoon salt (optional)
Freshly ground black pepper to taste
1½ cups White Sauce (see page 256)

Preheat oven to 350° F.

Spray a nonstick skillet with vegetable oil spray. Heat
skillet over medium-high heat, add chicken pieces a few at
a time and lightly brown on all sides. Remove pieces to an
ovenproof casserole or Dutch oven. Repeat process with
remaining chicken. Pour wine or stock over warm chicken
pieces, toss to cover and allow to stand for 10 minutes.

Mix herbs, onions, parsley and seasonings into White
Sauce. Pour over chicken pieces. Cover and bake 45 to 60
minutes, or until chicken pieces are tender.

If making ahead, refrigerate; reheat before serving.

NUTRIENT ANALYSIS*

Calories	293.56 kcal
Protein	39.99 g
Carbohydrate	6.58 g
Total Fat	10.92 g
Saturated	2.67 g
Polyunsaturated	3.88 g
Monounsaturated	3.13 g
Cholesterol	106.51 mg
Sodium	281.38 mg

* Using wine.

CHICKEN FAJITAS

This delicious dish is fun to make
and good for you, too. Enjoy it with
shredded lettuce, sliced tomatoes,
Guacamole, Refried Beans, and
Salsa (see pages 91, 222, and 260).

SERVES 4
2 FAJITAS PER SERVING

1 clove garlic, finely minced
1 tablespoon acceptable vegetable oil
1½ tablespoons fresh lemon or lime juice
3 tablespoons Worcestershire sauce
⅛ teaspoon freshly ground black pepper, or to taste
1¼ pounds boneless chicken breasts, skinned, all visible fat
*   removed*
1 large onion
1 large green pepper
2 teaspoons acceptable vegetable oil
8 corn tortillas

P reheat broiler.

To make marinade, combine garlic, oil, lemon or lime
juice, Worcestershire sauce and pepper in a bowl.

Cut chicken lengthwise into thin ⅜-inch strips. Add to
marinade, toss to coat evenly and let chicken marinate in
refrigerator 10 to 20 minutes, turning at least once.

Slice the onion and pepper into thin ⅛-inch strips.

In a nonstick skillet, heat 2 teaspoons oil over medium-
high heat. Add onion and pepper slices and sauté, stirring
constantly, about 5 minutes, or until onion is slightly
brown.

Wrap tortillas in foil and place on lower shelf of oven.
Heat thoroughly.

Line broiler pan with foil. Place chicken on the foil and
broil about 3 inches from heat for 4 minutes.

To serve, place three cooked chicken strips on each tortilla, top with onions, peppers and assorted garnishes as desired. Roll tortilla around chicken strips and eat with fingers.

NUTRIENT ANALYSIS*

Calories	346.19 kcal
Protein	34.03 g
Carbohydrate	23.58 g
Total Fat	13.06 g
Saturated	3.48 g
Polyunsaturated	5.23 g
Monounsaturated	3.37 g
Cholesterol	74.95 mg
Sodium	315.75 mg

* Including garnishes.

CHICKENWICH

SERVES 4
I PER SERVING

Our Chickenwich is made with ham. Yes, ham! Ham is leaner than you may think. Modern farming methods make it possible to produce pork that is low in fat. Ham is still high in sodium because of the salt and sodium nitrate used in processing, so you may want to balance your diet by having a low-sodium entree at your next meal.

4 boneless chicken breasts, about 4 ounces each, skinned, all
*   visible fat removed*
4 slices part-skim mozzarella cheese, about 4 ounces
4 slices ham, about 4 ounces, visible fat removed
3 tablespoons whole-wheat or all-purpose flour
1 teaspoon dry mustard
½ teaspoon paprika
2 teaspoons olive oil

P lace chicken breasts, smooth-side up, between two sheets of plastic wrap. Using a meat mallet or a rolling pin, pound chicken to twice its original diameter and set aside.

Fold each slice of cheese in half and place it on a slice of ham. Fold the ham over the cheese to form a packet that is about half as big as the piece of chicken and place one packet on top of each chicken piece. Fold the chicken in half over the mozzarella ham packet to enclose it.

Mix flour, mustard powder and paprika. Dip chicken into mixture and tap lightly to remove excess.

In a nonstick skillet, heat oil over medium heat. When oil is hot, add chicken to pan, sauté on each side for about 4 or 5 minutes, then sauté each seam side for about 20 seconds to seal. Serve immediately.

NUTRIENT ANALYSIS

Calories	280.31 kcal
Protein	37.41 g
Carbohydrate	3.74 g
Total Fat	11.96 g
Saturated	4.74 g
Polyunsaturated	1.22 g
Monounsaturated	4.97 g
Cholesterol	93.87 mg
Sodium	362.80 mg

CRISPY OVEN-FRIED CHICKEN

This is a heart-healthy alternative to traditional fried chicken. It's spicy, crispy and easy to make.

SERVES 6
2 PIECES CHICKEN
PER SERVING

12 pieces chicken, about 3½ pounds, skinned, all visible fat removed
¼ cup acceptable vegetable oil
¼ teaspoon salt (optional)
Freshly ground black pepper to taste
1 teaspoon ground ginger, or to taste
1 clove garlic, crushed (optional)
1 teaspoon paprika
4 cups wheat-flake cereal, lightly crushed

NUTRIENT ANALYSIS

Calories	373.49 kcal
Protein	39.30 g
Carbohydrate	15.40 g
Total Fat	16.47 g
Saturated	3.31 g
Polyunsaturated	7.23 g
Monounsaturated	4.49 g
Cholesterol	105.28 mg
Sodium	413.61 mg

Preheat oven to 350° F.

Rinse chicken and pat dry.

Combine oil, salt, pepper, ginger, garlic and paprika in a small bowl. Place cereal in a pie plate or on a piece of foil. Brush each piece of chicken on both sides with oil mixture, then dip in cereal crumbs, pressing lightly to get an even coating on all sides. Place on an ungreased baking sheet. Bake 45 to 60 minutes, or until chicken is golden brown and tender. Timing will vary according to the thickness of the chicken pieces.

HEARTY CHICKEN STEW

This is a good recipe to make
ahead and refrigerate or freeze
until needed. The herbs and spices
give this dish a wonderful Oriental
flavor.

SERVES 8
1½ CUPS PER SERVING

2 tablespoons acceptable vegetable oil
1 medium onion, finely chopped
1 tablespoon minced fresh ginger or 1 teaspoon ground ginger
3 cloves garlic, minced
2 tablespoons all-purpose flour
2 medium tomatoes, diced
8 to 10 peppercorns, or to taste
6 whole cloves
1 cinnamon stick
8 pieces chicken, about 2½ pounds, skinned, all visible fat
    removed
2 cups water
1 tablespoon Worcestershire sauce
¾ pound baby carrots, fresh or frozen
6 ounces green peas, fresh or frozen
8 ounces red or white new potatoes, scrubbed and unpeeled

In a deep skillet or Dutch oven, heat oil over medium-high heat. Sauté onions, ginger and garlic until onions are soft, about 3 minutes. Add flour and cook 1 minute, stirring quickly to prevent sticking. Stir in tomatoes and allow to cook another 2 minutes.

Wrap peppercorns, cloves and cinnamon in a small piece of cheesecloth. Add chicken, cheesecloth package, water and Worcestershire sauce to onion mixture. Reduce heat and simmer, covered, 20 minutes. Add carrots, peas and potatoes. Continue to simmer, covered, until chicken and vegetables are cooked, 20 to 25 minutes. Remove cheese-cloth package and serve the stew steaming hot.

NUTRIENT ANALYSIS

Calories	215.25 kcal
Protein	18.49 g
Carbohydrate	19.97 g
Total Fat	6.68 g
Saturated	1.11 g
Polyunsaturated	1.76 g
Monounsaturated	3.07 g
Cholesterol	42.47 mg
Sodium	94.31 mg

BRUNSWICK STEW

1 tablespoon olive oil
1 medium onion, chopped
1 pound boneless chicken breasts, skinned, all visible fat
    removed and cut into 1-inch cubes
1½ cups chopped tomatoes
1 6-ounce can no-salt-added tomato paste
10 ounces baby lima beans, fresh or frozen
10 ounces corn kernels, fresh or frozen
3 cups homemade Chicken Stock (see page 352)
1 tablespoon Worcestershire sauce
3 tablespoons fresh lemon juice

In a deep skillet or Dutch oven, heat oil over medium-high
heat. Add onion and sauté until soft, about 3 minutes. Add
chicken pieces and remaining ingredients. Reduce heat to
low, cover and simmer 1 hour.

NUTRIENT ANALYSIS

Calories	255.20 kcal
Protein	23.80 g
Carbohydrate	31.40 g
Total Fat	5.29 g
Saturated	0.98 g
Polyunsaturated	1.11 g
Monounsaturated	2.36 g
Cholesterol	43.20 mg
Sodium	250.58 mg

TANDOORI CORNISH HENS

SERVES 6
½ HEN PER SERVING

One of the most popular Indian dishes, tandoori chicken is spicy but not hot. This easy and attractive lowfat dish is marinated in yogurt and spices. The recipe works equally well with chicken parts, a whole chicken or Cornish hens. Cornish hens are preferable because of their low fat content.

3 Cornish hens, approximately 1 pound each
1 teaspoon chili powder, or to taste
½ teaspoon salt (optional)
Freshly ground black pepper to taste
3 tablespoons fresh lime juice

Marinade
1 cup plain nonfat yogurt
3 cloves garlic
1-inch piece fresh ginger, coarsely chopped
1 small onion, coarsely chopped
1 teaspoon cumin seeds
½ teaspoon ground turmeric
½ teaspoon chili powder, or to taste
1 teaspoon sugar

Garnish
1 lime, cut into wedges
Few sprigs fresh cilantro or parsley

Thaw the hens if frozen. Rinse, remove giblets and necks and pat dry. Make several slits in the skin, then split each hen in half along the breastbone.

Mix together chili powder, salt, pepper and lime juice.

Rub mixture all over poultry and set aside for about 15 minutes.

In a blender, puree all marinade ingredients. Place poultry pieces in a bowl and add marinade. Mix well to coat all the pieces. Cover and refrigerate for at least 8 hours, turning occasionally.

Preheat oven to 400° F.

Place hens, skin-side up, on a rack in a roasting pan and spoon marinade over the pieces. Bake, basting frequently with marinade, until thoroughly cooked, 45 to 60 minutes, or until hens are very tender. Test for doneness by pricking the skin of the thigh; the juice should run clear. Serve hot. Remove skin before eating and garnish with lime and cilantro or parsley.

NUTRIENT ANALYSIS

Calories	208.95 kcal
Protein	27.23 g
Carbohydrate	8.16 g
Total Fat	7.97 g
Saturated	2.24 g
Polyunsaturated	1.82 g
Monounsaturated	2.93 g
Cholesterol	80.27 mg
Sodium	281.32 mg

ROAST CORNISH HENS

For that special occasion, serve this
with Savory Brown Rice (see page
241). Add a dash of color with
steamed vegetables.

SERVES 6
½ HEN PER SERVING

3 Cornish hens, approximately 1 pound each
1 tablespoon whole peppercorns, coarsely crushed
3 tablespoons chopped fresh tarragon or 1 tablespoon dried
    tarragon
1 medium pear, cut into thirds
1 cup fresh parsley sprigs, rinsed
2 tablespoons acceptable vegetable oil
Water

Thaw hens if frozen.
   Preheat oven to 425° F.
   Remove giblets and discard. Save the necks for making
stock. Rinse hens and pat dry. Gently loosen skin from meat
on breast and legs by breaking the membrane that holds the
skin to the meat and sliding your hand between the two to
loosen the skin. Spread pepper and tarragon under the skin
and in the cavity. Stuff each cavity with pieces of pear and
parsley.
   Place the hens on a rack, breast-side up, on the top of a
3-inch-deep roaster pan. Soak a cheesecloth in oil and cover
hens with the oiled cloth. This keeps the meat from drying
out. Put water in the pan to a depth of 1 to 1½ inches to
provide moisture and pan drippings for gravy. Place hens in
oven, reduce heat immediately to 325° F. and bake 45 to
60 minutes. Test for doneness by pricking the skin of the
thigh; the juice should run clear. Defat the drippings and
make Pan Gravy (see page 261). Cut each hen in half before
serving.

NUTRIENT ANALYSIS

Calories	228.76 kcal
Protein	24.84 g
Carbohydrate	5.58 g
Total Fat	12.31 g
Saturated	2.74 g
Polyunsaturated	4.42 g
Monounsaturated	3.99 g
Cholesterol	79.12 mg
Sodium	66.36 mg

ROAST TURKEY

Eating healthfully on holidays is
made easier with recipes like this.
For a traditional meal, serve it with
Green Beans Almondine,
Cornbread Dressing, and Pumpkin
Pie (pages 221, 286–287, and 305).

SERVES 12
APPROXIMATELY 4 OUNCES
BONELESS TURKEY
PER SERVING

1 11- to 12-pound fresh or frozen turkey
2 tablespoons whole black, white or green peppercorns, or a
    mixture, coarsely crushed
1 large apple, quartered
1 cup fresh parsley sprigs, rinsed
¼ cup acceptable vegetable oil (canola oil works well)
Water

T haw turkey if frozen.

Preheat oven to 425° F.

Remove giblets and discard. Save the neck for making
stock. Rinse turkey and pat dry. Gently loosen skin from
meat on breast and legs by breaking the membrane that
holds the skin to the meat and sliding your hand between
the two to loosen the skin.

Spread peppercorns under the skin and in the cavity.
Stuff the cavity with apple and parsley.

Place the turkey on a rack, breast-side up, on the top of
a 3-inch-deep roaster pan. Soak a cheesecloth in oil and
cover turkey with the oiled cloth. This keeps the meat from
drying out. Put water in the pan to a depth of 1 to 1½
inches to provide moisture and pan drippings for gravy.
Place turkey in oven and reduce heat immediately to
325° F. Bake 2 to 3 hours, or 12 to 15 minutes per pound.
Test for doneness by pricking the skin of the thigh; the
juice should run clear. Or use a thermometer inserted

in the thigh; it should register 185° F. when the turkey is fully cooked.

Let the turkey rest 20 minutes before serving. Defat the drippings and make Pan Gravy (see page 261). Serve turkey on a large heated platter and carve, removing the skin.

NUTRIENT ANALYSIS

Calories	355.15 kcal
Protein	48.56 g
Carbohydrate	6.04 g
Total Fat	14.13 g
Saturated	3.05 g
Polyunsaturated	3.71 g
Monounsaturated	5.78 g
Cholesterol	135.85 mg
Sodium	121.49 mg

TURKEY TETRAZZINI

This is a great way to use turkey
leftovers.

SERVES 8
1½ CUPS PER SERVING

1 14- to 15-ounce box macaroni and cheese (with powdered
  cheese-sauce packet)
1 tablespoon acceptable vegetable oil
1 cup coarsely chopped onion
½ cup chopped green bell pepper
2 cloves garlic, finely minced
8 ounces fresh mushrooms, sliced
Vegetable oil spray
12 ounces cooked breast of turkey, cubed, about 2 cups
1½ cups skim milk
2 tablespoons dry sherry

Topping (optional)
½ cup grated lowfat cheddar cheese

Preheat oven to 350° F.

Cook macaroni according to package directions, omitting salt.

While macaroni is cooking, heat oil in a large skillet.
Sauté onion, green pepper and garlic over medium-high
heat 2 to 3 minutes, or until soft. Add mushrooms and cook
2 more minutes, or until soft.

Spray a 3-quart casserole with vegetable oil spray, if desired. Drain the macaroni and combine with cheese packet,
sautéed vegetables, turkey, milk and sherry. Pour into prepared casserole dish. Cover and bake 35 to 40 minutes, or
until most of the liquid is absorbed.

Remove from oven and sprinkle with cheddar cheese.
Cover and allow casserole to sit for about 5 minutes, or just
until cheese melts.

NUTRIENT ANALYSIS

Calories	204.65 kcal
Protein	18.41 g
Carbohydrate	22.32 g
Total Fat	4.38 g
Saturated	1.17 g
Polyunsaturated	1.57 g
Monounsaturated	1.20 g
Cholesterol	33.14 mg
Sodium	297.57 mg

MEATS

Marinated Steak
Swedish Meatloaf with Dill Sauce
Shepherd's Pie
Bulgar and Ground Beef Casserole
Beef Ragout
Sloppy Joes
Mexican Beef and Cornbread Pie
Vegetable-Beef Burgers
Chili
Beef or Venison Stroganoff
Lamb and Red Beans
Pork with Savory Sauce
Pork and Tofu Stir-Fry
Scrambled Eggs and Ham in Sweet Potato Boat

MARINATED STEAK

Steak on a cholesterol-lowering
diet? Sure. Just select the meat
carefully and trim all visible fat. This
marinade is a favorite among steak
lovers. One taste will convince you,
too!

SERVES 6
APPROXIMATELY 3 OUNCES
PER SERVING

1½ *pounds flank steak, 1 inch thick, all visible fat removed*
Freshly ground pepper to taste

Marinade
2 *tablespoons acceptable vegetable oil*
3 *tablespoons tarragon or wine vinegar*
½ *cup dry red wine*
3 *cloves garlic, crushed*
3 *tablespoons minced fresh parsley*
1 *tablespoon chopped fresh oregano or 1 teaspoon dried*
   oregano
1 *tablespoon chopped fresh tarragon or 1 teaspoon dried*
   tarragon
1 *bay leaf*
½ *teaspoon freshly ground black pepper*

Place steak in a baking dish. In a small bowl, combine
ingredients for marinade. Pour over steak and turn to coat.
Cover and refrigerate for at least 8 hours, turning occasionally.
   Preheat broiler.
   Remove steak from marinade, pat dry and sprinkle with
additional freshly ground pepper. Broil 4 to 6 inches from

heat 4 to 7 minutes on each side for medium-well done, or 3 to 5 minutes on each side for medium-rare. Slice thin diagonally across the grain. Serve warm.

NUTRIENT ANALYSIS

Calories	198.96 kcal
Protein	25.19 g
Carbohydrate	1.94 g
Total Fat	9.72 g
Saturated	2.82 g
Polyunsaturated	2.98 g
Monounsaturated	3.31 g
Cholesterol	72.38 mg
Sodium	50.08 mg

SWEDISH MEATLOAF WITH DILL SAUCE

If you like Swedish meatballs, you'll love this moist and flavorful meatloaf.

SERVES 6
APPROXIMATELY 4 OUNCES OF MEATLOAF AND ¼ CUP OF SAUCE PER SERVING

Vegetable oil spray
1 teaspoon acceptable vegetable oil
½ medium onion, finely minced
2 cloves garlic, finely minced
¾ cup rye bread crumbs, about 4 slices
⅓ cup buttermilk
1 large egg white, lightly beaten
⅛ teaspoon freshly ground black pepper
¼ teaspoon ground nutmeg
¼ teaspoon ground ginger
⅛ teaspoon ground allspice
1 tablespoon chopped fresh dill or 1 teaspoon dried dill
¾ pound very lean ground sirloin
½ pound ground chicken breast (skin and all visible fat removed before grinding)

Sauce
1 tablespoon acceptable margarine, unsalted
2 tablespoons all-purpose flour
1 cup homemade Beef Stock (see pages 353–354)
3 tablespoons dry sherry
¾ cup evaporated skim milk
⅛ teaspoon freshly ground pepper
¼ teaspoon ground nutmeg
¼ teaspoon ground allspice
¼ teaspoon ground ginger
3 tablespoons chopped fresh dill or 1½ tablespoons dried dill

P reheat oven to 425° F. Spray a 9 × 5-inch ovenproof loaf pan with vegetable oil spray; set aside.

To make the loaf, heat oil in a large, nonstick skillet at medium setting. Add onion and sauté, stirring frequently, about 4 minutes. Add garlic and continue to sauté, stirring constantly, 1 minute more, or until onion is soft.

Mix bread crumbs and buttermilk in a large bowl and let soak 5 minutes. Add sautéed onion and garlic, egg white, pepper, nutmeg, ginger, allspice and dill. Use your hands to lightly mix. Add ground beef and chicken. Mix well to evenly distribute ingredients. Lightly pat into prepared loaf pan. Place in oven and reduce temperature to 350° F. Bake 30 minutes.

While meatloaf is cooking, make the sauce. In heavy saucepan, melt margarine over medium heat. Remove pan from heat and blend in flour. Return to heat and gradually add beef stock, sherry and milk. Stir constantly with a wire whisk until fully blended and mixture thickens, about 6 to 8 minutes. Remove from heat and blend in remaining ingredients.

Remove meatloaf from oven and pour off fat. Pour sauce over meatloaf, cover with foil and return to oven. Continue to cook 15 minutes more or until done. Serve hot.

NUTRIENT ANALYSIS OF SWEDISH MEATLOAF		NUTRIENT ANALYSIS OF DILL SAUCE	
Calories	209.07 kcal	Calories	47.97 kcal
Protein	24.11 g	Protein	1.79 g
Carbohydrate	14.22 g	Carbohydrate	5.81 g
Total Fat	5.25 g	Total Fat	2.31 g
Saturated	1.90 g	Saturated	0.43 g
Polyunsaturated	0.94 g	Polyunsaturated	0.69 g
Monounsaturated	1.88 g	Monounsaturated	0.95 g
Cholesterol	58.03 mg	Cholesterol	1.65 mg
Sodium	195.24 mg	Sodium	15.41 mg

SHEPHERD'S PIE

Assemble this easy entree ahead of
time and bake it just before serving.

SERVES 6
1 3 × 5-INCH PORTION
PER SERVING

1½ pounds potatoes, peeled
¼ cup skim milk
Freshly ground pepper to taste
1 pound very lean ground sirloin
1 large onion, finely chopped
1 large bell pepper, chopped
3 medium carrots, chopped
½ cup green peas, fresh or frozen
1 medium tomato, chopped
¼ cup chopped fresh parsley
¾ cup homemade Chicken Stock (see page 352)
½ teaspoon salt
Freshly ground black pepper to taste
2 tablespoons Worcestershire sauce
1 tablespoon cornstarch
2 tablespoons cold water

B oil potatoes until tender. Mash together with skim milk
and pepper until smooth; keep warm.

Preheat oven to 350° F.

Heat a heavy, nonstick skillet, at least 10 inches in diameter, over medium-high heat. Add ground beef and sauté,
stirring occasionally, 4 to 5 minutes, or until meat is no
longer pink. Pour contents of pan into a strainer or colander
lined with paper towels. Allow fat to drain out. Return meat
to pan, add onion and cook until onions are translucent, 4
to 5 minutes. Add bell pepper, carrots, peas, tomato, parsley, chicken stock, salt, pepper and Worcestershire sauce.
Simmer, uncovered, 15 minutes.

Dissolve cornstarch in water and stir into meat mixture. Spoon into an ungreased 10 × 10 × 2-inch or 9 × 11 × 2-inch baking dish. Spread mashed potatoes over the surface, using a fork for texture. Bake 30 to 35 minutes, or until lightly browned.

NUTRIENT ANALYSIS

Calories	256.67 kcal
Protein	21.38 g
Carbohydrate	30.53 g
Total Fat	4.55 g
Saturated	1.84 g
Polyunsaturated	0.39 g
Monounsaturated	1.77 g
Cholesterol	49.01 mg
Sodium	314.96 mg

BULGUR AND GROUND BEEF CASSEROLE

Bulgur or cracked wheat is available
in most supermarkets and health
food stores. It has a delicious, nutty
flavor and is an excellent substitute
for rice.

SERVES 6
1 3 × 5-INCH PORTION
PER SERVING

1 cup bulgur
1½ cups cold water
1 pound very lean ground sirloin
2 medium onions, chopped
¼ teaspoon salt
Freshly ground black pepper to taste
½ cup finely chopped fresh cilantro or parsley
1 tablespoon chopped fresh dill weed or ½ teaspoon dried dill
    weed
4 medium tomatoes, chopped
2 tablespoons fresh lemon juice
½ cup canned low-sodium vegetable juice

Garnish
2 tomatoes, cut into wedges
1 lemon, sliced thin

P reheat oven to 350° F.

In a medium bowl, soak bulgur in cold water 15 to 30
minutes, or until soft. Set aside.

Heat a heavy, nonstick skillet, at least 10 inches in diameter, over medium-high heat. Add ground beef and sauté,
stirring occasionally, 4 to 5 minutes, or until meat is no
longer pink. Pour contents of pan into a strainer or colander
lined with paper towels. Allow fat to drain out. Return meat

to pan, add onions, and cook until onions are translucent, 3 to 4 minutes. Add salt, pepper and herbs. Drain bulgur and add to meat. Add tomatoes, lemon juice and vegetable juice. Stir lightly.

Place mixture in a 10 × 10 × 2-inch or 9 × 11 × 2-inch baking dish or ovenproof casserole. Bake, uncovered, 15 to 20 minutes, or until heated thoroughly. Garnish with tomato and lemon.

NUTRIENT ANALYSIS

Calories	267.52 kcal
Protein	21.83 g
Carbohydrate	32.32 g
Total Fat	4.91 g
Saturated	1.84 g
Polyunsaturated	0.43 g
Monounsaturated	1.79 g
Cholesterol	48.25 mg
Sodium	138.27 mg

BEEF RAGOUT

This hearty ground beef dish is quick and easy to prepare. Instead of buying ground beef in a package, have your butcher grind a sirloin steak for you. Ask him to remove all visible fat beforehand and to clean the grinder to remove any fat from previous grindings.

1½ pounds very lean ground sirloin
1 large onion, chopped
½ cup water
¾ cup dry red wine or ¾ cup additional water
1 red chili pepper, seeded and chopped (optional)
3 cloves garlic, minced
2 large tomatoes, chopped
1 8-ounce can no-salt-added tomato sauce
1 teaspoon chili powder, or to taste
1 teaspoon ground cumin
1 tablespoon fresh oregano or 1 teaspoon dried oregano
½ teaspoon salt (optional)
Freshly ground black pepper to taste
2 15-ounce cans kidney beans, rinsed and drained

Garnish
¼ cup chopped fresh parsley

Heat a heavy, nonstick skillet, at least 10 inches in diameter, over medium-high heat. Add ground beef and sauté, stirring occasionally, 4 to 5 minutes, or until meat is no longer pink. Pour contents of pan into a strainer or colander lined with paper towels. Allow fat to drain out. Return meat to the pan, add onions and sauté 4 to 5 minutes, or until onions are translucent. Stir in water, wine, hot pepper, garlic, tomatoes, tomato sauce, chili powder, cumin, oregano, salt and pepper. Bring mixture to a boil, reduce heat and simmer, partially covered, about 45 minutes, stirring occasionally. Add kidney beans and simmer 10 to 15 minutes, or until beans are heated thoroughly. Sprinkle with parsley before serving.

NUTRIENT ANALYSIS

Calories	394.25 kcal
Protein	37.76 g
Carbohydrate	41.81 g
Total Fat	8.63 g
Saturated	3.13 g
Polyunsaturated	1.33 g
Monounsaturated	2.81 g
Cholesterol	72.38 mg
Sodium	262.03 mg

SLOPPY JOES

You can eat to lower your blood
cholesterol and still enjoy some old
favorites. Here's a pared-down
version of Sloppy Joes with perked-
up flavor.

SERVES 6
½ CUP PER SERVING

Sauce

1 8-ounce can no-salt-added tomato sauce
½ cup ketchup
1½ tablespoons Worcestershire sauce
1 teaspoon prepared yellow mustard
½ teaspoon dry mustard
1 teaspoon molasses
1 clove garlic, finely minced
¼ teaspoon freshly grated orange peel
Pinch ground cloves
Hot pepper sauce to taste

1 pound very lean ground sirloin
½ small onion, finely chopped
6 whole-wheat hamburger buns, toasted if desired

In a saucepan over low heat, combine sauce ingredients.
Mix well and simmer while preparing meat.

Next, heat a heavy, nonstick skillet, at least 10 inches in
diameter, over medium-high heat. Add ground beef and
sauté, stirring occasionally, 4 to 5 minutes, or until meat is
no longer pink. Pour contents of pan into a strainer or
colander lined with paper towels. Allow fat to drain out.

Add onion to pan and sauté, stirring frequently, about 5
minutes, or until translucent. Return meat to pan and add

sauce. Heat 3 minutes, stirring occasionally. Add additional hot pepper sauce, if desired. Spoon ½ cup mixture over each bun. Serve immediately.

The sauce and meat mixture freezes well.

NUTRIENT ANALYSIS

Calories	260.28 kcal
Protein	21.89 g
Carbohydrate	30.19 g
Total Fat	5.61 g
Saturated	2.05 g
Polyunsaturated	0.73 g
Monounsaturated	2.05 g
Cholesterol	48.82 mg
Sodium	549.99 mg

MEXICAN BEEF AND CORNBREAD PIE

A blend of the Old South and
South-of-the-Border makes this a
real winner. Serve with your
favorite green salad for a hearty
family meal.

SERVES 6
1 3 × 5-INCH PORTION
PER SERVING

Meat Mixture

1 pound very lean ground sirloin
1 large onion, chopped, about 1 cup
2 large tomatoes, chopped, about 2 cups
1 10-ounce package frozen whole kernel corn
1 large green bell pepper, chopped, about 1 to 1½ cups
1 teaspoon cumin powder
1 teaspoon chili powder, or to taste
½ teaspoon salt (optional)
1 tablespoon Worcestershire sauce
1 cup homemade Chicken or Beef Stock (see pages 352, 353–354)

Cornbread Mixture

1 ½ cups yellow cornmeal
¼ cup all-purpose flour
1 teaspoon sugar (optional)
¼ teaspoon salt (optional)
2 teaspoons baking powder
3 large egg whites, lightly beaten
½ cup skim milk
1 tablespoon acceptable vegetable oil

P reheat oven to 400° F.

Heat a heavy, nonstick skillet, at least 10 inches in diameter, over medium-high heat. Add ground beef and sauté, stirring occasionally, 4 to 5 minutes, or until meat is no longer pink. Pour contents of pan into a strainer or colander lined with paper towels. Allow fat to drain out. Return meat to the pan, add onions and cook until onions are translucent, about 3 minutes. Add tomatoes, corn, bell pepper, cumin, chili powder, salt, Worcestershire sauce and stock. Simmer, uncovered, 20 to 25 minutes.

In a bowl, mix together cornmeal, flour, sugar, salt and baking powder. In another bowl, combine egg whites, milk and oil; add to cornmeal mixture. Mix lightly.

Place meat mixture in a 10 × 10 × 2-inch baking dish. Spoon cornbread mixture over meat and spread lightly to cover surface. Bake, uncovered, 30 to 40 minutes, or until cornbread is golden brown.

NUTRIENT ANALYSIS*

Calories	370.70 kcal
Protein	25.28 g
Carbohydrate	49.16 g
Total Fat	8.66 g
Saturated	2.09 g
Polyunsaturated	1.30 g
Monounsaturated	3.36 g
Cholesterol	49.98 mg
Sodium	478.57 mg

* Based on canola oil.

VEGETABLE-BEEF BURGERS

If you thought your lowfat diet
meant never eating another
hamburger, think again. This recipe
is low in fat and will be high on
your list of favorites.

SERVES 6

Meat Mixture
1 pound very lean ground sirloin
1 small tomato, finely chopped
1 medium onion, finely chopped
1 small green bell pepper, finely chopped
1/2 teaspoon freshly ground black pepper, or to taste
1 teaspoon Worcestershire sauce
Vegetable oil spray

Accompaniments
6 whole-wheat hamburger buns
1 large tomato, sliced
6 lettuce leaves
Mustard to taste
Ketchup to taste

Combine ground beef, tomato, onion, green pepper, freshly ground pepper and Worcestershire sauce. Mix well. Divide mixture into six portions and shape each into a patty about 1/2 inch thick.

Spray a heavy, nonstick skillet with vegetable oil spray and heat over medium-high heat. Add beef patties and cook

5 to 7 minutes on each side, or until done as desired. Handle meat patties very carefully to prevent breaking.

Place cooked patties on paper towels and blot to absorb fat. Serve on buns with tomato, lettuce, mustard and ketchup.

NUTRIENT ANALYSIS*

Calories	238.40 kcal
Protein	21.54 g
Carbohydrate	24.77 g
Total Fat	5.46 g
Saturated	2.04 g
Polyunsaturated	0.71 g
Monounsaturated	2.02 g
Cholesterol	48.52 mg
Sodium	278.33 mg

* For burger with lettuce, tomato slice, mustard and ketchup on whole-wheat bun.

CHILI

For that four-alarm taste, add a
jalapeño pepper or two! This
recipes tastes best when made the
day before, allowing the flavors to
mingle.

SERVES 6
1¼ CUPS PER SERVING

1 pound very lean ground sirloin
2 large onions, chopped
2 to 4 cloves garlic, minced
2 8-ounce cans no-salt-added tomato sauce
1½ cups water
3 tablespoons chili powder
⅛ teaspoon cayenne pepper, or to taste
1 teaspoon ground cumin
1 tablespoon fresh oregano or 1 teaspoon dried oregano
Freshly ground black pepper to taste
½ teaspoon salt (optional)
2 15-ounce cans pinto beans, rinsed and drained
2 tablespoons cornstarch
¼ cup cold water

Garnish
Corn Crisps (see page 288)

H eat a heavy, nonstick skillet over medium-high heat. Add
ground beef and sauté, stirring occasionally, 4 to 5 minutes,
or until meat is no longer pink. Pour contents of pan into a
strainer or colander lined with paper towels. Allow fat to
drain out.

In a large, heavy saucepan or Dutch oven, heat oil over
medium-high heat. Add onions and sauté 2 to 3 minutes,
or until translucent. Add meat, garlic, tomato sauce and 1½
cups water. Simmer 20 minutes. Stir in chili powder, cay-

enne pepper, cumin, oregano, pepper, salt and pinto beans. Allow to simmer an additional 30 to 40 minutes. Combine cornstarch and cold water. Stir into chili mixture to thicken, and cook an additional 3 to 4 minutes. Serve hot, garnished with Corn Crisps.

NUTRIENT ANALYSIS

Calories	374.46 kcal
Protein	30.02 g
Carbohydrate	46.07 g
Total Fat	9.38 g
Saturated	2.68 g
Polyunsaturated	2.34 g
Monounsaturated	2.99 g
Cholesterol	47.96 mg
Sodium	286.83 mg

BEEF OR VENISON STROGANOFF

The long, slow cooking tenderizes
the meat and gives the stroganoff a
chance to develop its full flavor.
Use beef or venison in this recipe.

SERVES 10
¾ CUP STROGANOFF AND
¾ CUP MACARONI
PER SERVING

½ cup all-purpose flour
½ teaspoon freshly ground black pepper
2 pounds boneless beef round steak or venison, all visible fat
    removed, cut into bite-size pieces
2 tablespoons acceptable vegetable oil
1 large onion, sliced ¼-inch thick
1¾ cups homemade Beef Stock (see pages 353–354)
¼ cup dry sherry
1 pound fresh mushrooms, thickly sliced
1 12-ounce package macaroni
1 cup Double-Thick Yogurt (see page 351)
2 tablespoons ketchup
1 tablespoon Worcestershire sauce
¼ teaspoon salt

In a large bowl, mix flour and pepper. Add meat and toss
to coat evenly.

In a large, nonstick skillet or Dutch oven, heat oil over
medium-high heat. Add meat and onions and sauté, stirring
frequently, until meat is nearly browned on all sides, about
5 minutes. Add stock and sherry; stir well. Partially cover
and simmer over low heat, stirring occasionally, 1½ hours,
or until meat is tender.

While meat simmers, sauté mushrooms in a nonstick
skillet over medium heat, stirring occasionally. Cook 20
minutes. Add mushrooms to the meat.

Cook macaroni according to package directions, omitting salt; drain.

Place Double-Thick Yogurt, ketchup, Worcestershire sauce and salt in a medium bowl. Whisk together to mix well and set aside.

When meat is fully cooked, add yogurt mixture. Stir and heat about 5 minutes. Serve over macaroni.

The meat mixture freezes well. Just omit the Double-Thick Yogurt, and add it after reheating.

NUTRIENT ANALYSIS OF BEEF STROGANOFF	
Calories	340.01 kcal
Protein	29.31 g
Carbohydrate	37.50 g
Total Fat	7.64 g
Saturated	2.33 g
Polyunsaturated	2.10 g
Monounsaturated	2.54 g
Cholesterol	60.28 mg
Sodium	292.67 mg

NUTRIENT ANALYSIS OF VENISON STROGANOFF	
Calories	345.73 kcal
Protein	31.66 g
Carbohydrate	37.50 g
Total Fat	7.64 g
Saturated	2.21 g
Polyunsaturated	3.16 g
Monounsaturated	1.58 g
Cholesterol	43.77 mg
Sodium	309.18 mg

LAMB AND RED BEANS

Make a double batch and freeze
some for later.

SERVES 8
1½ CUPS PER SERVING

2 tablespoons olive oil
2 medium onions, chopped
3 cloves garlic, finely chopped
2 pounds lean lamb, all visible fat removed, cut into bite-size
    pieces
6 medium tomatoes, chopped
2 15-ounce cans red kidney beans, rinsed and drained
1 teaspoon turmeric
1 teaspoon freshly ground black pepper, or to taste
1 tablespoon fresh lemon juice
¼ cup finely chopped fresh parsley
1 tablespoon finely chopped fresh mint or 1 teaspoon dried mint
¾ cup homemade Chicken Stock (see page 352)
½ cup plain nonfat yogurt, lightly beaten

Garnish
2 tablespoons fresh parsley, chopped

Preheat oven to 350° F.

In Dutch oven or ovenproof casserole, heat oil over medium-high heat. Add onions and garlic, and sauté until onions are soft. Stir in lamb pieces and allow to brown on all sides, about 5 to 7 minutes. Add tomatoes, kidney beans, turmeric, pepper, lemon juice, parsley, mint and chicken stock. Bring to a boil, cover and transfer to oven. Bake 1 to

1½ hours, or until lamb pieces are tender. Remove from oven. Stir in yogurt, and garnish with parsley.

This dish freezes well for up to two months. If freezing, omit yogurt and garnish. Reheat in a preheated 350° F. oven until heated thoroughly, 30 to 35 minutes, then add yogurt and garnish.

NUTRIENT ANALYSIS

Calories	361.92 kcal
Protein	31.82 g
Carbohydrate	30.02 g
Total Fat	12.72 g
Saturated	4.04 g
Polyunsaturated	1.37 g
Monounsaturated	5.59 g
Cholesterol	80.27 mg
Sodium	84.04 mg

PORK WITH SAVORY SAUCE

The raspberry or balsamic vinegar gives this dish a dash of elegance.

SERVES 4
APPROXIMATELY 4 OUNCES
PER SERVING

¾ cup homemade Chicken
   Stock (see page 352)
¼ cup raspberry or balsamic
   vinegar
4 teaspoons olive oil
2 tablespoons port wine
½ teaspoon coarsely ground
   black pepper
½ teaspoon dried oregano
1 garlic clove, minced
1 teaspoon cornstarch
2 tablespoons cold water
1¼ pounds pork tenderloin,
   all visible fat removed, cut
   into ¼-inch medallions

NUTRIENT ANALYSIS

Calories	215.39 kcal
Protein	29.22 g
Carbohydrate	1.89 g
Total Fat	9.42 g
Saturated	2.29 g
Polyunsaturated	0.99 g
Monounsaturated	5.49 g
Cholesterol	93.55 mg
Sodium	73.03 mg

In a small saucepan, combine stock, vinegar, 2 teaspoons oil, wine, pepper, oregano and garlic. Cook, uncovered, over medium-high heat about 20 minutes, or until liquid is reduced to ½ cup.

Mix cornstarch and water and stir to fully dissolve. Add to the pan, stirring to mix well. Heat over medium heat, stirring until mixture thickens, about 1 minute. Cover, remove from heat and set aside.

Heat 2 teaspoons oil in a nonstick skillet over medium-high heat. Add pork and sauté 3 to 4 minutes on each side, or until pork is no longer pink. Pour 2 tablespoons of sauce over each piece. Serve hot.

PORK AND TOFU STIR-FRY

SERVES 6
1½ CUPS PER SERVING

This dish is wonderful served on a Pasta Pancake (see page 229). It can also be served with ordinary noodles or rice. If you marinate the pork and slice the vegetables in advance, the meal can be put together quickly.

Tofu is an excellent high-protein, lowfat food made from soy milk. It is extremely versatile and can be used creatively in several ways—salads, dips, sandwiches, casseroles, burgers and even desserts like ice cream. Over the years, tofu has gained great popularity and is now considered an important protein source in a lowfat diet. It is available in health food stores and most supermarkets.

1 pound lean, boneless pork, all visible fat removed

Marinade
1 tablespoon homemade Chicken Stock (see page 352)
1 tablespoon dry sherry (optional)
1 tablespoon low-sodium soy sauce
2 tablespoons minced fresh ginger or 1 teaspoon ginger powder
2 cloves garlic, minced

Sauce
½ cup water
2 teaspoons low-sodium soy sauce
1 tablespoon honey
1 tablespoon Worcestershire sauce
1 tablespoon cornstarch

Vegetables
3 teaspoons acceptable vegetable oil, to be used 1 teaspoon at a time
1 small green bell pepper, cut into 1-inch strips
1 small red or yellow bell pepper, cut into 1-inch strips

1 small onion, cut into wedges
6 green onions with tops, sliced diagonally
2 stalks celery, sliced diagonally
20 snow peas, trimmed
1 cup finely sliced red cabbage

8 ounces firm tofu, drained and cut into ½-inch cubes
10 to 12 cherry tomatoes, halved

S lice pork into thin 1-inch strips.

In a small bowl, combine all ingredients for marinade; add sliced pork and toss to coat. In another bowl, combine all ingredients for sauce; stir to blend and set aside.

Heat 1 teaspoon of the oil in a large, nonstick skillet or wok over high heat. Add vegetables and stir-fry 2 minutes. Remove vegetables from pan; set aside.

Heat another teaspoon of oil and stir-fry tofu 1 to 2 minutes, or until light golden brown. Remove and set aside with vegetables.

Heat remaining teaspoon of oil, add pork and marinade. Stir-fry until meat loses its pink color. Stir in tomatoes and reserved sauce. Cook until sauce starts to bubble and thicken. Add reserved vegetables and heat thoroughly, 1 to 2 minutes.

NUTRIENT ANALYSIS

Calories	196.95 kcal
Protein	20.72 g
Carbohydrate	14.96 g
Total Fat	6.64 g
Saturated	1.45 g
Polyunsaturated	2.60 g
Monounsaturated	2.08 g
Cholesterol	49.09 mg
Sodium	281.18 mg

SCRAMBLED EGGS AND HAM IN SWEET POTATO BOAT

This dish is great for a light meal, including breakfast. The ham or Canadian bacon offers lots of flavor with very little fat.

SERVES 2
1 BOAT PER SERVING

4 large egg whites
2 teaspoons skim milk
2 ounces Canadian bacon or ham, visible fat removed, diced
Vegetable oil spray
2 medium sweet potatoes, baked

Garnish (optional)
1 tablespoon grated lowfat cheddar cheese
Freshly ground black pepper to taste

NUTRIENT ANALYSIS

Calories	201.16 kcal
Protein	15.42 g
Carbohydrate	27.89 g
Total Fat	2.82 g
Saturated	0.95 g
Polyunsaturated	0.36 g
Monounsaturated	1.17 g
Cholesterol	16.54 mg
Sodium	551.34 mg

In a small bowl, whisk together egg whites and milk. Add Canadian bacon or ham.

Spray a small, nonstick frying pan with vegetable oil spray and place over medium heat. Add egg mixture and stir. Cook until semi-firm.

Cut each potato in half, lengthwise. Top potato halves with scrambled eggs. Garnish with cheese and pepper. Serve hot.

VEGETARIAN DISHES

Vegetarian Sauce with Whole-Wheat Pasta
Pasta Primavera
Macaroni and Cheese
Spinach-Stuffed Pizza
Spicy Lentil Curry
Chilled Stuffed Artichokes
Eggplant Parmigiana
Tofu Quiche
Spanish-Style Scrambled Eggs
Shredded Wheat with Banana-Milk Topping

VEGETARIAN SAUCE WITH WHOLE-WHEAT PASTA

SERVES 6
1½ CUPS PER SERVING

The whole-wheat pasta used in this recipe gives this dish a wonderful, nutty flavor. The sauce can be made in advance and reheated at serving time. The flavors improve with age. Leftovers or the whole recipe can be frozen.

2 tablespoons olive oil
6 green onions, with tops, chopped
1 large red or white onion, chopped
4 cloves garlic, minced
8 ounces mushrooms, sliced
2 ribs celery with leaves, chopped
2 medium red, green or yellow bell peppers, chopped
1 16-ounce can vegetarian beans or 1 16-ounce can kidney
   beans
1 16-ounce can no-salt-added tomatoes
1 cup water
½ cup dry red wine (optional)
¼ cup minced fresh parsley
1 bay leaf
1 tablespoon chopped fresh oregano or 1 teaspoon dried
   oregano
1 tablespoon chopped fresh basil or ½ teaspoon dried basil
Freshly ground black pepper to taste
12 ounces whole-wheat pasta
4 ounces part-skim mozzarella cheese, shredded

In a large saucepan or Dutch oven, heat oil over medium-high heat. Add onions and garlic and sauté until onions are soft, 2 to 3 minutes. Add remaining ingredients, except pasta and cheese, and bring to a boil. Reduce heat and simmer, covered, about 1 hour, stirring frequently. Remove bay leaf before serving.

Cook noodles according to package directions, omitting salt. Rinse and drain. Serve sauce over hot pasta. Sprinkle with 1 to 2 tablespoons shredded cheese per serving.

NUTRIENT ANALYSIS

Calories	449.00 kcal
Protein	24.09 g
Carbohydrate	73.74 g
Total Fat	9.32 g
Saturated	2.94 g
Polyunsaturated	1.16 g
Monounsaturated	4.40 g
Cholesterol	10.21 mg
Sodium	142.08 mg

PASTA PRIMAVERA

SERVES 4
2 CUPS PER SERVING

This is a wonderful and simple one-dish meal. Make the sauce a day ahead of time and prepare the vegetables a few hours before serving. The pasta is best when prepared "al dente," cooked until tender, yet still firm. Try using freshly grated Parmesan cheese, which releases the cheese's full flavor.

3 cups broccoli florets, cut into bite-size pieces
½ pound fresh mushrooms, quartered
2 small zucchini, sliced into ¼-inch rounds
1 tablespoon olive oil
3 cloves garlic, minced
1 pint cherry tomatoes, stemmed and cut in half
8 ounces fettuccine

Sauce
¾ cup skim milk
3 tablespoons nonfat "butter" granules
⅔ cup part-skim ricotta cheese
¼ cup grated Parmesan cheese
2 tablespoons chopped fresh basil or 1 tablespoon dried basil
2 teaspoons dry sherry

Garnish
2 tablespoons grated Parmesan cheese
Freshly ground black pepper to taste

In a large saucepan fitted with a steamer basket, layer broccoli, mushrooms and zucchini. Steam for about 3 minutes, or until just tender-crisp. Set aside.

In a large, nonstick skillet or nonstick wok, heat olive oil over medium-high heat. Add garlic and sauté for 1 minute, stirring frequently. Add tomatoes and sauté for 2 minutes, stirring frequently, until tomatoes are slightly cooked, but not wilted. Set aside.

Cook fettuccine according to package directions, omitting salt. Drain well.

Combine milk, "butter" granules, ricotta cheese, Parmesan cheese, basil and sherry in a blender. Process until smooth. In a small saucepan, heat sauce over low heat, stirring occasionally, until warm.

In a large serving dish, toss the drained pasta, vegetables and sauce to coat well. Garnish each portion with Parmesan cheese and pepper. Serve immediately.

NUTRIENT ANALYSIS

Calories	383.96 kcal
Protein	18.51 g
Carbohydrate	61.14 g
Total Fat	8.08 g
Saturated	2.67 g
Polyunsaturated	0.75 g
Monounsaturated	3.52 g
Cholesterol	9.81 mg
Sodium	418.48 mg

MACARONI AND CHEESE

SERVES 3
I CUP PER SERVING

This recipe starts with a favorite packaged food. The great cheese flavor and very little fat will surprise you. That's because lowfat sour cream is used instead of butter or margarine. Try it as a main dish for a light meal.

1 7-ounce package macaroni and cheese (with powdered cheese-sauce packet)
2 tablespoons skim milk
¹⁄₃ cup lowfat sour cream

Cook the noodles according to package directions, omitting salt. Drain, then add milk and sour cream instead of the butter or margarine called for on the package. Mix well to coat evenly. Add contents of the cheese-sauce packet; mix well. Serve hot.

NUTRIENT ANALYSIS

Calories	283.85 kcal
Protein	9.99 g
Carbohydrate	45.39 g
Total Fat	5.42 g
Saturated	2.64 g
Polyunsaturated	0.79 g
Monounsaturated	1.59 g
Cholesterol	12.39 mg
Sodium	680.03 mg

SPINACH-STUFFED PIZZA

The fresh spinach gives this pizza a
delightful taste. Don't expect
leftovers!

SERVES 6
⅙ OF 9-INCH
DOUBLE-CRUST PIE

Dough

¾ cup very warm water (105° to 115° F.)
1 teaspoon sugar
1 package rapid-rise yeast
1½ cups whole-wheat flour
¾ cup all-purpose flour
Vegetable oil spray

Filling

6 ounces fresh spinach
1½ cups shredded part-skim mozzarella cheese, about 6 ounces
⅓ cup grated Parmesan cheese, about 1 ounce

Topping

4 ounces fresh mushrooms, thinly sliced
2 teaspoons olive oil
1 cup prepared pizza or spaghetti sauce

To make the dough, combine sugar and water. Add yeast
and stir to dissolve. Let sit for about 5 minutes. The yeast
will bubble and develop a frothy head.

In a large bowl, mix the flours. Make a well in the center
and slowly pour in the yeast mixture, while mixing. Knead
the dough 6 to 8 minutes, or until a ball of smooth-yet-
elastic dough forms. If dough is sticky, add more all-purpose flour as you knead. Lighly dust the ball of dough with
all-purpose flour, put into the bowl and cover with plastic
wrap and a towel. Place in a warm, draft-free place and
allow to rise until doubled in bulk, about 30 minutes.

Preheat oven to 475° F.

Punch down and divide dough into two balls. Keep one in the bowl, covered with plastic wrap, and place the other on a lightly floured surface. Use a lightly floured rolling pin to roll the ball into an 11-inch circle. Spray the bottom and sides of a 9-inch glass pie plate with vegetable oil spray. Place the rolled dough in the plate so that it covers the bottom and sides. With a fork, generously prick the dough on the bottom. Bake 4 minutes, remove to a rack and let cool.

To prepare the filling, rinse, stem, dry and chop the spinach. Mix with cheeses and spread in the prebaked crust.

Roll the second dough ball into an 11-inch circle, place over the filling and tuck the edges of dough around the bottom crust layer. Compress the filling by applying light pressure to the dough with the palms of your hands. Cut a 1-inch slit in the center of the top crust.

To make the topping, heat oil in a small nonstick skillet over medium-high heat. Add mushrooms and sauté 3 to 4 minutes, or until soft, stirring occasionally. Evenly spread the topping over the top crust and top with pizza sauce. Place on middle rack of oven, reduce temperature to 450° F. and bake 15 minutes. Reduce temperature to 400° F. and bake another 5 to 10 minutes, or until edges are deep golden brown.

NUTRIENT ANALYSIS

Calories	304.43 kcal
Protein	16.71 g
Carbohydrate	39.98 g
Total Fat	9.90 g
Saturated	4.30 g
Polyunsaturated	1.37 g
Monounsaturated	3.62 g
Cholesterol	20.10 mg
Sodium	514.38 mg

SPICY LENTIL CURRY

This makes a good vegetarian meal
when served with rice and yogurt.
Leftovers are delicious with pita
bread. You'll want to make extra to
freeze.

SERVES 6
I CUP PER SERVING

1½ cups lentils, washed and drained
6 cups water
1 tablespoon acceptable vegetable oil
1 teaspoon cumin seeds
1 large onion, chopped
1 medium tomato, chopped
1 red hot chili pepper (optional)
1 tablespoon grated fresh ginger or 1 teaspoon powdered ginger
1 clove garlic, minced
½ teaspoon ground turmeric
½ teaspoon salt

Garnish
2 tablespoons chopped fresh cilantro or parsley

In a heavy saucepan, heat lentils and water over medium-
high heat. Bring to a boil, then reduce heat. Simmer, partially covered, 45 to 50 minutes, or until lentils are tender,
occasionally skimming off the foam. Stir to prevent sticking.

In a nonstick skillet, heat oil over medium-high heat.
Sauté cumin seeds for just a minute, taking care not to burn
them. Add onions and cook until light brown, 4 to 5 minutes. Add tomato and hot pepper and continue to cook
until tomato is reduced to a pulp, about 5 minutes, stirring
frequently. Remove hot pepper.

When lentils are tender, stir in onion mixture, ginger,

garlic, turmeric and salt and cook another 10 to 15 minutes. Serve hot, garnished with cilantro or parsley.

NUTRIENT ANALYSIS

Calories	218.05 kcal
Protein	13.23 g
Carbohydrate	36.35 g
Total Fat	4.27 g
Saturated	0.54 g
Polyunsaturated	2.16 g
Monounsaturated	0.85 g
Cholesterol	0.00 mg
Sodium	201.93 mg

CHILLED STUFFED ARTICHOKES

This elegant and different main dish
is fun to eat. The combination of
artichokes and assorted vegetables
with a smooth, creamy sauce is
delightful.

SERVES 4

4 artichokes
1 tablespoon fresh lemon juice
3 cups Steamed Vegetables with Ginger (see page 251)

Sauce
5 ounces tofu, drained
1/2 cup tomato puree
1/4 cup prepared horseradish
2 teaspoons fresh lemon juice
2 teaspoons white vinegar
1/2 teaspoon Lemon Herb Seasoning (see page 34)
1/2 teaspoon onion powder
1/2 teaspoon sugar
A few drops hot pepper sauce
Freshly ground white pepper to taste

Remove stem and tough leaves from the base of each artichoke. Cut off top third of leaves. Place the prepared artichokes and lemon juice in a deep saucepan. Add boiling
water to cover. Cover and cook 30 minutes, or until one of
the lower artichoke leaves pulls off easily. Remove from
water, turn upside down to drain, then refrigerate to cool.

Remove the center, fuzzy portion of each artichoke and
fill with 3/4 cup chilled Steamed Vegetables with Ginger.

In a blender or the workbowl of a food processor fitted
with a metal blade, process sauce ingredients until fully
blended. Pour 1/3 cup of sauce over each serving.

NUTRIENT ANALYSIS

Calories	77.87 kcal
Protein	6.55 g
Carbohydrate	17.20 g
Total Fat	1.81 g
Saturated	0.24 g
Polyunsaturated	0.87 g
Monounsaturated	0.35 g
Cholesterol	0.00 mg
Sodium	57.58 mg

EGGPLANT PARMIGIANA

We've lifted the fat—but kept the
flavor—of this Italian favorite. To
complete the meal, add garden
salad and Whole-Wheat French
Bread (see pages 269–270).

SERVES 6
1 4×4-INCH PORTION
PER SERVING

Sauce

1 14-ounce can artichoke hearts, drained
2 8-ounce cans no-salt-added tomato sauce
1 6-ounce can no-salt-added tomato paste
1 tablespoon olive oil
1/4 teaspoon fennel seeds, crushed (optional)
1 tablespoon Italian herb seasoning
2 cloves garlic, finely minced
1/8 teaspoon freshly ground black pepper
Dash hot pepper sauce

Eggplant-Cheese Layers

1 eggplant, about 1 pound, sliced into 3/8-inch rounds
10 ounces tofu, drained
1 large egg white
1 cup part-skim mozzarella cheese, shredded, about 4 ounces
1 tablespoon all-purpose flour (if needed)
1/3 cup grated Parmesan cheese, about 1 ounce
1/3 cup bread crumbs from French or sourdough bread

In a blender or the workbowl of a food processor fitted
with a metal blade, blend sauce ingredients for about 30
seconds, or until no lumps remain. Set aside.

Preheat broiler. Place eggplant slices on baking sheet; do
not overlap. Broil 4 inches from heat, 3 to 4 minutes per
side, being careful not to burn the eggplant. Remove from
oven and let cool.

Preheat oven to 350° F.

Place tofu between two thick layers of paper towels. Place between two plates and press down on the top plate. Pour off the liquid. In a blender, process tofu and egg white until smooth; set aside.

To keep mozzarella from sticking together, it may be necessary to mix it with flour.

In a 2-quart ovenproof glass $8 \times 11\frac{1}{2} \times 2$-inch pan, assemble the layers in order from bottom to top: a third sauce, half eggplant slices, a third sauce, mozzarella, tofu-egg mixture, remaining eggplant slices, remaining sauce, Parmesan cheese and bread crumbs.

Bake, uncovered, 35 minutes. Let sit 5 minutes before serving.

NUTRIENT ANALYSIS

Calories	235.21 kcal
Protein	16.46 g
Carbohydrate	28.05 g
Total Fat	9.50 g
Saturated	3.47 g
Polyunsaturated	1.50 g
Monounsaturated	3.45 g
Cholesterol	14.72 mg
Sodium	284.07 mg

TOFU QUICHE

Do you love quiche but realize that all the cream and butter in it aren't for you? Here's a creamy, yet cream-free, quiche. Enjoy!

SERVES 8
⅛ PIE PER SERVING

Crust
Vegetable oil spray
2 shredded wheat biscuits, crushed

Filling
1 teaspoon olive oil
1 medium onion, finely chopped
2 cups frozen chopped vegetables (a good mixture is broccoli, corn and red bell peppers)
4 large egg whites
10 ounces firm tofu, drained
1 tablespoon fresh lemon juice
1 tablespoon nonfat "butter" granules (optional)
Pinch ground nutmeg
Pinch freshly ground black pepper
8 ounces lean ham, visible fat removed

Garnish
Ground nutmeg

P reheat oven to 350° F.

Spray a 9-inch pie pan with vegetable oil spray and add crushed shredded wheat biscuits evenly to bottom of pan.

In a large, nonstick skillet, heat oil at medium setting. Add onion and sauté, stirring frequently, until onion is soft. Add vegetables, mix thoroughly, remove from heat and set aside.

In a blender or the workbowl of a food processor fitted

with a metal blade, process egg whites, tofu, lemon juice, "butter" granules, nutmeg and pepper until smooth and creamy. Cut ham into eight pieces and add to tofu mixture. Process just until ham is diced.

Evenly place the onion-vegetable mixture over the biscuit crust. Pour tofu-ham mixture over vegetables, spreading evenly with a spatula. Bake 40 to 45 minutes, or until a knife inserted in the center comes out clean. Top with a light dusting of nutmeg. Serve hot or at room temperature.

NUTRIENT ANALYSIS

Calories	127.90 kcal
Protein	11.77 g
Carbohydrate	11.56 g
Total Fat	4.46 g
Saturated	1.07 g
Polyunsaturated	1.28 g
Monounsaturated	1.74 g
Cholesterol	18.26 mg
Sodium	242.96 mg

SPANISH-STYLE SCRAMBLED EGGS

SERVES 3
⅓ CUP PER SERVING

1 teaspoon acceptable
   vegetable oil
1 green onion, finely chopped
1 small ripe tomato, finely
   chopped
6 large egg whites
1 tablespoon Salsa (see page
   260) or picante sauce
Freshly ground black pepper
   to taste
1 tablespoon minced fresh
   cilantro or parsley

Garnish
Cilantro or parsley sprigs
1 tomato, cut into wedges

NUTRIENT ANALYSIS	
Calories	68.07 kcal
Protein	7.63 g
Carbohydrate	5.31 g
Total Fat	1.70 g
Saturated	0.20 g
Polyunsaturated	0.89 g
Monounsaturated	0.37 g
Cholesterol	0.00 mg
Sodium	155.34 mg

In nonstick skillet, heat oil over medium-high heat. Add onions and tomato; sauté until onions are soft, 1 to 2 minutes. Reduce heat to low.

In a bowl, combine egg whites, Salsa or picante sauce and pepper; beat until frothy. Add to the skillet. Cook over low heat, stirring occasionally, until almost set. Add cilantro or parsley and stir until eggs are fully set. Garnish with cilantro or parsley and tomato.

SHREDDED WHEAT WITH BANANA-MILK TOPPING

This makes a quick, nutritious breakfast.

**SERVES 2
APPROXIMATELY 1 CUP
PER SERVING**

*1 ripe banana
2 cups bite-size shredded wheat biscuits
¼ cup wheat bran (unprocessed miller's bran)
2 tablespoons sliced almonds
1½ cups skim milk
1 or 2 drops vanilla extract*

Peel banana and place in a heavy plastic bag. Freeze at least 6 hours. Remove from freezer and cut into eighths.

Divide shredded wheat biscuits into two serving bowls. Top with wheat bran and almonds. In blender, process banana slices, milk and vanilla until slightly frothy. Pour over cereal. Serve immediately.

NUTRIENT ANALYSIS

Calories	350.77 kcal
Protein	14.91 g
Carbohydrate	67.21 g
Total Fat	5.95 g
Saturated	0.86 g
Polyunsaturated	1.56 g
Monounsaturated	2.98 g
Cholesterol	3.68 mg
Sodium	102.10 mg

VEGETABLES

Green Beans Almondine
Refried Beans
Beets in Orange Sauce
Stir-Fried Broccoli
Honey Carrots
Sautéed Carrots
Corn on the Cob
Sautéed Greens
Pasta Pancake
Southern-Style Black-eyed Peas
Green Peas with Lettuce
Baked Potatoes with Vegetable Topping
Herbed Baby Potatoes
Home-Fried Potatoes
Favorite Mashed Potatoes
Scalloped Potatoes
Steamed New Potatoes with Garlic Sauce
Golden Rice
Savory Brown Rice
Spaghetti Squash
Spinach Cheese Strudel
Sautéed Cherry Tomatoes
Sautéed Zucchini
Ratatouille
Chinese Vegetable Stir-Fry
Steamed Vegetables with Ginger

GREEN BEANS ALMONDINE

SERVES 6
½ CUP PER SERVING

1 pound fresh green beans
1 teaspoon acceptable margarine
1 tablespoon chopped fresh oregano or 1 teaspoon dried
   oregano
Freshly ground black pepper to taste
3 tablespoons sliced almonds

Trim and slice green beans into 2-inch sections. In non-stick skillet, heat margarine over medium-high heat. Add green beans and sauté 2 to 3 minutes, stirring constantly so beans cook evenly. Add oregano and pepper; sauté 20 to 30 seconds. Beans should be tender-crisp. Sprinkle with almonds and serve immediately.

NUTRIENT ANALYSIS

Calories	47.03 kcal
Protein	1.92 g
Carbohydrate	5.24 g
Total Fat	2.69 g
Saturated	0.28 g
Polyunsaturated	0.63 g
Monounsaturated	1.62 g
Cholesterol	0.00 mg
Sodium	9.44 mg

REFRIED BEANS

Many canned refried beans contain lard. This recipe has only a small amount of vegetable oil, so it fits right into a healthful diet.

SERVES 5
½ CUP PER SERVING

1 teaspoon acceptable
   vegetable oil
2 tablespoons finely chopped
   onion
2 cloves garlic, minced
2 15-ounce cans no-salt-
   added pinto beans
1 tablespoon reduced-sodium
   ketchup
2 tablespoons canned, diced
   green chili peppers

NUTRIENT ANALYSIS

Calories	192.91 kcal
Protein	11.61 g
Carbohydrate	34.08 g
Total Fat	2.99 g
Saturated	0.56 g
Polyunsaturated	1.47 g
Monounsaturated	0.41 g
Cholesterol	0.00 mg
Sodium	13.67 mg

In large, nonstick skillet, heat oil over medium heat. Add onion and sauté about 5 minutes, or until soft. Add garlic and sauté another 2 to 3 minutes. Set aside. Drain beans well, reserving liquid. Put beans in shallow bowl and mash with a potato masher or fork. Add ½ cup of reserved bean liquid and ketchup, and mash again. Add bean mixture and chili peppers to the sautéed garlic and onion. Mix well.

Heat over medium heat, stirring constantly, until beans are thoroughly heated.

BEETS IN ORANGE SAUCE

SERVES 6
¾ CUP PER SERVING

The smooth orange sauce adds zest and flair to brightly colored beets. To prevent the color of beets from "bleeding" during cooking and also to preserve nutrients, leave about 2 inches of stem on the beets. Peel beets only after they have been cooked.

2 pounds fresh beets
1 tablespoon sugar
1 tablespoon cornstarch
¼ teaspoon salt (optional)
⅔ cup fresh orange juice
2 teaspoons grated orange
    rind, or to taste
1 teaspoon acceptable
    margarine

Garnish
1 orange, peeled and
    divided into sections

NUTRIENT ANALYSIS	
Calories	92.00 kcal
Protein	2.05 g
Carbohydrate	20.30 g
Total Fat	0.85 g
Saturated	0.12 g
Polyunsaturated	0.23 g
Monounsaturated	0.30 g
Cholesterol	0.00 mg
Sodium	159.91 mg

Cook beets until tender. Drain, peel and slice.

To prepare sauce, combine sugar, cornstarch and salt. Slowly add orange juice and orange rind, stirring until smooth. Cook over medium heat, stirring constantly, until thickened, 5 to 8 minutes. Add margarine and stir until melted.

Pour sauce over warm beets, garnish with orange sections and serve.

STIR-FRIED BROCCOLI

This recipe uses only the broccoli
florets. Use the stems in soups, or
cook and serve them as a vegetable
side dish.

SERVES 6
½ CUP PER SERVING

1½ pounds broccoli
4 green onions with tops, cut into 1-inch strips
1 tablespoon acceptable margarine
1 teaspoon Lemon Herb Seasoning (see page 34)

Trim broccoli, reserving stems for use in another recipe.
Rinse and break broccoli florets into bite-size pieces. In a
nonstick skillet, stir-fry broccoli and onions 2 to 3 minutes
over medium-high heat. Add margarine, sprinkle with seasoning and toss to coat evenly. Broccoli should be tender-
crisp. Serve immediately.

NUTRIENT ANALYSIS

Calories	61.60 kcal
Protein	4.65 g
Carbohydrate	8.13 g
Total Fat	2.41 g
Saturated	0.32 g
Polyunsaturated	0.65 g
Monounsaturated	0.87 g
Cholesterol	0.00 mg
Sodium	49.15 mg

HONEY CARROTS

Carrots fixed this way will be a
favorite—even among the young
ones in your family.

SERVES 6
½ CUP PER SERVING

1½ pounds baby carrots, fresh or frozen
½ cup water
1 tablespoon acceptable margarine
½ tablespoon brown sugar
2 tablespoons honey
2 to 3 tablespoons minced fresh parsley

R inse and trim carrots, if fresh. Bring water to a boil in a
medium saucepan. Add carrots, reduce heat, cover and simmer about 10 minutes, or until carrots are tender-crisp.
Drain.

If using frozen carrots, follow package directions for
cooking.

In a nonstick skillet, melt margarine over medium-high
heat. Add sugar, honey and carrots. Reduce heat and turn
carrots frequently until well glazed, 1 to 2 minutes. Sprinkle
with parsley before serving.

NUTRIENT ANALYSIS

Calories	88.27 kcal
Protein	1.41 g
Carbohydrate	17.36 g
Total Fat	2.19 g
Saturated	0.31 g
Polyunsaturated	0.64 g
Monounsaturated	0.86 g
Cholesterol	0.00 mg
Sodium	74.81 mg

SAUTÉED CARROTS

Tired of plain carrots? Try these for
a distinctive change of pace. The
apple and lemon juices make the
difference.

SERVES 6
½ CUP PER SERVING

1 pound carrots, peeled and grated
1 tablespoon fresh lemon juice
2 tablespoons frozen apple juice concentrate, defrosted
1 teaspoon margarine or 1½ teaspoons nonfat "butter"
    granules

Garnish
1 teaspoon poppy seeds

In a nonstick skillet, combine carrots, lemon juice and
apple juice concentrate. Place over medium-high heat and
sauté about 3 minutes, stirring constantly. Add margarine
or "butter" granules and stir to coat evenly. Garnish with
poppy seeds and serve hot.

NUTRIENT ANALYSIS

Calories	43.77 kcal
Protein	0.93 g
Carbohydrate	7.90 g
Total Fat	1.00 g
Saturated	0.13 g
Polyunsaturated	0.36 g
Monounsaturated	0.31 g
Cholesterol	0.00 mg
Sodium	44.56 mg

CORN ON THE COB

How can anyone improve on plain,
fresh corn? Try just a little curry
powder, and see for yourself.

SERVES 4

4 ears fresh corn, husked
4 teaspoons nonfat "butter" granules
1/4 teaspoon curry powder

In a large saucepan, bring 5 quarts of water to a boil. Add
corn and return to a boil. Boil uncovered 2 minutes; remove
from heat. Let stand uncovered 10 minutes. Remove corn
from water.

While corn cooks, follow directions on the package to
reconstitute the nonfat "butter" granules with water. Mix
with curry powder. Drizzle over corn and serve immediately.

NUTRIENT ANALYSIS

Calories	76.48 kcal
Protein	2.58 g
Carbohydrate	17.69 g
Total Fat	0.86 g
Saturated	0.10 g
Polyunsaturated	0.45 g
Monounsaturated	0.18 g
Cholesterol	0.02 mg
Sodium	88.15 mg

SAUTÉED GREENS

Good nutrition and good taste—all in one dish. This cooking method leaves the greens tender-crisp, and the spices add a dash of flavor.

SERVES 6
½ CUP PER SERVING

1 bunch collard greens, about
   ¾ pound, rinsed, stems
   removed and coarsely
   shredded
⅓ medium head cabbage,
   coarsely shredded
2 tablespoons olive oil
1 clove garlic, minced
1 medium onion, cut into
   quarters and sliced
1 to 2 teaspoons rice vinegar
   (optional)

NUTRIENT ANALYSIS	
Calories	68.34 kcal
Protein	2.12 g
Carbohydrate	5.57 g
Total Fat	4.88 g
Saturated	0.61 g
Polyunsaturated	0.38 g
Monounsaturated	3.32 g
Cholesterol	0.00 mg
Sodium	18.94 mg

In a large saucepan, boil 3 quarts of water. Add collard greens, return to a boil and cook 3 to 4 minutes, or until greens are tender-crisp. With a slotted spoon, remove greens, leaving the water in the pan. Place greens in a colander and set aside.

Return water to a boil, add cabbage and cook 1 minute. Pour into the colander and let drain. Set aside.

In a large skillet, heat olive oil over medium-low setting. Sauté garlic and onions 3 to 4 minutes, or until tender-crisp. Add greens and cabbage, and sauté 2 to 3 minutes, stirring occasionally. Add vinegar. Toss and serve immediately.

PASTA PANCAKE

Try this for a tasty alternative to
plain noodles. The recipe can be
made from freshly cooked or
leftover noodles.

SERVES 8
1 WEDGE PER SERVING

16 ounces fine linguine, vermicelli or thin spaghetti
2 tablespoons acceptable vegetable oil, divided
Vegetable oil spray
1 teaspoon sesame seeds, toasted

P reheat oven to 400° F.

Cook noodles according to package directions, omitting salt. Drain, add 1 tablespoon oil and toss to coat.

Grease a large 12-inch pizza or round baking pan with vegetable oil spray. Heat pan in preheated oven 3 to 4 minutes. Arrange noodles on heated pan and press down lightly. Drizzle the remaining tablespoon of oil on top. Bake 15 to 20 minutes, or until the edges are crisp and lightly browned. Sprinkle with sesame seeds. Cut into eight wedges and serve.

NUTRIENT ANALYSIS

Calories	224.42 kcal
Protein	6.59 g
Carbohydrate	39.16 g
Total Fat	4.23 g
Saturated	0.56 g
Polyunsaturated	2.36 g
Monounsaturated	0.97 g
Cholesterol	0.00 mg
Sodium	166.60 mg

SOUTHERN-STYLE BLACK-EYED PEAS

SERVES 4 (AS A MAIN DISH)
1½ CUPS PER SERVING
SERVES 12 (AS A SIDE DISH)
½ CUP PER SERVING

Make this mainstay of Southern cuisine in a crockpot or on top of the stove. Black-eyed peas are rich in protein and contain a soluble fiber that may help lower blood cholesterol slightly. Seasoning the peas with ham instead of the traditional salt pork lowers the fat content considerably.

*1 pound dried black-eyed
  peas*
½ medium onion, diced
1 medium carrot, thinly sliced
*1 serrano pepper, seeded and
  thinly sliced (optional)*
*4 ounces smoke-flavored lean
  ham, visible fat removed,
  diced*
5 cups water

NUTRIENT ANALYSIS*

Calories	665.79 kcal
Protein	39.46 g
Carbohydrate	107.56 g
Total Fat	10.31 g
Saturated	1.57 g
Polyunsaturated	3.98 g
Monounsaturated	2.71 g
Cholesterol	18.26 mg
Sodium	219.81 mg

*For a main-dish serving.

Crockpot directions: Rinse peas under cold running water. Place all ingredients in crockpot. Cook on low setting 8 to 10 hours, or until peas are tender.

Stove-top directions: Rinse peas under cold running water. Place all ingredients in a large saucepan or Dutch oven. Add two additional cups of water. Bring to a boil and skim off any foam. Reduce heat to medium-low. Cover and simmer 2 hours, or until peas are tender.

GREEN PEAS WITH LETTUCE

This classic French vegetable dish goes well with meat, fish or poultry dishes.

SERVES 6
½ CUP PER SERVING

2 pounds fresh or 1 pound
    frozen green peas
1 tablespoon acceptable
    margarine
1 small onion, finely chopped
¼ teaspoon salt (optional)
½ teaspoon freshly ground
    black pepper, or to taste
1 to 2 tablespoons homemade
    Chicken Stock (see page
    352)
½ head lettuce, iceberg or
    romaine, rinsed, dried and
    finely shredded
½ tablespoon chopped fresh thyme or ½ teaspoon dried thyme
1 tablespoon minced fresh parsley

NUTRIENT ANALYSIS

Calories	81.61 kcal
Protein	4.62 g
Carbohydrate	11.77 g
Total Fat	2.25 g
Saturated	0.41 g
Polyunsaturated	0.68 g
Monounsaturated	0.95 g
Cholesterol	0.14 mg
Sodium	159.39 mg

Shell peas if fresh, defrost if frozen.

In a nonstick skillet, heat margarine over medium-high heat. Sauté onion until transparent, 2 to 3 minutes. Add peas, salt, pepper and stock. Cover and cook 1 minute. Top peas with lettuce. Cover tightly and cook over low heat 4 to 8 minutes, or until peas are tender. Sprinkle with herbs; toss and serve hot.

BAKED POTATOES WITH VEGETABLE TOPPING

SERVES 6
1 POTATO PER SERVING

6 medium baking potatoes, about 2 pounds
1 small onion, finely chopped
2 green onions with tops, finely chopped
1 small carrot, shredded
2 radishes, shredded
¼ cup cucumber, peeled, finely chopped
2 tablespoons cider vinegar
1 tablespoon chopped fresh basil or ½ teaspoon dried basil
½ cup plain nonfat yogurt
¼ cup grated Parmesan cheese
¼ cup skim milk
1 teaspoon nonfat "butter" granules
Freshly ground black pepper to taste

Preheat oven to 400° F.

Bake potatoes for 50 to 60 minutes, or until tender.

Combine onion, green onions, carrot, radishes, cucumber, vinegar and basil. Toss to mix well; set aside.

Cut a 1-inch-thick slice off the top of each potato, carefully scoop out the pulp and reserve the shells. Mash potato pulp with yogurt, Parmesan cheese, skim milk, "butter" granules and pepper. Mix until smooth. Stuff potato mixture into reserved shells. Place on baking sheet and bake at 350° F. for 25 to 30 minutes. Serve hot, topped with vegetable mixture.

NUTRIENT ANALYSIS

Calories	199.19 kcal
Protein	7.82 g
Carbohydrate	39.49 g
Total Fat	1.58 g
Saturated	0.85 g
Polyunsaturated	0.19 g
Monounsaturated	0.38 g
Cholesterol	3.84 mg
Sodium	124.55 mg

HERBED BABY POTATOES

Take simple kitchen staples, add to new potatoes, and you have a tasty side dish that goes well with almost anything.

SERVES 6
½ CUP PER SERVING

1½ pounds small red or new
    potatoes, scrubbed,
    unpeeled and quartered
2 tablespoons olive oil
2 tablespoons minced fresh
    parsley
1 tablespoon chopped fresh
    oregano or 1 teaspoon
    dried oregano
½ teaspoon paprika
½ teaspoon garlic powder
Freshly ground black pepper
    to taste

NUTRIENT ANALYSIS

Calories	129.97 kcal
Protein	2.59 g
Carbohydrate	20.22 g
Total Fat	4.70 g
Saturated	0.63 g
Polyunsaturated	0.50 g
Monounsaturated	3.33 g
Cholesterol	0.00 mg
Sodium	4.68 mg

Garnish
2 tablespoons minced fresh parsley

Preheat oven to 350° F.

In a 2-quart casserole, toss potatoes in oil to coat each piece. Add remaining ingredients, except parsley for garnish. Toss to coat evenly. Bake 30 to 40 minutes, or until lightly browned. Garnish with parsley.

HOME-FRIED POTATOES

These potatoes are a family favorite
and are delicious with Chicken with
Mustard and Herbs or Crispy
Oven-Fried Chicken (see pages 147
and 158).

SERVES 6
¾ CUP PER SERVING

1 tablespoon acceptable vegetable oil
1½ pounds small red or new potatoes, scrubbed, unpeeled,
    cooked and quartered
1 teaspoon paprika
Freshly ground black pepper to taste
¼ teaspoon salt (optional)

In a heavy, nonstick skillet, heat oil over medium-high
heat. Sauté potatoes until golden brown, 5 to 8 minutes.
Stir and shake pan frequently to prevent potatoes from
sticking. Add paprika, pepper and salt. Toss to mix. Serve
immediately.

NUTRIENT ANALYSIS

Calories	107.13 kcal
Protein	2.44 g
Carbohydrate	19.58 g
Total Fat	2.43 g
Saturated	0.31 g
Polyunsaturated	1.45 g
Monounsaturated	0.55 g
Cholesterol	0.00 mg
Sodium	92.01 mg

FAVORITE MASHED POTATOES

Here's a recipe for creamy and
buttery-tasting mashed potatoes.

SERVES 10
APPROXIMATELY ¾ CUP
PER SERVING

10 medium potatoes, unpeeled, about 3 pounds
1 cup skim milk
6 tablespoons nonfat "butter" granules
Freshly ground black pepper to taste

S team potatoes until they can easily be pierced with a fork.
In a small saucepan, heat milk until warm and set aside.
Peel potatoes. Place potatoes, milk and "butter" granules in
a large bowl and mash with a potato masher until smooth.
Add pepper to taste. Serve warm.

NUTRIENT ANALYSIS

Calories	133.51 kcal
Protein	4.02 g
Carbohydrate	29.49 g
Total Fat	0.33 g
Saturated	0.05 g
Polyunsaturated	0.12 g
Monounsaturated	0.01 g
Cholesterol	0.52 mg
Sodium	170.27 mg

SCALLOPED POTATOES

How can you make lowfat scalloped
potatoes? Use lowfat ingredients and
"butter" granules. Your heart—and your
taste buds—will love you for it.

SERVES 6
1 4×4-INCH PORTION
PER SERVING

Vegetable oil spray
1 cup lowfat sour cream
1¾ cups skim milk
3 tablespoons nonfat "butter"
   granules
1 tablespoon cornstarch
⅛ teaspoon freshly ground
   black pepper
4 medium potatoes, about 1½
   pounds, scrubbed,
   unpeeled, and cut into ⅛-
   to ¼-inch-thick slices
½ medium onion, diced
Paprika to taste

NUTRIENT ANALYSIS	
Calories	190.77 kcal
Protein	6.10 g
Carbohydrate	31.65 g
Total Fat	3.08 g
Saturated	1.77 g
Polyunsaturated	0.23 g
Monounsaturated	0.80 g
Cholesterol	10.76 mg
Sodium	207.97 mg

Preheat oven to 350° F. Spray an 8 × 11½ × 2-inch baking pan with vegetable oil spray.

In a medium bowl, whisk together sour cream, skim
milk, "butter" granules, cornstarch and pepper. Set aside.

Line pan with a third of the potatoes. Pour a third of the
sour cream mixture over the potatoes. Sprinkle half of the
onion over the sour cream mixture. Repeat the layers in
order: a third of the potatoes, a third of the sour cream
mixture and the remaining onions. Place the rest of the
potatoes on top and pour the remaining sour cream mixture
over the contents of the pan. Cover with aluminum foil and
bake 1 hour. Uncover and bake an additional 20 minutes.
Sprinkle with paprika. Let stand 5 minutes before serving.

STEAMED NEW POTATOES WITH GARLIC SAUCE

The steamed garlic used in this sauce has a surprisingly mild flavor. The dish is easy to fix and offers a nice change of pace.

SERVES 4
1 LARGE OR 2 SMALL POTATOES PER SERVING

8 small or 4 large new potatoes, about 1¼ pounds, unpeeled, scrubbed and, if large, cut in half
2 heads garlic
2 teaspoons skim milk
1 teaspoon acceptable vegetable oil
1 teaspoon nonfat "butter" granules
2 teaspoons chopped fresh parsley
Freshly ground black pepper to taste

In a medium saucepan, place a steamer basket and add water to a depth of 1 to 2 inches. Be sure the water does not reach the bottom of the basket. Cover saucepan and bring to a boil over medium-high heat. Place potatoes in steamer basket. Separate cloves of garlic, but do not peel the paper-thin skins surrounding each clove. Scatter cloves around potatoes. Cover and steam about 20 minutes, or until a fork can be easily inserted into potatoes.

Remove garlic from pan. Remove skins from garlic cloves by peeling them off with your hands or by pushing the garlic pulp out of the cloves. Discard skins and mash garlic pulp with milk, oil and "butter" granules.

Remove potatoes from pan and cut them in half. Serve with a dollop of garlic sauce, parsley and pepper.

NUTRIENT ANALYSIS

Calories	146.38 kcal
Protein	3.84 g
Carbohydrate	30.62 g
Total Fat	1.34 g
Saturated	0.17 g
Polyunsaturated	0.81 g
Monounsaturated	0.28 g
Cholesterol	0.05 mg
Sodium	28.33 mg

GOLDEN RICE

SERVES 6
½ CUP PER SERVING

This dish is known as "pilau" in Indian cuisine and as "pilaf" in Middle Eastern and Greek cuisine. It can be made from long-grain rice or, for an exotic flavor, from basmati rice. Basmati is an aromatic, long-grain rice from India and Pakistan.

1 cup long-grain basmati rice
1 cup homemade Chicken
*   Stock (see page 352)*
1 cup water
1 cinnamon stick
1 bay leaf
¼ teaspoon salt (optional)
¼ teaspoon ground turmeric
*   or ½ teaspoon saffron*
2 tablespoons slivered
*   almonds*

NUTRIENT ANALYSIS

Calories	129.01 kcal
Protein	3.02 g
Carbohydrate	26.22 g
Total Fat	1.49 g
Saturated	0.16 g
Polyunsaturated	0.30 g
Monounsaturated	0.91 g
Cholesterol	1.14 mg
Sodium	274.17 mg

Rinse rice in several changes of water before cooking.

In a 2-quart saucepan over medium-high heat, bring chicken stock and water to a boil. Add rice, cinnamon, bay leaf and salt; stir. Reduce heat and simmer, covered, 20 minutes. Add turmeric or saffron and stir lightly with a fork. Continue to cook, covered, over low heat, another 10 minutes, or until rice is tender and liquid is absorbed. Remove cinnamon stick and bay leaf. Sprinkle with almonds and serve hot.

SAVORY BROWN RICE

Try this in place of the usual white rice for a nutritious side dish that is a tasty accompaniment to almost any entree.

SERVES 6
½ CUP PER SERVING

1 cup brown rice
1 tablespoon acceptable
   vegetable oil
2 green onions with tops,
   thinly sliced
1 teaspoon caraway seeds
1 cinnamon stick
1 cup homemade Chicken
   Stock (see page 352)
1½ cups water

NUTRIENT ANALYSIS

Calories	116.30 kcal
Protein	2.48 g
Carbohydrate	20.51 g
Total Fat	4.00 g
Saturated	0.28 g
Polyunsaturated	0.82 g
Monounsaturated	1.57 g
Cholesterol	1.13 mg
Sodium	5.69 mg

R inse rice in several changes of water.

In 2- or 3-quart saucepan, heat oil over medium-high heat. Add onions, caraway and cinnamon. Sauté, stirring frequently, until onions are soft, about 3 minutes. Stir in the rice and sauté for an additional minute. Add stock and water, bring mixture to a boil. Reduce heat and simmer, covered, 30 to 40 minutes, or until rice is tender and liquid is absorbed.

Fluff rice with fork, remove cinnamon stick and serve immediately.

SPAGHETTI SQUASH

Is it spaghetti or is it squash? Whatever, you'll love the taste and texture of one of nature's surprise packages.

SERVES 6
½ CUP PER SERVING

3 pounds spaghetti squash
2 teaspoons nonfat "butter" granules

Preheat oven to 350° F.

Cut squash lengthwise and scrape with a spoon to remove seeds. Place water in a shallow baking dish to a depth of ½ inch. Place squash, cut-side down, in the dish. Bake 35 to 40 minutes, or until squash gives under slight pressure. While still warm, remove squash pulp and place it in a serving bowl. Using a fork, separate squash into strands. Sprinkle on "butter" granules, mix well and serve immediately.

NUTRIENT ANALYSIS

Calories	43.03 kcal
Protein	1.14 g
Carbohydrate	10.42 g
Total Fat	0.36 g
Saturated	0.00 g
Polyunsaturated	0.00 g
Monounsaturated	0.00 g
Cholesterol	0.01 mg
Sodium	57.70 mg

SPINACH CHEESE STRUDEL

SERVES 6
2 1½-INCH SLICES PER SERVING

Phyllo is a paper-thin dough, available frozen in 1-pound packages of about 24 sheets in most large supermarkets and specialty groceries. Phyllo should be defrosted in the refrigerator. Unopened, the defrosted dough will keep for a month, if refrigerated. Refreezing can make the dough crumbly. When working with the dough, keep it covered with a damp cloth to prevent drying.

Feta cheese is made from sheep's milk and is lower in fat than most cow's milk cheese. Soaking the cheese in cold water and then draining it removes some of the salt.

8 ounces fresh spinach
1 tablespoon acceptable margarine
6 green onions with tops, chopped
8 sheets phyllo dough
3 tablespoons acceptable margarine, melted
1½ ounces feta cheese
½ teaspoon caraway seeds
¼ teaspoon freshly ground black pepper, or to taste
1 tablespoon honey

P reheat oven to 350° F.

Rinse, stem, hand-tear spinach and put in a bowl.

In a nonstick skillet, heat 1 tablespoon margarine over medium-high heat. Add green onions and sauté until soft, about 1 to 2 minutes. Pour cooked onions over spinach and mix while still hot enough to wilt spinach.

Lightly brush every other sheet of phyllo with melted margarine and stack the sheets on top of each other. Spread spinach-onion mixture over the phyllo, leaving a 1-inch border on all sides.

Crumble the feta cheese. Sprinkle cheese, caraway and pepper over spinach mixture. Drizzle honey over the top.

Roll lengthwise, jelly-roll fashion, and place on a non-stick baking sheet, making sure that the ends of the roll are tucked under and seam-side faces down. Brush the top lightly with remaining margarine. Cut through the pastry to the spinach, at 1½-inch intervals, to provide vents for steam to escape. Bake 20 to 30 minutes, or until a light golden brown. Slice, using vent lines as guides.

This recipe freezes well. Prepare as above but omit the final brushing with margarine, and the baking. Freeze overnight on a baking sheet, then wrap well in freezer paper or foil. To prevent the pastry from getting soggy, do not defrost before baking. Place on a baking sheet, brush with margarine and bake 35 to 45 minutes, or until golden brown.

NUTRIENT ANALYSIS

Calories	205.58 kcal
Protein	6.01 g
Carbohydrate	23.60 g
Total Fat	10.29 g
Saturated	2.76 g
Polyunsaturated	2.68 g
Monounsaturated	4.12 g
Cholesterol	7.44 mg
Sodium	172.73 mg

SAUTÉED CHERRY TOMATOES

Don't put all the cherry tomatoes in your salad—save some for this creative side dish. It adds color and variety to any meal.

SERVES 5
½ CUP PER SERVING

1 pint cherry tomatoes
1 tablespoon olive oil
1 clove garlic, finely minced
3 tablespoons finely chopped fresh parsley
½ shredded wheat biscuit, crushed
⅛ teaspoon freshly ground black pepper, or to taste

Rinse, stem and halve the tomatoes. In a nonstick skillet, heat oil over medium-high heat. Add garlic and sauté 30 seconds. Add tomatoes and parsley and sauté 20 to 30 seconds, or until tomato skins just begin to wilt. Stir constantly so all surfaces of tomatoes cook evenly. Toss with biscuit crumbs and pepper. Serve immediately.

NUTRIENT ANALYSIS

Calories	43.82 kcal
Protein	0.79 g
Carbohydrate	4.10 g
Total Fat	2.85 g
Saturated	0.37 g
Polyunsaturated	0.26 g
Monounsaturated	2.00 g
Cholesterol	0.00 mg
Sodium	2.43 mg

SAUTÉED ZUCCHINI

Add a touch of Italy to your menu.   **SERVES 6**
The herbs and spices blend for a   **¾ CUP PER SERVING**
unique-tasting side dish.

1 tablespoon acceptable vegetable oil
2 pounds zucchini, sliced into ½-inch-thick rounds
½ cup whole-wheat bread crumbs, toasted
2 tablespoons minced almonds
1 tablespoon grated Parmesan cheese
¼ cup fresh parsley, finely chopped
1 tablespoon chopped fresh oregano or ½ teaspoon dried
   oregano
1 clove garlic, minced (optional)
Freshly ground black pepper to taste

In a nonstick skillet, heat oil over medium-high heat. Add
zucchini and sauté until just tender and lightly browned, 5
to 8 minutes. Combine remaining ingredients and add to
zucchini. Remove from heat, toss gently and serve immediately.

NUTRIENT ANALYSIS

Calories	107.95 kcal
Protein	4.60 g
Carbohydrate	14.45 g
Total Fat	4.57 g
Saturated	0.54 g
Polyunsaturated	1.08 g
Monounsaturated	2.52 g
Cholesterol	1.06 mg
Sodium	110.23 mg

RATATOUILLE

SERVES 6
I CUP PER SERVING

This recipe for French stew uses a simple, lowfat method that results in a delicious blend of textures and flavors. Ratatouille is an excellent accompaniment to chicken or fish. It also tastes wonderful served hot on a baked potato or cold with chunks of crusty French bread.

1 large eggplant, cut into 1-inch cubes
4 medium zucchini, sliced ½ inch thick
1 teaspoon salt
2 tablespoons olive oil
2 medium onions, sliced
2 medium red, green or yellow bell peppers, chopped
2 large tomatoes, chopped
2 cloves garlic, minced
Freshly ground black pepper to taste
1 tablespoon chopped fresh thyme or 1 teaspoon dried thyme
1 tablespoon chopped fresh oregano or 1 teaspoon dried
    oregano
1 tablespoon chopped fresh basil or 1 teaspoon dried basil

Put eggplant and zucchini in a colander, sprinkle with salt and toss lightly. Allow to drain for at least 30 minutes. Rinse and pat dry with paper towels.

In a heavy, nonstick skillet, heat oil over medium-high heat. Sauté onions until translucent, 2 to 3 minutes. Stir in peppers, tomatoes, eggplant, zucchini, garlic, salt, pepper, thyme, oregano and basil. Reduce heat, cover and simmer 30 to 45 minutes, or until vegetables are thoroughly cooked. Stir occasionally to prevent sticking. Uncover and cook another 5 minutes to reduce liquid.

Ratatouille is best made a day ahead to allow flavors to blend. Serve warm or cold.

NUTRIENT ANALYSIS

Calories	119.80 kcal
Protein	4.15 g
Carbohydrate	17.04 g
Total Fat	5.11 g
Saturated	0.65 g
Polyunsaturated	0.47 g
Monounsaturated	3.31 g
Cholesterol	0.00 mg
Sodium	370.36 mg

CHINESE VEGETABLE STIR-FRY

SERVES 6
I CUP PER SERVING

This is a wonderful side dish. The secret is to prepare all the vegetables ahead of time and stir-fry them just before serving. This keeps the texture crisp and crunchy. The combinations can be changed to accommodate seasonal vegetables.

1½ tablespoons low-sodium soy sauce
2 tablespoons acceptable vegetable oil
¼ cup homemade Chicken Stock (see page 352)
2 cups finely shredded red cabbage
1 large carrot, finely sliced on the diagonal and then cut into
    very thin strips
1 cup snow peas, stems and strings removed
2 medium green, red or yellow bell peppers, cut into 1-inch
    strips
4 ounces fresh mushrooms, thinly sliced
4 green onions with tops, cut into fine 1-inch strips
1 tablespoon grated fresh ginger or 1 teaspoon powdered ginger

Garnish
1 tablespoon sesame seeds, toasted

Combine soy sauce, oil and chicken stock.

Heat a nonstick wok or skillet over high heat and add soy sauce mixture. Over high heat, stir-fry cabbage, carrots, snow peas, bell peppers, mushrooms and onions, stirring constantly, 2 minutes. Add ginger, stir to mix well and remove from heat. Vegetables should be tender-crisp.

Garnish with toasted sesame seeds and serve immediately.

NUTRIENT ANALYSIS

Calories	100.52 kcal
Protein	3.51 g
Carbohydrate	11.02 g
Total Fat	5.61 g
Saturated	0.74 g
Polyunsaturated	3.06 g
Monounsaturated	1.41 g
Cholesterol	0.28 mg
Sodium	187.49 mg

STEAMED VEGETABLES
WITH GINGER

This vegetable combo bears little
resemblance to mixed vegetables
of old. The ginger makes the
difference.

SERVES 8
APPROXIMATELY ¾ CUP
PER SERVING

2 medium carrots, sliced into ¼-inch-thick rounds
1 cup cauliflower florets
1 cup broccoli florets
2 small zucchini, sliced into ½-inch-thick rounds
1½-inch piece fresh ginger root, julienned

In the bottom of a medium saucepan, place steamer basket
and water to a depth of 1 inch. Bring to a boil. Layer steamer
basket, in order, with carrots, cauliflower, broccoli, zucchini
and ginger. Cover and steam 5 to 7 minutes, or until barely
tender. Remove steamer basket from saucepan. Remove ginger. Pour vegetables into serving dish and serve immediately.

NUTRIENT ANALYSIS

Calories	21.11 kcal
Protein	1.29 g
Carbohydrate	4.34 g
Total Fat	0.14 g
Saturated	0.00 g
Polyunsaturated	0.00 g
Monounsaturated	0.00 g
Cholesterol	0.00 mg
Sodium	13.43 mg

SAUCES

CAPER SAUCE FOR FISH

This recipe uses reduced-calorie
mayonnaise, which has about half
the fat of regular mayonnaise.

MAKES 1 CUP
SERVES 8
2 TABLESPOONS PER SERVING

1 cup tofu, about 7 ounces, drained and crumbled
2 tablespoons reduced-calorie mayonnaise
2 tablespoons fresh lemon juice
2 tablespoons capers, drained
2 tablespoons chopped fresh dill or 2 teaspoons dried dill
2 tablespoons chopped fresh parsley

In a blender or the workbowl of a food processor fitted
with a metal blade, process all ingredients until smooth.
Serve hot or cold.

NUTRIENT ANALYSIS

Calories	32.54 kcal
Protein	2.05 g
Carbohydrate	1.38 g
Total Fat	2.33 g
Saturated	0.41 g
Polyunsaturated	1.11 g
Monounsaturated	0.75 g
Cholesterol	2.50 mg
Sodium	79.86 mg

WHITE SAUCE (BÉCHAMEL)

This basic French sauce can be used
with poultry, meat or vegetables.

MAKES 2 CUPS
SERVES 4
½ CUP PER SERVING

2 tablespoons acceptable vegetable oil
3 tablespoons all-purpose flour
2 cups skim milk
¼ teaspoon salt (optional)
Freshly ground black pepper to taste
1 bay leaf (optional)

In a 1-quart saucepan, heat oil over medium-high heat.
Blend in flour. Cook, stirring constantly, 1 minute, or until
mixture becomes foamy. Gradually add milk. Stir in seasonings and bay leaf. Stir vigorously with a wooden spoon until
mixture thickens, 5 to 8 minutes. Remove bay leaf before
serving.

NUTRIENT ANALYSIS

Calories	61.79 kcal
Protein	2.38 g
Carbohydrate	5.15 g
Total Fat	3.55 g
Saturated	0.51 g
Polyunsaturated	2.02 g
Monounsaturated	0.85 g
Cholesterol	1.22 mg
Sodium	98.55 mg

CUCUMBER RAITA

Raita (rah-eé-ta) is an Indian yogurt sauce. It makes a cool and refreshing accompaniment to any spicy dish.

MAKES 1½ TO 2 CUPS
SERVES 6–8
¼ CUP PER SERVING

8 ounces plain nonfat yogurt
1 small cucumber, peeled, seeded and finely diced
¼ cup finely diced green bell pepper
2 tablespoons finely chopped fresh parsley or cilantro
¼ teaspoon ground cumin
Freshly ground black pepper to taste

In a bowl, whisk the yogurt until smooth. Add remaining ingredients except pepper. Stir well, cover and chill until ready to serve. Can be made up to 1 hour in advance. Sprinkle with pepper before serving.

NUTRIENT ANALYSIS

Calories	155.18 kcal
Protein	14.55 g
Carbohydrate	23.70 g
Total Fat	0.79 g
Saturated	0.29 g
Polyunsaturated	0.10 g
Monounsaturated	0.09 g
Cholesterol	4.00 mg
Sodium	189.92 mg

TOMATO MINT RAITA

MAKES 1½ TO 2 CUPS
SERVES 6–8
¼ CUP PER SERVING

8 ounces plain nonfat yogurt
2 medium tomatoes, peeled
    and finely chopped
4 green onions with tops,
    finely chopped
1 red chili pepper, seeded and
    finely chopped (optional)
¼ cup finely chopped fresh
    mint
¼ teaspoon ground cumin
¼ teaspoon salt (optional)
Paprika to taste

Garnish
Sprig mint

NUTRIENT ANALYSIS

Calories	155.18 kcal
Protein	14.55 g
Carbohydrate	23.70 g
Total Fat	0.79 g
Saturated	0.29 g
Polyunsaturated	0.10 g
Monounsaturated	0.09 g
Cholesterol	4.00 mg
Sodium	189.92 mg

Place yogurt in a bowl and whisk until smooth. Add remaining ingredients except paprika. Stir well, cover and chill until ready to serve. Can be made up to 1 hour in advance. Sprinkle with paprika before serving. Garnish with mint.

PESTO

MAKES 2 CUPS
SERVES 32
1 TABLESPOON PER SERVING

This versatile sauce is excellent as a topping for pasta or baked potatoes, or as a dip or salad dressing. Because of the fat content, limit a serving to 1 to 2 tablespoons. For a change of flavor, try using cilantro leaves instead of basil.

2 cups fresh basil leaves,
*   loosely packed*
¹/₃ cup olive oil
1 clove garlic
¹/₃ cup freshly grated
*   Parmesan cheese*
¹/₂ cup pecans or pine nuts
¹/₄ to ¹/₂ cup homemade
*   Chicken Stock (see page*
*   352)*

NUTRIENT ANALYSIS	
Calories	39.13 kcal
Protein	0.55 g
Carbohydrate	0.49 g
Total Fat	3.95 g
Saturated	0.64 g
Polyunsaturated	0.54 g
Monounsaturated	2.57 g
Cholesterol	1.10 mg
Sodium	18.69 mg

In a blender or the workbowl of a food processor fitted with a metal blade, combine basil, oil, garlic, Parmesan and nuts. Process until smooth, occasionally scraping down the sides of the container. If mixture does not move during processing, slowly drizzle chicken stock to loosen it.

Pesto can be made well in advance, covered with plastic wrap and refrigerated. It can also be frozen.

SALSA

This spicy Mexican sauce is
excellent as a topping or a dip. It
can also be used to perk up dishes
from scrambled eggs to grilled
chicken. Make it several hours in
advance to allow flavors to blend.

MAKES 1 TO 1½ CUPS
SERVES 4–6
¼ CUP PER SERVING

6 small ripe tomatoes,
  chopped
1 to 2 jalapeño peppers,
  seeded and minced, or to
  taste*
2 tablespoons finely chopped
  red onion
2 tablespoons finely chopped
  fresh cilantro or parsley
⅓ cup fresh lime juice
2 teaspoons red wine vinegar
⅛ teaspoon salt (optional)
Freshly ground black pepper
  to taste

NUTRIENT ANALYSIS*

Calories	179.71 kcal
Protein	7.56 g
Carbohydrate	36.31 g
Total Fat	1.55 g
Saturated	0.04 g
Polyunsaturated	0.08 g
Monounsaturated	0.02 g
Cholesterol	0.00 mg
Sodium	307.11 mg

* For entire recipe.

For a smooth sauce, thoroughly process all ingredients in
blender or food processor. If you prefer a chunky sauce,
simply combine the ingredients. Cover and refrigerate.

*Note: Wear rubber gloves when handling hot peppers or wash hands
thoroughly after handling. Skin, especially around the eyes, is very sensitive
to oil from peppers.

PAN GRAVY

1 tablespoon cornstarch
2 tablespoons cold water
2 cups pan juices, defatted*
Freshly ground black pepper to taste
½ teaspoon dried thyme (optional)

In a small bowl, mix cornstarch with water. Heat pan juices over medium-high heat. Add mixture to pan juices while stirring constantly to prevent lumps from forming. Cook until smooth and thickened, about 3 minutes. Add pepper and thyme. Strain if a smooth consistency is desired. Serve hot.

*See page 28.

NUTRIENT ANALYSIS

Calories	7.58 kcal
Protein	0.60 g
Carbohydrate	0.85 g
Total Fat	0.18 g
Saturated	0.05 g
Polyunsaturated	0.04 g
Monounsaturated	0.08 g
Cholesterol	0.00 mg
Sodium	10.54 mg

CREAMY DESSERT TOPPING

This topping is luscious when drizzled over a bowl of fruit, spread on muffins or poured over a slice of angel food cake. It has a fraction of the calories and fat of whipped cream or butter.

SERVES 8
2 TABLESPOONS PER SERVING

½ cup plain nonfat yogurt
½ cup part-skim ricotta cheese
2 tablespoons honey

Combine ingredients and stir until light and creamy. Refrigerate. Serve chilled.

NUTRIENT ANALYSIS

Calories	41.84 kcal
Protein	2.40 g
Carbohydrate	6.13 g
Total Fat	1.15 g
Saturated	0.71 g
Polyunsaturated	0.04 g
Monounsaturated	0.33 g
Cholesterol	4.64 mg
Sodium	28.61 mg

CHEESECAKE SAUCE

This sauce is delicious when poured
over a fruit salad or sorbet.

SERVES 6
2 TABLESPOONS PER SERVING

¼ *cup nonfat plain yogurt*
½ *cup lowfat cottage cheese*
2 *tablespoons honey*
½ *teaspoon vanilla extract*

▌n a blender, process all ingredients about 1 minute, or
until smooth and creamy. Refrigerate. Serve chilled.

NUTRIENT ANALYSIS

Calories	41.21 kcal
Protein	2.91 g
Carbohydrate	7.26 g
Total Fat	0.21 g
Saturated	0.13 g
Polyunsaturated	0.01 g
Monounsaturated	0.05 g
Cholesterol	0.93 mg
Sodium	84.49 mg

BERRY SAUCE

Pour Berry Sauce over Cheesecake
Sauce (see page 263) for a colorful
and flavorful topping for fruit salads,
yogurt, sorbet or even cottage
cheese.

SERVES 6
¼ CUP PER SERVING

1 16-ounce bag unsweetened frozen strawberries, raspberries
*   or other berries*
1 teaspoon cornstarch

Defrost berries and puree in a blender. Mix berry puree
and cornstarch in a saucepan. Place over medium-high heat
and bring to a boil, stirring frequently until mixture thickens. Refrigerate. Serve chilled.

NUTRIENT ANALYSIS*

Calories	177.15 kcal
Protein	3.18 g
Carbohydrate	40.36 g
Total Fat	2.28 g
Saturated	0.00 g
Polyunsaturated	0.01 g
Monounsaturated	0.00 g
Cholesterol	0.00 mg
Sodium	4.53 mg

* For entire recipe.

BLUEBERRY SAUCE

This sauce can be served hot or cold. It's great over vanilla ice milk, pancakes or Vanilla Cheesecake (a variation of Mocha Cheesecake, see pages 316–317).

SERVES 6
⅓ CUP PER SERVING

1 pint fresh blueberries or 2 cups frozen no-sugar-added blueberries
½ cup water
¼ cup sugar
1 tablespoon fresh lemon juice
1 tablespoon cornstarch
2 tablespoons cold water

NUTRIENT ANALYSIS

Calories	64.40 kcal
Protein	0.35 g
Carbohydrate	16.14 g
Total Fat	0.20 g
Saturated	0.00 g
Polyunsaturated	0.01 g
Monounsaturated	0.00 g
Cholesterol	0.00 mg
Sodium	3.52 mg

In a medium saucepan over medium-high heat, bring blueberries, water, sugar and lemon juice to a boil. If using fresh blueberries, reduce heat and simmer 1 to 2 minutes, or until berries soften. If using frozen berries, there's no need to simmer.

In a small bowl, combine cornstarch and water. Add to blueberry mixture and cook over low heat 1 to 2 minutes more, stirring until thick and smooth. Serve hot or cold.

APPLE-RAISIN SAUCE

Try this deliciously refreshing sauce
over Whole-Grain Oatmeal
Pancakes (page 282).

SERVES 6
½ CUP PER SERVING

3 medium apples
2 cups apple juice
¼ cup raisins
1 teaspoon ground cinnamon
1 tablespoon cornstarch
2 tablespoons cold water

Peel apples, if desired; core and coarsely chop. In a large
saucepan, combine apples, juice, raisins and cinnamon over
medium-high heat. Bring to a boil, reduce heat and simmer
15 minutes, or until apples are tender.

Meanwhile, combine cornstarch and water in a small
bowl. Add to apple-raisin mixture and cook an additional 1
to 2 minutes, stirring until thick and smooth. Serve warm.

NUTRIENT ANALYSIS

Calories	93.48 kcal
Protein	0.37 g
Carbohydrate	23.71 g
Total Fat	0.30 g
Saturated	0.06 g
Polyunsaturated	0.09 g
Monounsaturated	0.02 g
Cholesterol	0.00 mg
Sodium	4.52 mg

BREADS

Whole-Wheat French Bread
Honey-Nut Bread
Southern-Style Cornbread
Potato Bread
Zucchini Bread
Oat Bran Muffins
Cardamom Lemon-Peel Muffins
Whole-Grain Oatmeal Pancakes
French Toast
Breakfast Toast
Cheese Danish
Cornbread Dressing
Corn Crisps
Pita Crisps
Croutons
Seasoned Bread Crumbs

WHOLE-WHEAT FRENCH BREAD

This dense bread has a wonderful
texture. Make up an extra batch
and freeze it. These loaves
disappear fast!

MAKES 4 LOAVES
12 SLICES PER LOAF
2 SLICES PER SERVING

Vegetable oil spray
1½ teaspoons active dry yeast, ½ envelope
2 tablespoons honey
1 teaspoon salt
2 cups very warm water (110° to 115° F.)
4 cups whole-wheat flour
3 cups all-purpose flour
1 large egg white, lightly beaten

Topping
1 teaspoon sesame seeds (optional)

Grease two large baking sheets and one large bowl with
vegetable oil spray. Set aside.

In a large bowl, mix together yeast, honey, salt and
water. In another bowl, combine whole-wheat and all-purpose flours; mix well. Add 2 cups flour to the yeast mixture
and stir well. Stir in 3 more cups of flour. Turn the dough
onto a floured board. Knead in as much of the remaining 2
cups of flour as necessary to make a soft, but not sticky,
dough. Knead the dough for 8 to 10 minutes or until
smooth and elastic. Shape into a ball, and place in the
greased bowl, turning to coat all sides. Cover the bowl with
a clean towel and set in a warm, draft-free place to rise, 1½
hours or until doubled in bulk.

Turn dough onto a lightly floured surface, punch down
and knead out large air bubbles. Divide dough into four
equal pieces. Shape each piece into a skinny loaf, about 12

inches long. Arrange on the greased baking sheets and cover with a clean towel. Allow to rise again in a warm, draft-free place for 45 minutes, or until doubled in bulk.

Preheat oven to 350° F.

Brush each loaf with egg white and bake 40 to 50 minutes, or until loaves are golden brown and sound hollow when tapped.

During the last 5 minutes, loaves can be reglazed with egg white and sprinkled with sesame seeds. For a crisp, flaky crust, put a pan of boiling water on the lowest oven shelf during baking.

NUTRIENT ANALYSIS

Calories	126.85 kcal
Protein	4.45 g
Carbohydrate	26.58 g
Total Fat	0.72 g
Saturated	0.12 g
Polyunsaturated	0.36 g
Monounsaturated	0.15 g
Cholesterol	0.00 mg
Sodium	92.15 mg

HONEY-NUT BREAD

Freeze single slices of this delicious
bread for a nutritious lunch-box
addition. When packed frozen, a
slice will thaw in less than an hour.

**MAKES 2 LOAVES
10 SLICES PER LOAF
1 SLICE PER SERVING**

1 cup skim milk
1 cup honey
1¼ cups whole-wheat flour
1¼ cups all-purpose flour
1 tablespoon baking powder
½ teaspoon salt
¼ cup acceptable margarine
   (½ stick)
1 whole egg plus 2 egg whites,
   lightly beaten
½ cup chopped walnuts
Vegetable oil spray

NUTRIENT ANALYSIS

Calories	152.08 kcal
Protein	3.32 g
Carbohydrate	25.90 g
Total Fat	4.69 g
Saturated	0.72 g
Polyunsaturated	2.17 g
Monounsaturated	1.47 g
Cholesterol	13.95 mg
Sodium	91.59 mg

Preheat oven to 325° F.

In a small saucepan, heat milk and honey over medium-high heat until very warm, 120° to 130° F.

In a large bowl, combine whole-wheat and all-purpose flours, baking powder and salt. Add liquid mixture and beat. Add margarine and eggs, and continue beating until well blended. Fold in nuts.

Lightly grease two 9 × 5 × 3-inch loaf pans with vegetable oil spray. Pour in bread mixture and bake 45 to 60 minutes, or until a cake tester inserted into the center of the loaf comes out moist, but not wet. Cool on a rack.

To store, wrap each loaf in foil to preserve moisture. The loaves can be frozen for later use.

SOUTHERN-STYLE CORNBREAD

This cornbread has a crispy crust
and a flavorful, moist center. For a
simple yet satisfying meal, serve
with Sautéed Greens and Southern-
Style Black-Eyed Peas (see pages
228, 230).

SERVES 12
1 WEDGE OR SQUARE
PER SERVING

¼ cup acceptable vegetable oil
1½ cups yellow cornmeal, whole-grain if possible
1½ cups whole-wheat flour
⅓ cup instant powdered nonfat milk
½ teaspoon salt
1½ tablespoons baking powder
3 tablespoons sugar (optional)
3 large egg whites
1½ cups skim milk

Preheat oven to 450° F.

Pour 1 tablespoon of oil into a 10½-inch cast-iron skillet
or into a 9 × 11-inch ovenproof glass casserole dish. Set
aside.

In a bowl, mix cornmeal, flour, powdered milk, salt,
baking powder and sugar. Set aside. In another bowl, beat
egg whites with a whisk until slightly frothy. Add milk and
remaining oil and whisk again.

Pour liquid ingredients into dry ingredients and mix, but
do not overmix (some lumps will remain).

Place skillet or dish in oven 3 or 4 minutes to heat the
oil. **Be careful not to let it burn!** Watch the time carefully.

Pour batter into hot skillet or dish. Bake 20 minutes.
Immediately remove from pan by turning onto a cutting
board.

Cut into twelve wedges or squares. Serve immediately.

NUTRIENT ANALYSIS

Calories	185.36 kcal
Protein	5.87 g
Carbohydrate	29.90 g
Total Fat	5.10 g
Saturated	0.69 g
Polyunsaturated	2.93 g
Monounsaturated	1.20 g
Cholesterol	0.95 mg
Sodium	236.14 mg

POTATO BREAD

This bread freezes well.

MAKES 4 LOAVES
12 SLICES PER LOAF
2 SLICES PER SERVING

Vegetable oil spray
4 cups whole-wheat flour
4 cups all-purpose flour
2 tablespoons active dry yeast, 2 envelopes
2 tablespoons honey
2½ teaspoons salt
1½ cups mashed potatoes (leftovers are perfect)
1½ cups skim milk
¼ cup acceptable margarine (½ stick)
½ cup water
4 large egg whites

Glaze
¼ cup skim milk

Grease two large baking sheets and one large bowl with vegetable oil spray. Set aside.

In another large bowl, combine whole-wheat and all-purpose flours. In another large bowl, mix together yeast, honey, salt and 1½ cups of combined flour. In a 2-quart saucepan, combine mashed potatoes, milk, margarine and water. Heat over medium-high heat until very warm, 120° to 130° F., stirring frequently. The margarine does not need to melt completely.

With electric mixer at low speed, beat liquid ingredients into dry ingredients. Add egg whites, increase mixer speed to medium and beat 2 minutes, scraping bowl occasionally. Beat in 1 cup flour to make a thick batter; beat 2 minutes longer. Stir in 3 more cups of flour. Turn the dough onto a well-floured board. Knead in as much of the remaining 2½ cups of flour as necessary to make a soft, but not sticky, dough. Knead the dough for about 10 minutes, or until smooth and elastic. Shape into a ball and place in the greased bowl, turning to coat all sides. Cover the bowl with a clean towel and set in a warm, draft-free place to rise, about 1½ hours, or until doubled in bulk.

Turn the dough onto a lightly floured surface, punch down and knead out the large air bubbles. Divide the dough into four equal pieces. Shape each piece into an oval, about 10 inches long. Cut two parallel slashes on top of each loaf, place on the greased baking sheet (two loaves per sheet) and cover with a clean towel. Allow to rise in a warm, draft-free place for 1 hour, or until doubled in bulk.

Preheat oven to 350° F.

Brush each loaf with skim milk. Bake 35 to 45 minutes, or until loaves are golden brown and sound hollow when tapped. Serve warm or at room temperature.

NUTRIENT ANALYSIS

Calories	172.71 kcal
Protein	6.11 g
Carbohydrate	31.58 g
Total Fat	2.84 g
Saturated	0.54 g
Polyunsaturated	1.02 g
Monounsaturated	1.07 g
Cholesterol	0.84 mg
Sodium	293.19 mg

ZUCCHINI BREAD

A perfect luncheon bread is hard to
find, but this comes close. Good
nutrition and great taste rolled
into one!

MAKES I LOAF
12 SLICES PER LOAF
I SLICE PER SERVING

Vegetable oil spray
1½ cups whole-wheat flour
1½ cups all-purpose flour
1 cup brown sugar, lightly packed
1 tablespoon baking powder
¼ teaspoon salt (optional)
1 teaspoon ground cinnamon
2 cups shredded, unpeeled zucchini (about 2 small)
1 cup raisins
¼ cup finely chopped walnuts
2 large egg whites
1½ cups skim milk
¼ cup acceptable vegetable oil
1 teaspoon vanilla extract

Preheat oven to 350° F. Grease a 9 × 5 × 3-inch loaf pan
with vegetable oil spray.

In a large bowl, combine whole-wheat and all-purpose
flours, sugar, baking powder, salt and cinnamon. Stir in
zucchini, raisins and nuts; set aside.

In a smaller bowl, beat together egg whites, milk, oil and
vanilla. Add liquid ingredients to flour mixture and stir
lightly to moisten.

Pour into greased pan and bake 1 hour, or until a cake
tester inserted into the center of the loaf comes out moist,
but not wet. Remove from pan and allow to cool.

To store, wrap loaf in foil to preserve moisture. Loaf can
be frozen for later use.

NUTRIENT ANALYSIS

Calories	318.04 kcal
Protein	6.80 g
Carbohydrate	53.85 g
Total Fat	9.88 g
Saturated	0.93 g
Polyunsaturated	4.67 g
Monounsaturated	3.64 g
Cholesterol	0.61 mg
Sodium	151.59 mg

OAT BRAN MUFFINS

SERVES 18
1 2½-INCH MUFFIN
PER SERVING

You've heard about the healthfulness of oat bran—now taste how good it can be. These delicious, moist muffins are welcome at breakfast, lunch or snack time. Make up an extra batch to freeze. Oat bran is available in some supermarkets and most health food stores. The almond extract gives the muffins a slightly sweet, nutty flavor.

2½ cups oat bran, uncooked
¼ cup brown sugar, firmly packed
¼ cup chopped nuts
¼ cup currants
1 tablespoon baking powder
¼ teaspoon salt (optional)
4 large egg whites, lightly beaten
¾ cup skim milk
¼ cup honey
2 tablespoons acceptable vegetable oil
1 teaspoon almond extract
1 teaspoon vanilla extract
Vegetable oil spray

P reheat oven to 350° F.

In a bowl, combine oat bran, sugar, nuts, currants, baking powder and salt. Mix well.

In a small bowl, combine egg whites, milk, honey, oil, almond and vanilla extracts. Add to dry ingredients and mix to blend.

Spray two muffin tins lightly with vegetable oil spray or use paper muffin cups. Spoon mixture evenly into muffin cups. Bake 20 to 25 minutes, or until light brown. Serve warm or at room temperature.

NUTRIENT ANALYSIS

Calories	107.07 kcal
Protein	4.45 g
Carbohydrate	14.92 g
Total Fat	3.72 g
Saturated	0.45 g
Polyunsaturated	1.45 g
Monounsaturated	1.60 g
Cholesterol	0.22 mg
Sodium	104.08 mg

CARDAMOM LEMON-PEEL MUFFINS

SERVES 12
2 2½-INCH MUFFINS
PER SERVING

The spices in these muffins make them smell and taste wonderful. The cardamom adds a distinctive flavor and enhances the sweetness. Instead of using a lot of fat, applesauce is used to help keep the muffins moist. Oat bran is sometimes called oat bran cereal and is available in some supermarkets and most health food stores. It contains soluble fibers that may help to lower blood cholesterol slightly.

Vegetable oil spray
2½ cups oat bran, uncooked
2 cups whole-wheat flour
1 teaspoon ground cardamom
2 teaspoons baking powder
1½ teaspoons baking soda
2 cups unsweetened applesauce
½ cup acceptable vegetable oil
½ cup honey
4 large egg whites
¼ teaspoon almond extract
Grated rind of 1 lemon

Preheat oven to 400° F.

Spray two muffin tins with vegetable oil spray or use paper muffin cups. In a medium bowl, combine bran, flour, cardamom, baking powder and baking soda. Mix well. In a large bowl, combine applesauce, oil, honey, egg whites, almond extract and lemon peel. Mix well.

Stir dry ingredients into wet ingredients. Mix well, but

do not overmix. Fill prepared muffin cups almost full. Place in oven and reduce heat to 375° F. Bake 18 to 20 minutes, or until golden brown. Serve warm or at room temperature.

If you prefer lighter muffins, use 1 cup of white flour to replace 1 cup of the whole-wheat flour.

NUTRIENT ANALYSIS

Calories	271.44 kcal
Protein	8.32 g
Carbohydrate	37.67 g
Total Fat	11.02 g
Saturated	1.51 g
Polyunsaturated	6.16 g
Monounsaturated	2.80 g
Cholesterol	0.00 mg
Sodium	169.47 mg

WHOLE-GRAIN OATMEAL PANCAKES

Short stack or tall—these hearty pancakes are sure to please. The high-fiber goodness of whole grains and oatmeal is a great way to start the day. Serve them with Blueberry Sauce or Apple-Raisin Sauce (pages 265 and 266).

SERVES 4
3 4-INCH PANCAKES
PER SERVING

1¾ cups skim milk
1 tablespoon honey
1½ cups rolled oats (not instant oatmeal)
1 cup whole-wheat flour
2 teaspoons baking powder
4 large egg whites
¼ cup acceptable vegetable oil

NUTRIENT ANALYSIS

Calories	408.46 kcal
Protein	15.25 g
Carbohydrate	52.09 g
Total Fat	16.63 g
Saturated	2.31 g
Polyunsaturated	9.10 g
Monounsaturated	4.10 g
Cholesterol	2.14 mg
Sodium	252.67 mg

In a small bowl, mix milk and honey until honey is dissolved. Add oatmeal and stir to coat evenly; set aside. In another bowl, stir together flour and baking powder. Add oat mixture, egg whites and 3 tablespoons oil. Stir just until mixed.

In a large, nonstick skillet, heat remaining tablespoon of oil over medium-high heat. Pour batter, in ¼-cup portions, into skillet. When pancakes have a bubbly surface and have just begun to dry around the edges, turn to cook the other side. Serve immediately.

FRENCH TOAST

3 large egg whites, lightly beaten
6 slices cinnamon-raisin bread
Vegetable oil spray
2 tablespoons Apple-Almond Butter (see page 45)

Place egg whites in a medium pie plate. Place two slices of bread into pie plate and let soak 5 to 10 seconds; turn bread over and let soak another 5 to 10 seconds. Remove from plate and set aside. Repeat with remaining slices of bread.

Coat a nonstick skillet with vegetable oil spray. Heat skillet over medium-high heat. When skillet is hot, add the prepared slices of bread. Brown evenly on both sides. Serve with a teaspoonful of Apple-Almond Butter on each slice of bread.

NUTRIENT ANALYSIS*

Calories	132.14 kcal
Protein	7.07 g
Carbohydrate	22.09 g
Total Fat	1.37 g
Saturated	0.37 g
Polyunsaturated	0.40 g
Monounsaturated	0.46 g
Cholesterol	0.64 mg
Sodium	267.90 mg

* Without Apple-Almond Butter.

BREAKFAST TOAST

SERVES 1
2 SLICES PER SERVING

2 slices whole-wheat bread
1 teaspoon acceptable vegetable oil
½ teaspoon nonfat "butter" granules
Ground cinnamon to taste (optional)

P reheat broiler. Lightly toast bread. Brush one side of each slice with oil and sprinkle with "butter" granules. Add cinnamon if desired. Place 3 to 4 inches from broiler, "buttered"-side up, and toast again 30 to 60 seconds, or until nicely browned.

NUTRIENT ANALYSIS

Calories	166.13 kcal
Protein	5.28 g
Carbohydrate	25.04 g
Total Fat	6.10 g
Saturated	0.90 g
Polyunsaturated	3.23 g
Monounsaturated	1.46 g
Cholesterol	0.71 mg
Sodium	306.15 mg

CHEESE DANISH

This Cheese Danish will be filling
even to a person with a hearty
appetite. If you want to watch your
calories, just eat half the Danish.

SERVES I

1 whole-wheat pita, approximately 7 inches in diameter
½ cup lowfat cottage cheese, drained
1 tablespoon raisins
1 teaspoon honey
Pumpkin pie spice to taste

P reheat oven to 350° F.

Cut pita in half and toast lightly 3 to 4 minutes. In a small bowl, mix cottage cheese, raisins, honey and spice. Spoon into warm pita pockets. Place on baking sheet or aluminum foil and bake 3 to 4 minutes. Serve immediately.

NUTRIENT ANALYSIS*

Calories	355.75 kcal
Protein	23.41 g
Carbohydrate	57.12 g
Total Fat	3.37 g
Saturated	1.56 g
Polyunsaturated	0.59 g
Monounsaturated	0.73 g
Cholesterol	9.07 mg
Sodium	876.10 mg

* For entire recipe.

CORNBREAD DRESSING

When it comes to dressing, everyone seems to have a favorite recipe. Here's a winner with real Southern flavor.

SERVES 7
ABOUT ¾ CUP PER SERVING

¼ cup water
1½ cups chopped celery
1 cup chopped onion (about 1 medium)
3 cups cornbread crumbs, approximately half of the Southern-
    Style Cornbread recipe (see pages 272–273)
4 slices stale or toasted whole-grain bread, cut into cubes
1 teaspoon rubbed sage
¼ cup chopped fresh parsley
1 teaspoon poultry seasoning
1½ cups homemade Chicken Stock (see page 352)
2 large egg whites, lightly beaten
Vegetable oil spray
1 tablespoon acceptable margarine

Preheat oven to 350° F.

In a small saucepan, boil the water. Add celery and onion and cook 2 to 3 minutes, or until soft. In a medium bowl, toss cornbread crumbs, bread cubes, sage, parsley and poultry seasoning to mix well. Add chicken stock and egg whites and mix again. Pour the celery, onions and cooking liquid into the bowl and mix well.

Spray a 2-quart casserole with vegetable oil spray. Pour mixture into prepared casserole and dot with margarine. Bake, uncovered, 30 minutes. Serve immediately.

NUTRIENT ANALYSIS

Calories	230.25 kcal
Protein	8.66 g
Carbohydrate	36.14 g
Total Fat	6.50 g
Saturated	0.97 g
Polyunsaturated	3.18 g
Monounsaturated	1.86 g
Cholesterol	2.42 mg
Sodium	349.34 mg

CORN CRISPS

Try these in place of regular corn chips. But watch out, it's hard to stop at just a few!

SERVES 6
6 WEDGES PER SERVING

6 corn tortillas

Preheat oven to 350° F.

Stack the tortillas and cut into six wedges. Lay tortilla pieces on baking sheet so they do not overlap. Bake 15 to 20 minutes. Chips should be crisp and lightly brown. Serve warm or allow to cool and store in an airtight container.

NUTRIENT ANALYSIS

Calories	47.81 kcal
Protein	1.54 g
Carbohydrate	9.13 g
Total Fat	0.81 g
Saturated	0.09 g
Polyunsaturated	0.42 g
Monounsaturated	0.18 g
Cholesterol	0.00 mg
Sodium	37.99 mg

PITA CRISPS

Try these thin and crunchy Pita
Crisps for a nutritious snack.
They're easy to make and taste a
lot like crackers.

SERVES 4
8 WEDGES PER SERVING

2 whole-wheat pitas, approximately 7 inches in diameter

Preheat oven to 350° F.

Divide each pita into two circles. Stack pita circles on
top of each other. Cut the stack into eight wedges. Put pita
pieces on a baking sheet so they do not overlap. Bake 5 to
8 minutes, or until lightly browned. Watch carefully to prevent them from burning. Serve warm or allow to cool and
store in an airtight container.

NUTRIENT ANALYSIS

Calories	102.17 kcal
Protein	3.82 g
Carbohydrate	19.92 g
Total Fat	0.54 g
Saturated	0.08 g
Polyunsaturated	0.25 g
Monounsaturated	0.05 g
Cholesterol	0.00 mg
Sodium	207.64 mg

CROUTONS

These croutons add a special
crunch to soups and salads.

SERVES 16
2 TABLESPOONS PER SERVING

2 tablespoons olive oil
4 slices whole-wheat bread, cut into ¼-inch cubes (stale bread
    works well)
1 clove garlic, crushed

In a heavy, nonstick skillet, heat oil over medium-high
heat. Add bread cubes and garlic. Sauté cubes, stirring frequently and shaking the pan, until the cubes are golden
brown, 8 to 10 minutes. Remove and discard garlic.

Store croutons in an airtight container.

NUTRIENT ANALYSIS*

Calories	242.89 kcal
Protein	5.34 g
Carbohydrate	24.31 g
Total Fat	15.00 g
Saturated	2.14 g
Polyunsaturated	1.70 g
Monounsaturated	10.31 g
Cholesterol	0.70 mg
Sodium	263.79 mg

* For entire recipe.

SEASONED BREAD CRUMBS

This is a good staple to have on hand. It perks up ordinary steamed vegetables, adds crunch to broiled fish, and garnishes soups or salads. These bread crumbs also make a tasty topping for casseroles.

SERVES 16
1 TABLESPOON PER SERVING

4 slices whole-wheat bread
1 tablespoon dried parsley flakes
½ teaspoon dried basil
½ teaspoon dried oregano
1 teaspoon dried onion flakes
¼ cup grated Parmesan cheese

NUTRIENT ANALYSIS

Calories	24.11 kcal
Protein	1.43 g
Carbohydrate	3.24 g
Total Fat	0.73 g
Saturated	0.38 g
Polyunsaturated	0.08 g
Monounsaturated	0.20 g
Cholesterol	1.49 mg
Sodium	66.32 mg

Preheat oven to 275° F.

Arrange bread slices in a single layer on a baking sheet. Bake 15 to 20 minutes, or until crisp and dry. Break slices into pieces and reduce to crumbs using a blender or a food processor, or by placing bread pieces in a plastic bag and crushing with a rolling pin. Add remaining ingredients and stir to mix well.

Store refrigerated in an airtight container.

DESSERTS

Angel Food Cake
Fresh Apple Streusel Cake
Carrot Cake
Orange Snack Cake
Basic Pie Dough
Pumpkin Pie
French Apple Tart
Apple-Almond Flavored Yogurt Pie
Meringue Pie Shell with Sherbet
Baklava
Chocolate Soufflé with Vanilla Sauce
Mocha Cheesecake
Coffee Liqueur Clouds
Mock Whipped Cream
Orange Fluff
Strawberries Romanoff
Frozen Banana Mousse
Tapioca Pudding
Blueberry Pudding
White Grape Juice Gelatin Dessert
Coffee Shake
Frozen Orange Cream
Very Berry Sorbet
Melon with Sherbet
Yogurt-Fruit Cup
Cherries Jubilee
Broiled Grapefruit with Port Wine
Baked Apples
Meringues
Cocoa-Almond Meringue Kisses
Gingerbread Bars
Chewy Oatmeal Squares
Oatmeal Crisps

ANGEL FOOD CAKE

MAKES 1 CAKE
SERVES 12

1 cup cake flour
10 large egg whites*
1 teaspoon cream of tartar
1 teaspoon vanilla extract
½ teaspoon almond extract
1 cup sugar

Preheat oven to 350° F.

Sift flour and set aside.

In a large mixing bowl, beat egg whites until foamy. Add cream of tartar, vanilla and almond extracts. Beat until very stiff, but not dry. Add sugar, 2 tablespoons at a time, and continue to beat just until the mixture is smooth. Using a spatula, gently fold in flour.

Pour the batter into an ungreased, 10-inch tube pan. Draw a knife through the batter to remove any large air bubbles. Place the pan in the lower third of the oven and bake 45 minutes, or until cracks feel dry and top springs back when touched lightly.

When cake is done, remove it from the oven and invert the pan. If the tube in the center of the pan is not high enough for the inverted cake to be suspended in the air, use a heatproof funnel or a thin-necked soda bottle on which to rest the pan. Let the cake hang and cool for 1½ hours.

Remove the cake from its perch and slide a sharp knife inside the edges of the pan to release the cake.

* Remember, even a single drop of egg yolk will prevent egg whites from rising, so separate eggs very carefully, one at a time.

NUTRIENT ANALYSIS

Calories	106.78 kcal
Protein	3.36 g
Carbohydrate	22.74 g
Total Fat	0.06 g
Saturated	0.01 g
Polyunsaturated	0.03 g
Monounsaturated	0.00 g
Cholesterol	0.00 mg
Sodium	58.92 mg

FRESH APPLE STREUSEL CAKE

Lowfat cakes are hard to find, but you can make one yourself. One taste will convince you that it was well worth the effort!

MAKES I BUNDT CAKE
SERVES 20

Vegetable oil spray

Streusel Topping
1/4 cup pecans, chopped
3 tablespoons all-purpose flour
3 tablespoons sugar
2 tablespoons acceptable vegetable oil
1 teaspoon ground cinnamon

Cake
2 cups whole-wheat flour
2 cups all-purpose flour
1/2 teaspoon salt
1/2 teaspoon baking soda
1 tablespoon baking powder
1/2 teaspoon ground cloves
2 teaspoons ground cinnamon
3/4 cup acceptable vegetable oil
1 3/4 cups firmly packed brown sugar
6 large egg whites
1 4 1/2-ounce jar strained applesauce (baby food)
1 tablespoon vanilla extract
2 1/2 cups chopped fresh apples (about 3 medium)
2 tablespoons fresh lemon juice
1/4 cup chopped pecans

Preheat oven to 350° F. Spray a nonstick Bundt pan with vegetable oil spray.

In a small bowl, mix ingredients for streusel topping until crumbly. Sprinkle topping over the bottom of prepared Bundt pan and set aside.

In a large bowl, sift together flours, salt, baking soda, baking powder, cloves and cinnamon. Mix until evenly distributed. Set aside.

In another large bowl, mix oil, brown sugar, egg whites, applesauce and vanilla with an electric mixer until fully blended and smooth.

In a small bowl, mix together apples and lemon juice. Add the flour mixture and apple-lemon mixture alternately to the liquid mixture, beginning and ending with the flour. Fold nuts into the batter, being careful not to overmix.

Pour batter evenly into prepared pan. Bake on middle rack of oven for 55 minutes, or until a cake tester inserted into the center of the cake comes out moist, but not wet. Remove from oven and let cool on wire rack 5 minutes. Remove cake from pan, and after it has cooled, wrap with aluminum foil to retain moisture.

NUTRIENT ANALYSIS

Calories	289.06 kcal
Protein	4.25 g
Carbohydrate	42.53 g
Total Fat	12.09 g
Saturated	1.47 g
Polyunsaturated	6.34 g
Monounsaturated	3.63 g
Cholesterol	0.00 mg
Sodium	139.46 mg

CARROT CAKE

This cake tastes marvelous and is healthful too. Watch it disappear! Instead of a lot of fat, strained carrots add moisture.

MAKES I BUNDT CAKE WITH APPROXIMATELY 2 CUPS TOPPING SERVES 20

Cake
Vegetable oil spray
2 cups whole-wheat flour
2 cups all-purpose flour
1/2 teaspoon salt
1/2 teaspoon baking soda
1 tablespoon baking powder
1 teaspoon ground allspice
2 teaspoons ground cinnamon
3/4 cup acceptable vegetable oil
1 3/4 cups firmly packed brown sugar
6 large egg whites
1 4 1/2-ounce jar strained carrots (baby food)
1 tablespoon vanilla extract
2 cups grated carrots, packed (about 6 carrots)
1/2 cup crushed pineapple, drained
2 tablespoons fresh lemon juice
1/4 cup chopped walnuts

Topping
1 cup part-skim ricotta cheese
3/4 cup Double-Thick Yogurt (see page 351)
3/4 cup confectioners' sugar
Grated rind of 1 lemon
1 teaspoon vanilla extract

Preheat oven to 350° F. Spray a nonstick Bundt pan with vegetable oil spray.

In a large bowl, sift together flours, salt, baking soda, baking powder, allspice and cinnamon. Mix until evenly distributed. Set aside.

In another large bowl, combine oil, brown sugar, egg whites, strained carrots and vanilla. Mix until fully blended and no lumps remain.

Place the grated carrots, pineapple and lemon juice in another bowl. Mix well. Add the flour mixture and carrot-pineapple mixture alternately to the liquid mixture, beginning and ending with the flour. Stir in nuts, being careful not to overmix.

Pour batter evenly into prepared pan. Bake on middle rack of oven for 55 minutes, or until a cake tester inserted into the center comes out moist, but not wet. Remove from oven and let cool on wire rack 5 minutes. Remove cake from pan, and when completely cooled, wrap with aluminum foil to retain moisture.

Place all topping ingredients in a large bowl. Using an electric mixer, mix for about 1 minute, or until no lumps remain. Refrigerate for 30 minutes before serving. Place a dollop of topping on each slice of cake.

NUTRIENT ANALYSIS*

Calories	298.00 kcal
Protein	6.60 g
Carbohydrate	46.16 g
Total Fat	10.54 g
Saturated	1.83 g
Polyunsaturated	5.65 g
Monounsaturated	2.99 g
Cholesterol	4.11 mg
Sodium	175.01 mg

* Includes 1 tablespoon of topping.

ORANGE SNACK CAKE

MAKES 1 19 × 13-INCH CAKE
SERVES 12

Vegetable oil spray
1 cup quick-cooking oats
1½ cups boiling water
2 cups all-purpose flour
1 teaspoon baking powder
1 teaspoon baking soda
1 teaspoon ground cinnamon
¼ teaspoon salt (optional)
½ cup acceptable margarine, 1 stick, at room temperature
½ cup sugar
¾ cup lightly packed brown sugar
3 large egg whites
¼ cup frozen orange juice concentrate
1 teaspoon vanilla extract

Topping
¼ cup acceptable margarine, ½ stick
¾ cup lightly packed brown sugar
2 tablespoons orange juice concentrate
½ cup finely chopped walnuts or pecans

Preheat oven to 350° F. Grease a 9 × 13-inch cake pan
with vegetable oil spray.

In a small bowl, combine oats and boiling water; set
aside. In another bowl, mix flour, baking powder, baking
soda, cinnamon and salt. Set aside.

In a large bowl, cream together margarine and sugars
until light and fluffy. Beat in egg whites, orange juice concentrate and vanilla. Blend in flour mixture alternately with
oats, beginning and ending with flour.

Pour into greased pan and bake 25 to 30 minutes, or until cake springs back when lightly pressed. Remove cake from oven and preheat broiler.

To make the topping, combine margarine, brown sugar and orange juice concentrate in a small saucepan. Bring to a boil and cook 1 minute, over medium-high heat, stirring constantly. Remove from heat and stir in nuts. Spread topping evenly over warm cake; place under broiler for 1 minute, or until golden brown. Topping can burn easily. Watch it carefully! Allow to cool on rack before cutting.

NUTRIENT ANALYSIS

Calories	382.49 kcal
Protein	4.86 g
Carbohydrate	58.27 g
Total Fat	15.20 g
Saturated	2.34 g
Polyunsaturated	6.17 g
Monounsaturated	5.81 g
Cholesterol	0.00 mg
Sodium	310.71 mg

BASIC PIE DOUGH

If you need only one pie shell, just
cut this recipe in half.

**MAKES 2 9-INCH PIE SHELLS
OR I DEEP-DISH PIE SHELL
AND TOP CRUST**

2 cups all-purpose flour
¼ teaspoon salt
½ cup acceptable margarine, 1 stick
7 to 9 tablespoons ice water

In a large bowl, combine flour and salt. Using a pastry
blender, lightly cut the margarine into the flour until the
mixture resembles coarse meal. Add water, a few tablespoons at a time, and mix lightly and quickly until pastry
forms a ball.

Divide pastry into two balls and form into two flat circles
about 1-inch thick. Cover with plastic wrap and refrigerate
at least 1 hour.

On a floured surface, roll each ball into a 12-inch circle.
(The pastry can be rolled between sheets of floured wax
paper or on a pastry sheet.) Place pastry in pie dish. (Folding the pastry in half before lifting helps prevent stretching
or tearing.) Trim or flute the edges and prick the bottom of
each shell lightly with a fork.

For a baked pie shell (to be filled later), bake in a preheated 400° F. oven. For a partially baked crust, bake 8 to 10 minutes. For a fully baked crust, bake 10 to 15 minutes, or until edges are light brown.

To prevent the crust from puffing up or losing shape during baking, cover pastry with wax paper and weigh it down with dried beans or an aluminum-foil pie plate.

NUTRIENT ANALYSIS*

Calories	1644.85 kcal
Protein	25.05 g
Carbohydrate	176.05 g
Total Fat	92.88 g
Saturated	15.46 g
Polyunsaturated	31.67 g
Monounsaturated	41.40 g
Cholesterol	0.00 mg
Sodium	1753.51 mg

* For entire recipe.

PUMPKIN PIE

Evaporated skim milk is very low in fat, yet rich in taste and texture. Use it in cooking in place of whole milk or cream. To make this tasty dessert attractive, serve each slice with a dollop of Creamy Topping (see page 262).

9-inch unbaked pie shell (use
   ½ recipe Basic Pie Dough,
   see pages 303–304)
½ cup firmly packed dark
   brown sugar
1 teaspoon ground cinnamon
1 teaspoon ground ginger
¼ teaspoon ground nutmeg
Pinch of ground cloves
1 16-ounce can pumpkin
   puree
1¼ cups evaporated skim
   milk
3 large egg whites

NUTRIENT ANALYSIS

Calories	211.57 kcal
Protein	6.30 g
Carbohydrate	33.93 g
Total Fat	6.12 g
Saturated	1.04 g
Polyunsaturated	1.99 g
Monounsaturated	2.62 g
Cholesterol	0.22 mg
Sodium	177.11 mg

Preheat oven to 350° F.

Bake pie crust until lightly browned, about 10 minutes. Remove from oven and let cool to room temperature.

Preheat oven to 450° F.

In a large bowl, beat all filling ingredients until no lumps remain. Pour into pie shell and bake 10 minutes. Reduce heat to 325° F. and bake 50 minutes more, or until a knife inserted in the center comes out clean.

FRENCH APPLE TART

This elegant way to serve fruit is
easy to prepare. Since the tart must
be served immediately after baking,
it's a good idea to assemble it ahead
of time and refrigerate it. Then
bake it just before serving.

MAKES 1 12-INCH PASTRY
SERVES 8

*Pie dough for 1 pie shell (use ½ recipe Basic Pie Dough, see
    pages 303–304)*
½ cup unsweetened applesauce, divided
1 pound apples, quartered, cored and thinly sliced
2 tablespoons confectioners' sugar

Preheat oven to 350° F.

Prepare dough according to recipe. After chilling, roll the
dough into a 12½- to 13-inch circle. Place on a flat, 12-inch
round baking pan. Trim away extra dough from the sides.
Prick dough with a fork in several places.

Brush dough with half the applesauce. Begin to arrange
apple slices in a circular design, overlapping the pieces,
starting from the outer edge. Arrange a second inner ring
of apple slices overlapping the outer circle. Continue the
pinwheel design until the whole surface is covered. Apples
will flatten during baking. Brush surface of apples with remaining applesauce.

Bake 20 to 25 minutes, or until apples are golden and
crust edge is crisp. Sprinkle with confectioners' sugar and
serve immediately.

NUTRIENT ANALYSIS

Calories	150.82 kcal
Protein	1.71 g
Carbohydrate	23.40 g
Total Fat	6.02 g
Saturated	1.00 g
Polyunsaturated	2.03 g
Monounsaturated	2.60 g
Cholesterol	0.00 mg
Sodium	109.92 mg

APPLE-ALMOND FLAVORED YOGURT PIE

**MAKES I 9-INCH PIE
SERVES 8**

This pie looks beautiful and tastes much richer than it is. The apple juice concentrate gives it a sweet-but-not-too-sweet flavor. Of course it's great for dessert, but why not have a slice for breakfast, too?

Crust
1¼ cups whole-grain, wheat-and-barley nugget cereal
¼ cup frozen apple juice concentrate, defrosted
1 tablespoon ground cinnamon

Filling
1 envelope unflavored gelatin (1 tablespoon)
⅓ cup cold water
½ cup frozen apple juice concentrate, defrosted
2¼ cups plain nonfat yogurt
¼ cup honey
½ teaspoon ground cinnamon
½ teaspoon almond extract

Garnish
1 dozen red seedless grapes, halved
1 dozen green seedless grapes, halved

P reheat oven to 350° F.

In a bowl, combine cereal, juice concentrate and cinnamon; mix until all cereal nuggets are coated. Press onto the bottom and sides of a 9-inch pie plate. Bake 5 minutes, remove from oven and let cool to room temperature.

To make the filling, sprinkle unflavored gelatin over cold

water in a small bowl. Let stand for a few minutes. Pour juice concentrate into a small saucepan. Heat to boiling, add to gelatin and stir until completely dissolved. In another bowl, whisk together yogurt, honey, cinnamon and almond extract until well blended. Add gelatin-juice mixture to yogurt mixture and whisk together until thoroughly blended. Pour into crust, refrigerate overnight and serve cold.

Before garnishing, score the pie into eighths. That way you can avoid placing grape halves on the slicing lines—making slicing and serving much easier. Arrange grapes in two circles or any other pattern you like. If grapes are out of season, garnish with canned fruit such as mandarin oranges or dark, sweet, pitted cherries.

NUTRIENT ANALYSIS

Calories	175.13 kcal
Protein	6.48 g
Carbohydrate	38.66 g
Total Fat	0.90 g
Saturated	0.11 g
Polyunsaturated	0.04 g
Monounsaturated	0.03 g
Cholesterol	1.13 mg
Sodium	121.50 mg

MERINGUE PIE SHELL WITH SHERBET

This elegant dessert is light and delicious. Try substituting ice milk or fresh fruit fillings for a different effect.

MAKES 1 9-INCH PIE
SERVES 8

Vegetable oil spray
2 large egg whites*
⅛ teaspoon cream of tartar
½ cup sugar
½ teaspoon white vinegar
½ teaspoon vanilla extract
2 cups sherbet, any flavor

Preheat oven to 275° F. Lightly spray a 9-inch pie plate with vegetable oil spray.

In a large bowl, beat egg whites and cream of tartar with an electric beater until stiff peaks form. Add sugar 2 tablespoons at a time, beating well after each addition. To test if sugar is completely dissolved, rub meringue mixture between fingers; if grainy, continue beating. Add vinegar and vanilla; beat well to blend.

Spoon meringue into prepared pie plate, heaping the mixture higher along the sides so that it resembles a large nest. Bake 1 hour. Reduce heat to 250° F. and bake another 30 minutes, or until meringue is firm and crisp, but not brown.

Let cool to room temperature. Spoon sherbet evenly into pie shell. Serve immediately.

* Remember that even a single drop of egg yolk will prevent egg whites from rising, so separate eggs very carefully, one at a time.

NUTRIENT ANALYSIS

Calories	119.76 kcal
Protein	1.37 g
Carbohydrate	26.82 g
Total Fat	0.96 g
Saturated	0.59 g
Polyunsaturated	0.03 g
Monounsaturated	0.28 g
Cholesterol	3.38 mg
Sodium	38.05 mg

BAKLAVA

Ready for a new taste treat? Try this traditional Greek favorite. It is made with phyllo, a paper-thin dough that is available in most large supermarkets and specialty groceries. It is frozen in 1-pound packages of about 24 sheets. Phyllo should be defrosted in the refrigerator. Unopened, the defrosted dough will keep for a month, if refrigerated. Refreezing can make the dough crumbly. When working with the dough, keep it covered with a damp cloth to prevent drying.

1 cup raisins
⅓ cup finely chopped pecans or walnuts
8 sheets phyllo dough
¼ cup acceptable margarine, ½ stick, melted
½ cup honey
2 teaspoons ground cinnamon

Preheat oven to 350° F.

In a small bowl, mix raisins and nuts. Set aside.

Lightly brush every other sheet of phyllo with melted margarine and stack the sheets on top of each other. Spread raisin-nut mixture over the phyllo, leaving a 1-inch border on all sides. Drizzle honey over the top and sprinkle with cinnamon.

Roll lengthwise, jelly-roll fashion, and place on a non-stick baking sheet, making sure that the ends of the roll are tucked under and the seam-side faces down. Brush the top lightly with remaining margarine. Cut through the pastry to the raisin-nut mixture, at 1½-inch intervals, to provide vents for steam to escape. Bake 20 to 30 minutes, or until light golden brown. Slice, using vent lines as guides.

This recipe freezes well. Prepare as above but omit the final brushing with margarine, and the baking. Freeze overnight on a baking sheet, then wrap well in freezer paper or foil. To prevent the pastry from getting soggy, do not defrost before baking. Place on a baking sheet, brush with margarine and bake 35 to 45 minutes, or until golden.

NUTRIENT ANALYSIS

Calories	195.49 kcal
Protein	2.89 g
Carbohydrate	34.86 g
Total Fat	6.11 g
Saturated	0.88 g
Polyunsaturated	2.67 g
Monounsaturated	2.04 g
Cholesterol	0.00 mg
Sodium	54.84 mg

CHOCOLATE SOUFFLÉ WITH VANILLA SAUCE

SERVES 6
5 OUNCES PER SERVING

This wonderful chocolate soufflé uses cocoa instead of chocolate. Cocoa is a great way to get that chocolaty flavor without the fat. Its unique topping makes this dessert taste just like the high-fat counterpart.

Vegetable oil spray
1/3 cup fresh orange juice
1/3 cup sugar
4 large egg whites*
1/4 cup unsweetened cocoa powder
2 tablespoons orange liqueur
3/4 cup vanilla ice milk, softened

Preheat oven to 300° F. Grease six 5-ounce custard cups with vegetable oil spray.

In a small saucepan, cook orange juice and sugar over medium-high heat until mixture has a syrupy consistency, about 3 to 4 minutes, stirring occasionally. Remove from heat and reserve.

In a large bowl, beat egg whites until stiff, but stop before dry peaks form. Pour syrup over the egg whites and continue beating for 2 minutes. Add cocoa and liqueur and beat only until well mixed. Pour into prepared custard cups. Bake 12 minutes, or until soufflés are puffed. Do not overbake, or soufflés will become tough.

To serve, spoon 2 tablespoons softened vanilla ice milk into the center of each soufflé. Serve immediately.

* Remember, even a single drop of egg yolk will prevent egg whites from rising, so separate eggs very carefully, one at a time.

NUTRIENT ANALYSIS

Calories	116.95 kcal
Protein	3.68 g
Carbohydrate	22.14 g
Total Fat	1.74 g
Saturated	1.05 g
Polyunsaturated	0.06 g
Monounsaturated	0.55 g
Cholesterol	2.05 mg
Sodium	46.00 mg

MOCHA CHEESECAKE

MAKES I 9-INCH PIE
SERVES 10

With this recipe, you can indulge in cheesecake on a cholesterol-lowering diet. Double-Thick Yogurt and part-skim ricotta cheese replace the high-fat cream cheese found in most cheesecakes. Also, egg whites and cocoa powder are used instead of whole eggs and chocolate. The result is a delectable cake that tastes sinful but isn't. It freezes well if wrapped tightly before freezing.

To make a vanilla cheesecake with a hint of orange flavor, omit the cocoa and coffee liqueur.

Crust
Vegetable oil spray
4 slices whole-wheat bread, toasted
3 tablespoons wheat germ
2 tablespoons unsweetened cocoa powder
2 large egg whites
¼ cup honey
1½ teaspoons vanilla extract
1½ teaspoons coffee liqueur

Filling
2 cups Double-Thick Yogurt (see page 351)
2 cups part-skim ricotta cheese
2 large egg whites
2 tablespoons all-purpose flour
⅔ cup sugar
Grated rind of ½ navel orange
1 tablespoon vanilla extract
2 tablespoons unsweetened cocoa powder
1 tablespoon coffee liqueur

Garnish
Fresh fruit, thinly sliced (optional)

Preheat oven to 300° F. Spray a 9-inch springform pan with vegetable oil spray.

Break bread into quarters and place in the workbowl of a food processor fitted with a metal blade. Process into fine crumbs. In a medium bowl, mix bread crumbs, wheat germ, cocoa, egg whites, honey, vanilla and liqueur until coarse and moist. Using a fork, press mixture evenly in the bottom of the prepared pan. Bake 10 minutes, or until firm to the touch. Cool on wire rack.

In the workbowl of a food processor fitted with a metal blade, process yogurt, ricotta cheese, egg whites, flour, sugar, orange rind, vanilla, cocoa and liqueur until fully blended, scraping the sides of the bowl as needed.

Pour batter into prepared pan and bake on middle rack of oven 1 hour. Turn off the heat and let cake remain in the oven 15 minutes more. Remove from oven and let cool. Chill in refrigerator for at least 3 hours, or preferably overnight, before removing sides of pan.

Garnish with fresh fruit, if desired. Serve chilled or at room temperature.

NUTRIENT ANALYSIS*

Calories	301.51 kcal
Protein	19.13 g
Carbohydrate	97.71 g
Total Fat	5.11 g
Saturated	2.93 g
Polyunsaturated	0.40 g
Monounsaturated	1.43 g
Cholesterol	17.40 mg
Sodium	269.62 mg

* Excluding garnish.

COFFEE LIQUEUR CLOUDS

Go ahead—indulge in a rich dessert! Just make sure you use *this* recipe—all the flavor is here, but the fat isn't.

SERVES 5
ABOUT ½ CUP PER SERVING

¾ cup part-skim ricotta cheese
2 tablespoons Mock Whipped Cream (see page 319)
¼ teaspoon ground cinnamon
2 tablespoons coffee liqueur
3 tablespoons confectioners' sugar
1 11-ounce can mandarin oranges, drained

Garnish
Ground cinnamon

NUTRIENT ANALYSIS

Calories	124.00 kcal
Protein	5.08 g
Carbohydrate	17.95 g
Total Fat	3.50 g
Saturated	1.90 g
Polyunsaturated	0.39 g
Monounsaturated	0.98 g
Cholesterol	11.67 mg
Sodium	54.00 mg

In a blender or the workbowl of a food processor fitted with a metal blade, thoroughly mix ricotta cheese, Mock Whipped Cream, ¼ teaspoon cinnamon, confectioners' sugar and coffee liqueur. Blend until smooth. Set aside.

Divide mandarin oranges evenly into five dessert dishes, and top each with ½ cup of cheese mixture. Garnish with ground cinnamon. Serve chilled.

MOCK WHIPPED CREAM

Use this light, tasty topping in place
of whipped cream or prepackaged
nondairy whipped topping.

MAKES 2 CUPS
SERVES 32
1 TABLESPOON PER SERVING

1 teaspoon gelatin
2 teaspoons cold water
3 tablespoons boiling water
½ cup ice water
½ cup nonfat dry milk
3 tablespoons sugar
3 tablespoons acceptable
    vegetable oil

NUTRIENT ANALYSIS

Calories	20.00 kcal
Protein	0.44 g
Carbohydrate	1.68 g
Total Fat	1.28 g
Saturated	0.17 g
Polyunsaturated	0.75 g
Monounsaturated	0.31 g
Cholesterol	0.19 mg
Sodium	6.00 mg

Chill a small mixing bowl.

In another small bowl, soften gelatin with cold water.
Add boiling water, stirring constantly until gelatin is completely dissolved. Cool until tepid.

Place ice water and nonfat dry milk in chilled mixing
bowl. Beat at high speed of electric mixer until stiff peaks
form. Continue beating and add sugar, oil and gelatin.

Place in freezer for approximately 15 minutes, then
transfer to refrigerator until ready to use. Stir before using
to retain creamy texture.

ORANGE FLUFF

SERVES 6
½ CUP PER SERVING

1 envelope unflavored gelatin
   (1 tablespoon)
¼ cup cold water
½ cup boiling water
½ cup sugar
1 cup orange juice
8 tablespoons Mock Whipped
   Cream (see page 319)
1 tablespoon finely grated
   orange rind

Garnish
2 kiwis, 2 peaches or 6 fresh
   strawberries, sliced
6 small sprigs of mint (optional)

NUTRIENT ANALYSIS*	
Calories	109.00 kcal
Protein	1.89 g
Carbohydrate	22.75 g
Total Fat	1.55 g
Saturated	0.20 g
Polyunsaturated	0.89 g
Monounsaturated	0.37 g
Cholesterol	0.26 mg
Sodium	10.00 mg

* Based on recipe without garnish.

In a small bowl, sprinkle gelatin over cold water. Let stand 2 to 3 minutes.

In another small bowl, mix sugar and boiling water. Add gelatin mixture; stir until dissolved. Add orange juice. Place bowl in refrigerator or over ice water and allow to chill, stirring occasionally, until the mixture thickens, 8 to 10 minutes. Add Mock Whipped Cream and beat vigorously with a hand beater. Continue beating 8 to 10 minutes, or until mixture is fluffy and doubles in volume. Fold in orange peel.

Spoon mixture into a serving bowl or individual glasses and chill until set. Garnish with sliced fruit and mint before serving.

STRAWBERRIES ROMANOFF

This great dessert can also be served as a breakfast treat; just leave out the liqueur and top with crunchy whole-grain cereal. For flavor variety, try substituting other fresh fruit.

SERVES 4
I CUP PER SERVING

Sauce

1 cup Double-Thick Yogurt (see page 351)
1/4 cup firmly packed brown sugar
1/2 teaspoon ground cinnamon
1 teaspoon vanilla extract
2 tablespoons strawberry liqueur (optional)

2 pints fresh strawberries, about 24 ounces, washed, hulled and cut into bite-size pieces

NUTRIENT ANALYSIS

Calories	219.82 kcal
Protein	7.88 g
Carbohydrate	69.25 g
Total Fat	3.36 g
Saturated	0.33 g
Polyunsaturated	0.61 g
Monounsaturated	1.50 g
Cholesterol	2.00 mg
Sodium	92.79 mg

Garnish
2 tablespoons pecan pieces, lightly toasted

In a small bowl, whisk sauce ingredients until fully mixed. Refrigerate for at least 1 hour to make the sauce slightly firm.

Divide berries evenly in four dessert dishes. Spoon 1/4 cup sauce over each serving. Top with nuts and serve immediately.

FROZEN BANANA MOUSSE

SERVES 3
⅔ CUP PER SERVING

3 ripe bananas
¼ cup part-skim ricotta cheese
3 tablespoons skim milk
Pinch ground nutmeg

Peel and place bananas in a heavy plastic bag. Freeze at least 6 hours. Remove from freezer and cut each into five or six pieces. In the workbowl of a food processor fitted with a metal blade, process banana pieces and remaining ingredients, scraping sides occasionally, until smooth and creamy. Serve immediately.

NUTRIENT ANALYSIS

Calories	121.72 kcal
Protein	3.62 g
Carbohydrate	25.13 g
Total Fat	2.03 g
Saturated	1.16 g
Polyunsaturated	0.14 g
Monounsaturated	0.49 g
Cholesterol	6.16 mg
Sodium	32.57 mg

TAPIOCA PUDDING

SERVES 4
ABOUT ⅔ CUP PER SERVING

3 tablespoons quick-cooking tapioca
⅓ cup sugar
2 large egg whites, lightly beaten
2¾ cups skim milk
¾ teaspoon vanilla extract
Pinch ground nutmeg

Garnish

¼ cup slivered almonds, toasted

In a 2-quart saucepan, mix tapioca, sugar, egg whites and
milk and let stand 5 minutes. Bring mixture just to a boil
over medium heat, stirring constantly. Remove from heat
and stir in vanilla and nutmeg. Cover with plastic wrap and
let stand at room temperature 20 minutes. Stir and pour
into individual serving dishes.

Garnish with 1 tablespoon slivered almonds per serving.
Serve warm or chilled.

NUTRIENT ANALYSIS

Calories	203.78 kcal
Protein	8.88 g
Carbohydrate	32.37 g
Total Fat	4.55 g
Saturated	0.55 g
Polyunsaturated	0.80 g
Monounsaturated	2.94 g
Cholesterol	3.37 mg
Sodium	113.38 mg

BLUEBERRY PUDDING

The sweetener in this recipe is apple juice concentrate. That's a good way to cut down on processed sugar.

SERVES 4
ABOUT ⅔ CUP PER SERVING

1 tablespoon unflavored
   gelatin, 1 envelope
¼ cup boiling water
10 ounces tofu, drained
5 tablespoons apple juice
   concentrate, defrosted
½ teaspoon vanilla extract
1 tablespoon firmly packed
   brown sugar
½ teaspoon ground cinnamon
1 pint fresh blueberries,
   rinsed, drained and
   divided, about 16 ounces

NUTRIENT ANALYSIS

Calories	139.88 kcal
Protein	7.62 g
Carbohydrate	22.46 g
Total Fat	3.34 g
Saturated	0.47 g
Polyunsaturated	1.74 g
Monounsaturated	0.70 g
Cholesterol	0.00 mg
Sodium	13.75 mg

Dissolve gelatin in boiling water, stirring until crystals disappear.

In a blender or the workbowl of a food processor fitted with a metal blade, blend dissolved gelatin, tofu, apple juice concentrate, vanilla, brown sugar, cinnamon and 1 cup of blueberries until smooth. Pour pudding into a bowl; fold in remaining cup of blueberries. Cover with plastic wrap and refrigerate for 4 hours, or until set. Serve cold.

WHITE GRAPE JUICE GELATIN DESSERT

SERVES 4
½ CUP PER SERVING

2 to 3 dozen seedless green grapes, chilled
1 envelope unflavored gelatin (1 tablespoon)
1 tablespoon sugar
2 cups white grape juice

Divide the grapes among four dessert dishes or wine-glasses; set aside. In a medium bowl, mix gelatin with sugar. In a small saucepan, heat juice to boiling. Add to gelatin-sugar mixture and stir until gelatin is completely dissolved. Pour ½ cup gelatin liquid into each dessert dish or wine-glass. Refrigerate 3 to 4 hours, or until mixture is slightly set. Serve cold.

NUTRIENT ANALYSIS

Calories	116.77 kcal
Protein	2.46 g
Carbohydrate	27.96 g
Total Fat	0.23 g
Saturated	0.08 g
Polyunsaturated	0.06 g
Monounsaturated	0.00 g
Cholesterol	0.00 mg
Sodium	6.06 mg

COFFEE SHAKE

SERVES 4
1¼ CUPS PER SERVING

1 quart decaffeinated coffee
2 cups vanilla ice milk, tightly packed

In blender, process coffee and ice milk until fully mixed.
Serve, icy cold, in tall glasses.

NUTRIENT ANALYSIS

Calories	127.30 kcal
Protein	3.45 g
Carbohydrate	20.79 g
Total Fat	3.76 g
Saturated	2.34 g
Polyunsaturated	0.14 g
Monounsaturated	1.09 g
Cholesterol	12.25 mg
Sodium	70.00 mg

FROZEN ORANGE CREAM

The vanilla extract enhances the
sweetness of this dish without
adding calories.

SERVES 6
½ CUP PER SERVING

3 cups vanilla ice milk, tightly packed
½ cup frozen orange juice concentrate
1 teaspoon vanilla extract

In a blender or the workbowl of a food processor fitted with a metal blade, blend all ingredients until fully mixed. Spoon mixture into dessert cups. Cover with plastic wrap and freeze for about 2 hours. If you freeze it longer, remove the dish from the freezer 10 minutes before serving to allow it to thaw slightly.

NUTRIENT ANALYSIS

Calories	160.21 kcal
Protein	4.01 g
Carbohydrate	28.45 g
Total Fat	3.80 g
Saturated	2.34 g
Polyunsaturated	0.15 g
Monounsaturated	1.09 g
Cholesterol	12.20 mg
Sodium	70.55 mg

VERY BERRY SORBET

This slightly tart sorbet is a perfect complement to Frozen Banana Mousse (see page 322). For an elegant presentation, try combining them in alternating layers in parfait glasses.

SERVES 2
½ CUP PER SERVING

Sorbet
1½ cups frozen no-sugar-added blackberries, slightly defrosted
1 teaspoon frozen orange juice concentrate
2 teaspoons water
1 teaspoon brandy or cognac (optional)

Garnish
Fresh mint sprigs (optional)

NUTRIENT ANALYSIS

Calories	66.73 kcal
Protein	0.83 g
Carbohydrate	14.95 g
Total Fat	0.43 g
Saturated	0.00 g
Polyunsaturated	0.00 g
Monounsaturated	0.00 g
Cholesterol	0.00 mg
Sodium	0.13 mg

In a blender or the workbowl of a food processor fitted with a metal blade, process sorbet ingredients until smooth, scraping sides as needed. Garnish with mint, if desired. Serve immediately.

This dish can be frozen. About 15 minutes before serving, remove from freezer and let defrost until it's soft enough to serve.

MELON WITH SHERBET

Serve this dessert in glasses with
pretty frosted rims.

SERVES 6

1 small honeydew melon, cut in half and seeded
4 oranges or 2 cups strawberries
2 tablespoons confectioners' sugar, sifted
12 ounces rainbow sherbet, six 2-ounce scoops

Garnish
Mint sprigs

With a melon baller, scoop out flesh of melon. Section
oranges or slice strawberries. Combine melon and oranges
or stawberries in a bowl and chill.

Place confectioners' sugar in a pie plate. Dampen rims of
six dessert glasses and then dip rims individually in confectioners' sugar.

Divide fruit mixture among glasses, top each with a
scoop of sherbet and garnish with a sprig of mint.

Serve immediately.

NUTRIENT ANALYSIS

Calories	223.55 kcal
Protein	3.37 g
Carbohydrate	53.64 g
Total Fat	1.48 g
Saturated	0.72 g
Polyunsaturated	0.08 g
Monounsaturated	0.35 g
Cholesterol	3.97 mg
Sodium	54.62 mg

YOGURT-FRUIT CUP

This offers a new twist to a back-to-basics favorite. You'll like the fragrant touch of cardamom.

SERVES 6

1 16-ounce can sliced peaches or pears, packed in fruit juice
16 ounces lowfat vanilla yogurt
2 tablespoons finely chopped almonds
1/2 teaspoon ground cardamom

D rain and divide fruit among six small dessert bowls. Top with yogurt and sprinkle lightly with nuts and cardamom. Serve immediately.

NUTRIENT ANALYSIS

Calories	121.01 kcal
Protein	4.39 g
Carbohydrate	22.19 g
Total Fat	2.23 g
Saturated	0.67 g
Polyunsaturated	0.30 g
Monounsaturated	1.15 g
Cholesterol	3.21 mg
Sodium	46.59 mg

CHERRIES JUBILEE

What an elegant finale to a dinner
party!

SERVES 4
1 CUP PER SERVING

1 16-ounce can dark, sweet, pitted cherries
¼ cup apple juice
1 tablespoon cornstarch
2 tablespoons brandy or rum
3 cups vanilla ice milk

D rain syrup from cherries and mix with apple juice.

In a small bowl, mix cornstarch and 2 tablespoons of juice until no lumps remain.

In a small saucepan over high heat, bring remaining liquid to a boil and reduce heat to medium. Add cornstarch mixture, stirring constantly. Let mixture return to a boil and cook about 1 minute, or until thickened. Add brandy, stir in cherries, and ignite.

Pour over individual portions of ice milk. Serve immediately.

NUTRIENT ANALYSIS

Calories	299.13 kcal
Protein	5.79 g
Carbohydrate	53.88 g
Total Fat	5.82 g
Saturated	3.55 g
Polyunsaturated	0.27 g
Monounsaturated	1.67 g
Cholesterol	18.37 mg
Sodium	108.54 mg

BROILED GRAPEFRUIT WITH PORT WINE

Port wine adds a tantalizing flavor
to grapefruit. Try this dish as an
appetizer or dessert.

SERVES 4
½ GRAPEFRUIT PER SERVING

2 grapefruit
2 tablespoons port wine

P reheat broiler.

Cut grapefruit into halves. Trim a thin section off the
uncut end of each half so the grapefruit can sit without
wobbling. Section the grapefruit. Place grapefruit in a baking pan, sprinkle with wine, place pan about 2 inches from
the broiler and broil about 5 minutes. Watch carefully to
keep them from burning.

NUTRIENT ANALYSIS

Calories	57.64 kcal
Protein	0.90 g
Carbohydrate	12.64 g
Total Fat	0.15 g
Saturated	0.01 g
Polyunsaturated	0.03 g
Monounsaturated	0.01 g
Cholesterol	0.00 mg
Sodium	0.29 mg

BAKED APPLES

SERVES 4

1/4 cup port wine
1/4 cup frozen apple juice
   concentrate, defrosted
1/4 cup raisins
1/4 teaspoon ground cinnamon
4 baking apples, preferably
   red Rome apples

NUTRIENT ANALYSIS

Calories	120.30 kcal
Protein	0.77 g
Carbohydrate	27.67 g
Total Fat	0.37 g
Saturated	0.11 g
Polyunsaturated	0.11 g
Monounsaturated	0.01 g
Cholesterol	0.00 mg
Sodium	6.40 mg

Preheat oven to 350° F.

In a small saucepan, heat wine and juice concentrate until mixture begins to boil. Turn heat off and add raisins and cinnamon. Stir, cover and let sit for 15 minutes.

Core each apple, leaving the last half-inch on the bottom intact. If necessary, slice off a small section from the bottom of each apple so that it does not fall over. Take a paring knife and score around the apple, about 1/2-inch from the bottom. Peel from top down to scored line to prevent splitting. Place apples in a glass baking dish so they are not touching. Stuff with the juice-soaked raisins, spooning remaining juice evenly over apples. Put water in the dish to a depth of 1/3 inch, cover with aluminum foil and bake 20 minutes. Remove the foil and bake another 20 minutes. Serve warm.

MERINGUES

For an elegant dessert, fill these
with fresh fruit or vanilla ice milk
and Blueberry Sauce (see page
265).

**SERVES 20
1 SHELL PER SERVING**

Vegetable oil spray
4 large egg whites*
1/8 teaspoon cream of tartar
1 cup sugar
1 teaspoon white vinegar
1/2 teaspoon vanilla extract

Preheat oven to 275° F. Line two large baking sheets with
wax paper, then spray lightly with vegetable oil spray.

In a large bowl, beat egg whites and cream of tartar
with an electric beater until stiff peaks form. Add sugar, 2
tablespoons at a time, beating well after each addition. To
test if sugar is completely dissolved, rub meringue mixture
between fingers; if grainy, continue beating. Add vinegar
and vanilla; beat well to blend.

Drop mixture by heaping tablespoonfuls about 2 inches
apart on prepared baking sheets. Spread each spoonful into
a 2½-inch circle, pushing the mixture against the edges to
resemble a nest. Bake 45 minutes. Reduce heat to 250° F.
and bake about 15 minutes more, until each meringue is
firm and crisp, but not brown.

Remove from wax paper while warm, and allow to cool
on a rack. Store in an airtight container.

* Remember, even a single drop of egg yolk will prevent egg whites from
rising, so separate eggs very carefully, one at a time.

NUTRIENT ANALYSIS

Calories	41.61 kcal
Protein	0.67 g
Carbohydrate	9.67 g
Total Fat	0.00 g
Saturated	0.00 g
Polyunsaturated	0.00 g
Monounsaturated	0.00 g
Cholesterol	0.00 mg
Sodium	11.41 mg

COCOA-ALMOND MERINGUE KISSES

These meringues are crispy on the outside and chewy on the inside.

SERVES 14
2 KISSES PER SERVING

Vegetable oil spray
3 large egg whites*
1/8 teaspoon cream of tartar
3/4 cup sugar
3 tablespoons unsweetened
    cocoa powder
1/2 teaspoon vanilla extract
1/4 cup sliced almonds

NUTRIENT ANALYSIS

Calories	60.17 kcal
Protein	1.32 g
Carbohydrate	11.27 g
Total Fat	1.44 g
Saturated	0.29 g
Polyunsaturated	0.21 g
Monounsaturated	0.86 g
Cholesterol	0.00 mg
Sodium	12.59 mg

Preheat oven to 325° F. Spray two large baking sheets with vegetable oil spray.

In a large bowl, beat egg whites and cream of tartar until stiff peaks form. Add sugar, 2 tablespoons at a time, beating well after each addition. Add cocoa and vanilla, beat well to blend. Fold in almonds.

Drop mixture by tablespoonfuls onto prepared baking sheets. Bake 25 minutes, or until meringues are crisp on the outside. Remove from baking sheets immediately, and allow to cool on a rack. Store in an airtight container.

*Remember, even a single drop of egg yolk will prevent egg whites from rising, so separate eggs very carefully, one at a time.

GINGERBREAD BARS

The wonderful, spicy aroma of
these cookies baking will have the
whole family lined up in the kitchen.
They're great any time, and they
freeze well.

SERVES 15
2 BARS PER SERVING

Vegetable oil spray
6 tablespoons acceptable unsalted margarine, at room
    temperature
1 cup dark brown sugar, firmly packed
2 large egg whites
¼ cup molasses
1¼ cups all-purpose flour
1 cup whole-wheat flour
¼ cup dry skim milk powder
¾ teaspoon baking powder
¾ teaspoon baking soda
¾ teaspoon powdered ginger
½ teaspoon ground cinnamon
½ teaspoon ground nutmeg
⅛ teaspoon ground cloves
½ cup coarsely chopped walnuts

P reheat oven to 350° F. Spray a 12½ × 8-inch baking pan
with vegetable oil spray.

In a large bowl, beat margarine at medium speed until
creamy. Add brown sugar and beat at high speed until light,
1 to 2 minutes. Beat in egg whites. Add molasses and beat
until no lumps remain.

In a separate bowl, sift together flours, dry skim milk
powder, baking powder, baking soda, ginger, cinnamon,
nutmeg and cloves. Add sifted ingredients to margarine
mixture and blend thoroughly. Stir in nuts and mix well.
The dough will be sticky.

Place the dough in center of prepared pan. Using a spatula or wet hands, spread dough evenly in pan. Place pan on center rack of oven and bake 25 minutes.

Allow to cool at least 5 minutes. Cut into 30 bars and store in an airtight container.

NUTRIENT ANALYSIS

Calories	198.51 kcal
Protein	3.47 g
Carbohydrate	31.75 g
Total Fat	6.97 g
Saturated	1.10 g
Polyunsaturated	3.18 g
Monounsaturated	2.27 g
Cholesterol	0.20 mg
Sodium*	76.42 mg

* Will increase if using regular margarine.

CHEWY OATMEAL SQUARES

This recipe and the one following are two versions of a favorite. Make them both and see which you like best.

SERVES 18
2 SQUARES PER SERVING

Vegetable oil spray
½ cup acceptable vegetable oil
½ cup firmly packed brown sugar
1 4½-ounce jar strained applesauce (baby food)
1 teaspoon vanilla extract
2 cups quick-cooking oats
⅓ cup chopped walnuts
½ teaspoon baking powder
1 teaspoon ground cinnamon

NUTRIENT ANALYSIS

Calories	127.72 kcal
Protein	1.59 g
Carbohydrate	13.16 g
Total Fat	8.05 g
Saturated	1.02 g
Polyunsaturated	4.66 g
Monounsaturated	1.86 g
Cholesterol	0.00 mg
Sodium	10.21 mg

Preheat oven to 325° F. Spray a 9-inch square pan with vegetable oil spray.

In a mixing bowl, combine oil, brown sugar, applesauce and vanilla. Add oats, walnuts, baking powder and cinnamon. Mix until blended.

Press mixture evenly and firmly into prepared pan. Bake 20 to 25 minutes, or until edges are golden brown. Cut into 36 squares while hot. Allow to cool in pan. Store in an airtight container.

OATMEAL CRISPS

SERVES 18
2 SQUARES PER SERVING

Vegetable oil spray
1/2 cup acceptable vegetable oil
1/2 cup firmly packed brown sugar
1 teaspoon vanilla extract
2 cups quick-cooking oats
1/2 teaspoon baking powder
1 teaspoon ground cinnamon

Preheat oven to 325° F. Spray a 9-inch square pan with vegetable oil spray.

In a mixing bowl, combine oil, brown sugar and vanilla. Add oats, baking powder and cinnamon. Mix until blended.

Press mixture evenly and firmly into prepared pan. Bake 20 to 25 minutes, or until edges are golden brown. Cut into 36 squares while hot. Allow to cool in pan. Store in a container with a loose-fitting lid.

NUTRIENT ANALYSIS

Calories	114.59 kcal
Protein	1.25 g
Carbohydrate	12.03 g
Total Fat	6.65 g
Saturated	0.86 g
Polyunsaturated	3.74 g
Monounsaturated	1.65 g
Cholesterol	0.00 mg
Sodium	10.00 mg

BEVERAGES

Orange Juice and Club Soda Cooler
Orange-Strawberry Juice Froth
Orange-Banana Shake
Spiced Apple Cider

ORANGE JUICE AND CLUB SODA COOLER

SERVES 4
I CUP PER SERVING

¼ cup frozen orange juice concentrate
3 cups club soda
Crushed ice

Garnish
4 strawberries or 4 sprigs fresh mint

In a 2-quart pitcher, combine orange juice concentrate and club soda. Stir and serve immediately over crushed ice. Garnish each glass with a strawberry or a fresh mint sprig.

NUTRIENT ANALYSIS

Calories	24.73 kcal
Protein	0.40 g
Carbohydrate	5.89 g
Total Fat	0.08 g
Saturated	0.00 g
Polyunsaturated	0.00 g
Monounsaturated	0.00 g
Cholesterol	0.00 mg
Sodium	29.37 mg

ORANGE-STRAWBERRY JUICE FROTH

SERVES 6
¾ CUP PER SERVING

2 cups orange juice
1½ cups apricot nectar
1 cup frozen, sweetened strawberries

In blender, process ingredients for about 20 seconds, or until smooth and frothy. Serve immediately.

NUTRIENT ANALYSIS

Calories	113.53 kcal
Protein	1.05 g
Carbohydrate	29.07 g
Total Fat	0.16 g
Saturated	0.02 g
Polyunsaturated	0.05 g
Monounsaturated	0.04 g
Cholesterol	0.00 mg
Sodium	4.00 mg

ORANGE-BANANA SHAKE

Cool. Refreshing. Fruity. Delicious.   **SERVES 2**
And lowfat, too.   **I CUP PER SERVING**

1 cup orange juice
1 small, ripe banana
¼ cup instant nonfat milk powder
½ cup ice cubes
¼ cup club soda

In blender, process orange juice, banana, milk powder and ice cubes until mixture is thick and ice cubes are crushed. Add club soda, stir and serve immediately.

NUTRIENT ANALYSIS

Calories	132.54 kcal
Protein	4.36 g
Carbohydrate	29.59 g
Total Fat	0.38 g
Saturated	0.15 g
Polyunsaturated	0.06 g
Monounsaturated	0.05 g
Cholesterol	1.53 mg
Sodium	53.32 mg

SPICED APPLE CIDER

A warm fire. A cozy room. A comfy chair. This holiday favorite completes the scene.

SERVES 16
¾ CUP PER SERVING

12 whole allspice
6 whole cloves
2 quarts apple juice or apple cider
1 quart water
3 tea bags, regular or decaffeinated
½ orange with peel, thinly sliced
½ lemon with peel, thinly sliced
2 cinnamon sticks
Ground allspice to taste

NUTRIENT ANALYSIS

Calories	71.05 kcal
Protein	0.37 g
Carbohydrate	17.55 g
Total Fat	0.21 g
Saturated	0.04 g
Polyunsaturated	0.05 g
Monounsaturated	0.02 g
Cholesterol	0.00 mg
Sodium	4.36 mg

Garnish
1 orange with peel, thinly sliced
1 lemon with peel, thinly sliced

Place whole allspice and cloves in tied cheesecloth packet. In a saucepan, bring apple juice or cider, water, tea bags, orange, lemon, cinnamon and cheesecloth packet to a boil. Reduce heat and simmer 3 minutes. Remove cheesecloth packet, tea bags and orange and lemon slices. Simmer 5 additional minutes. Add ground allspice to taste.

Serve hot or chilled. Garnish with fresh slices of orange and lemon.

BASICS AND TECHNIQUES

Defatted Cheddar Cheese
Double-Thick Yogurt
Fish Stock—See Poached Fish and Fish Stock,
pages 115–116
Chicken Stock
Beef Stock

DEFATTED CHEDDAR CHEESE

MAKES 3½ OUNCES

This recipe shows how to separate cheese from some of its fat. You can do it in the oven or the microwave. Either way, this clever technique produces a tasty cheese that is lower in fat than regular cheese. Use it as a spread on Rice Cake and Cheese Snack or on Whole-Wheat French Bread (see pages 46 and 269–270).

Vegetable oil spray
4 ounces sharp cheddar cheese or another natural cheese such
*   as Monterey Jack or Gouda, cut into ½-inch cubes*

Oven Method: Preheat oven to 450° F.

Select an ovenproof 5- or 6-inch-diameter pan or bowl. Spray thoroughly with vegetable oil spray. Place cheese in greased bowl and add cool tap water to barely cover. Bake 20 minutes, stirring every 5 minutes. Remove from oven and let cool for about 15 minutes. Pour into a fine sieve and rinse under cool running water for about a minute to wash away remaining surface fat. Remove liquid by pressing the palm of your hand against the cheese in the sieve. Refrigerate and use within 3 to 4 days.

Microwave Method: Select a 5- or 6-inch-diameter bowl suitable for a microwave oven. Spray thoroughly with vegetable oil spray. Place cheese in greased bowl and add cool tap water to barely cover. Microwave on high setting 3 minutes, or until cheese is completely melted, stirring after each minute of cooking. Remove from oven and let cool for about 10 minutes. Pour into a fine sieve and rinse for about 15 seconds under cool running water to wash away remaining surface fat. Remove liquid by pressing the palm of your hand against the cheese in the sieve. Refrigerate and use within 3 to 4 days.

NUTRIENT ANALYSIS*

Calories	201.00 kcal
Protein	30.30 g
Carbohydrate	0.20 g
Total Fat	8.80 g
Saturated	6.90 g
Polyunsaturated	0.20 g
Monounsaturated	1.80 g
Cholesterol	20.60 mg
Sodium	163.00 mg

* For entire recipe, using cheddar cheese.

DOUBLE-THICK YOGURT

MAKES 2 CUPS

Yogurt is one of the staples of a heart-healthful way of cooking. It is used in the Mocha Cheesecake (see pages 316–317), the Beef or Venison Stroganoff (see pages 191–192) and other recipes in this book. This recipe works best when using a yogurt that contains no gelatin, so read the label carefully.

1 quart plain nonfat yogurt

P lace a double-thick layer of fine-mesh cotton cheesecloth or paper coffee filters inside a colander, which does not rust. Place the colander in a bowl, leaving enough space for about 2 cups of whey to drain out of the colander. Pour the yogurt into the cheesecloth-lined colander and refrigerate for 8 hours. This will yield 2 cups of firm yogurt and 2 cups of drained whey.

Reserve the whey and use it as a substitute in recipes calling for skim milk, such as in baking bread. (See Honey-Nut Bread, page 271, Potato Bread, pages 274–275, etc.)

NUTRIENT ANALYSIS*

Calories	504.00 kcal
Protein	52.16 g
Carbohydrate	69.76 g
Total Fat	1.60 g
Saturated	0.96 g
Polyunsaturated	0 g
Monounsaturated	0.32 g
Cholesterol	16.00 mg
Sodium	680.00 mg

* For entire recipe.

CHICKEN STOCK

MAKES 2½ QUARTS

Canned chicken stock is no match for homemade. This stock is more flavorful and lower in fat and sodium than canned is. Because good stock is essential to so many recipes, prepare a large batch, freeze it in ice cube trays and then transfer the cubes to plastic freezer bags to be used as needed.

3 pounds chicken, skinned
    and all visible fat removed
3 quarts water
1 medium onion, coarsely
    chopped
2 stalks celery, chopped
2 large carrots, chopped
1 teaspoon whole
    peppercorns, or to taste
½-inch piece peeled, fresh
    ginger, chopped (optional)
1 bay leaf
1 teaspoon dried thyme

NUTRIENT ANALYSIS*

Calories	318.70 kcal
Protein	29.70 g
Carbohydrate	38.30 g
Total Fat	5.70 g
Saturated	1.50 g
Polyunsaturated	1.30 g
Monounsaturated	1.50 g
Cholesterol	68.00 mg
Sodium	326.80 mg

* For entire recipe.

In a large stockpot, bring all ingredients to a boil over medium-high heat. Reduce heat and simmer, partially covered, for at least 1 hour, or until chicken is tender. Frequently skim the froth off the top. Remove chicken and strain stock. (The chicken meat can be used in salads.)

To defat stock, refrigerate until the fat hardens on the surface, then remove and discard. The stock may gel during refrigeration; this is natural.

To defat commercially prepared canned chicken stock, store cans in the refrigerator to allow fat to harden. Remove and discard the fat before using the stock.

BEEF STOCK

MAKES 2 QUARTS

Roasting the bones gives the stock a rich flavor and color. You can, however, skip this step and combine the bones with the remaining ingredients to make a good stock. Defat and freeze the stock for future use. After tasting this, you may never want to buy another can of stock!

4 pounds beef or veal bones
3 quarts water
1 medium onion, coarsely chopped
3 large carrots, chopped
6 sprigs fresh parsley
1 teaspoon whole peppercorns, or to taste
4 cloves garlic, halved
1 bay leaf
2 whole cloves
1 teaspoon thyme
½ teaspoon celery seeds

P reheat oven to 400° F.

Place bones in a roasting pan and bake 30 minutes, turning once. Discard accumulated fat.

Transfer bones and remaining ingredients to a large stockpot. Bring mixture to a boil over medium-high heat. Reduce heat and simmer, partially covered, at least 4 hours. Frequently skim the froth off the top.

Using a colander or a large sieve lined with a layer of cheesecloth, strain stock.

To defat stock, refrigerate until the fat hardens on the

surface, then remove and discard. The stock may gel during refrigeration; this is natural.

To defat commercially prepared canned beef stock, store cans in the refrigerator to allow fat to harden. Remove and discard fat before using the stock.

NUTRIENT ANALYSIS*

Calories	399.98 kcal
Protein	34.61 g
Carbohydrate	50.63 g
Total Fat	7.22 g
Saturated	2.66 g
Polyunsaturated	0.42 g
Monounsaturated	2.66 g
Cholesterol	80.26 mg
Sodium	235.55 mg

* For entire recipe.

APPENDIX

APPENDIX A.

LIPOPROTEINS:
THE VEHICLES OF CHOLESTEROL

Tiny particles in your blood called lipoproteins carry cholesterol and other fats to various parts of the body. Some are dangerous. Others are innocuous or even beneficial. The dangerous lipoproteins filter into the walls of your small arteries, allowing cholesterol to build up, a condition called atherosclerosis. Heavy buildup can cause the blood flow to become blocked, resulting in heart attack or stroke. Conversely, other lipoproteins may actually remove excess cholesterol from the arteries. That's why it's important to know which is which.

Low Density Lipoproteins (LDL)

In most people, the majority of blood cholesterol is carried in low density lipoproteins, or LDL. LDL is the "bad guy" of lipoproteins; it's the kind that enters artery walls to cause atherosclerosis. Your doctor can more accurately judge your coronary risk by determining the amount of cholesterol carried by your LDL. This is referred to as LDL-cholesterol.

If your LDL-cholesterol is over 160 milligrams per 100 ml of blood (mg/dl), it's considered high risk. If it's between 130 and 160, it's borderline high risk. A desirable LDL-cholesterol is below 130.

The relationship between the blood cholesterol level and LDL-cholesterol level varies. Your doctor can't predict your LDL-cholesterol from a blood cholesterol test. People with high blood cholesterol should have a lipoprotein analysis, too, especially since LDL-cholesterol level is a much more accurate predictor of coronary risk.

High Density Lipoproteins (HDL)

Typically, one third to one fourth of the cholesterol in the blood is carried in high density lipoproteins, or HDL. HDL is the "good guy" among lipoproteins; a high blood level seems to protect against heart attack.

We're not sure exactly how HDL works, but some authorities believe that it removes excess cholesterol from the arteries to prevent the buildup of cholesterol in the artery wall. So a high level of HDL-cholesterol reduces your risk of heart attack, while a low level increases it.

HDL-cholesterol levels for men usually range from 40 to 50 mg/dl. For women, levels of 50 to 60 mg/dl are normal. If your blood level is below 35 mg/dl, your HDL-cholesterol is abnormally low and is a major cardiac risk factor for you.

Reduced HDL-cholesterol levels can be caused by a number of factors. The most common are cigarette smoking, obesity and lack of exercise. Fortunately, all can be corrected, resulting in an increased HDL level and a reduced heart attack risk. Having a high level of triglycerides in your blood also reduces HDL-cholesterol, which may be why most people with high triglycerides are at increased risk for heart attack.

Some drugs (e.g., beta-blockers) used to treat high blood pressure lower blood HDL. Male sex hormones (androgens), progesterone and anabolic steroids all lower HDL levels. People who take anabolic steroids to build muscles may be setting themselves up for heart attacks later in life. Female sex hormones (estrogens) raise HDL-cholesterol. This difference between male and female sex hormones may be one reason why men are more prone to heart attack than women.

Very Low Density Lipoproteins (VLDL)

Blood cholesterol that is not present in LDL or HDL is found in very low density lipoproteins, VLDL for short. Very low density lipoproteins have the additional job of carrying most of the blood triglycerides. Chemically, triglycerides are what most people know as fat. In fact, most body fat occurs in the form of triglycerides. (Table fats like butter, margarine and vegetable oil are triglycerides, too.) Normally, triglycerides are removed from VLDL during circulation, and serve as a source of energy for muscle activity. After triglycerides are removed, the lipoprotein particles remaining are triglyceride-poor and are called VLDL remnants, which are further broken down to produce LDL. Thus, cholesterol-rich low density lipoproteins are the end products of VLDL metabolism.

Authorities are divided on whether very low density lipoproteins are "bad guys" in the sense of contributing to the buildup of cholesterol-laden plaque in the arteries. Many investigators believe that VLDL can enter the coronary arteries and deposit cholesterol. If they're right, it means that VLDL-cholesterol may contribute to atherosclerosis in the same way that LDL-cholesterol does.

The blood triglyceride level is an indirect measure of VLDL-cholesterol. A simple way to estimate VLDL-cholesterol is to divide the blood triglyceride by five. An increased blood triglyceride level could, therefore, reflect a high risk by indicating an elevated VLDL-cholesterol. Indeed, more than one fourth of all patients who've had heart attacks have triglyceride levels that are abnormally high (over 250). Authorities aren't certain whether that relationship is because of abnormally high VLDL-cholesterol levels or reduced levels of HDL-cholesterol, which often results from elevated triglyceride levels. The fact is, both may contribute to atherosclerosis.

Blood triglyceride levels can be high for any number of reasons, including overweight, high alcohol consumption, diabetes and various inherited disorders of triglyceride metabolism.

APPENDIX B.

HOW DIET AFFECTS YOUR CHOLESTEROL LEVEL

BLOOD CHOLESTEROL–RAISING FACTORS IN THE DIET

Three major factors in the diet raise the blood cholesterol level; these are saturated fats, cholesterol, and obesity. Each of these factors will be examined.

Saturated Fat

Fats are composed mainly of triglycerides, which in turn are composed mainly of fatty acids. The latter fall into three categories: saturated fatty acids, monounsaturated fatty acids and polyunsaturated fatty acids. Of these three, only the saturated fatty acids raise blood cholesterol. The term "saturated fat" is shorthand for the more accurate term "saturated fatty acid."

Foods high in saturated fatty acids come from both animal and plant sources. Animal-based foods containing lots of saturated fats include butter, beef tallow, lard and poultry fat. Fish also contains a small amount. Plant-based oils containing saturated fats are coconut oil, palm kernel oil and palm oil.

Research shows that, for an average person, the intake of 1 gram of saturated fatty acid increases blood cholesterol by about 1 milligram per deciliter of blood (mg/dl). This response, however, varies from person to person. Some people are unusually sensitive to saturated fatty acids and show striking increases in blood cholesterol when saturates are ingested. Others experience less dramatic increases. Many people with high blood cholesterol seem to be especially sensitive to saturated fats, which partially explains their cholesterol levels.

There are several different kinds of saturated fatty acids, and some types raise the blood cholesterol more than others. Fatty acids present in butter, coconut oil, palm oil and palm kernel oil are the worst offenders for raising blood cholesterol. The fatty acids in cocoa butter and meat fats such as beef tallow and lard raise the blood cholesterol less, but they still contain significant portions of blood cholesterol—raising saturates.

Dietary Cholesterol

Another dietary substance that raises blood cholesterol is the cholesterol found in many of the foods we eat. It is important to distinguish between dietary cholesterol and blood cholesterol; the two are not the same.

Cholesterol in the diet comes exclusively from animal products. The richest sources are egg yolks and organ meats. Some cholesterol is found in all meats, poultry, fish and animal fats, such as butter and lard. For most Americans, dietary cholesterol sources are divided evenly among eggs, meat and animal fats like butter.

The effect of dietary cholesterol on blood cholesterol levels has been a subject of much controversy and dispute. Many research studies show that a diet high in cholesterol raises the blood cholesterol level, but the amount of that increase varies from person to person. Moreover, the response can vary even within a single person from one time to another. On the average, however, for every 250 milligrams of cholesterol habitually consumed in the diet the blood cholesterol rises by about 10 mg/dl. Most of this increase occurs in the LDL-cholesterol, the type of cholesterol most likely to build up in your arteries.

Obesity

Another way that diet can raise blood cholesterol is by taking in more calories than the body burns, a situation that leads to obesity. When the cholesterol level of an obese person is elevated, the increase is usually found in both LDL-cholesterol and VLDL-cholesterol. In contrast, the level of HDL or "good guy" cholesterol is usually low. (For a discussion of these types of cholesterol and their significance, see Appendix A.)

The ways in which excessive intakes of saturated fatty acids, cholesterol and total calories raise the blood cholesterol are outlined in Figure 1. The left panel shows how the body reduces the amounts of LDL and VLDL in the blood: Both VLDL remnants and LDL are removed primarily through the function of LDL receptors in the liver, which are extremely important for reducing LDL or "bad guy" cholesterol. The receptors are special proteins located on the surface of liver cells. They work by binding both VLDL remnants and LDL and pulling them out of the blood.

FIGURE 1

= LDL Receptors

The right panel of Figure 1 shows how this LDL and VLDL removal process is changed by a cholesterol-raising diet. When the diet is rich in cholesterol, the excess cholesterol makes its way into the liver. As the liver receives more dietary cholesterol, it partially shuts down the production of LDL receptors, which leads to reduced removal of LDL-cholesterol from the blood.

Moreover, saturated fatty acids seem to increase the ability of dietary cholesterol to decrease the production of LDL receptors. That's how both dietary cholesterol and saturated fatty acids decrease LDL and VLDL removal and increase the blood's LDL-cholesterol level.

Obesity overloads the liver with calories, causing it to make more VLDL, which is transformed in excess into LDL. When obesity is combined with a high intake of saturated fatty acids and cholesterol, the blood level of LDL-cholesterol is doubly increased.

This combination of obesity and an excessive intake of cholesterol and saturated fatty acids is common among Americans. In some people it leads to a borderline cholesterol problem, whereas in others a serious one.

BLOOD CHOLESTEROL—LOWERING FACTORS IN THE DIET

In contrast to the nutrients that raise the blood cholesterol levels, there are others that have no effect on it. Nutrients that help reduce blood cholesterol levels include polyunsaturated fatty acids, monounsaturated fatty acids and carbohydrates. By substituting these nutrients for ones containing saturated fatty acids and dietary cholesterol, you can help decrease your blood cholesterol level.

Polyunsaturated Fatty Acids

There are two types of polyunsaturates. One is composed of Omega-6 fatty acids, found in many vegetable oils such as safflower oil, sunflower seed oil, soybean oil and corn oil. The other type is composed of Omega-3 polyunsaturates, which are found in high amounts in some fish and fish oils. The American diet is typically very low in Omega-3 polyunsaturates. Polyunsaturates of all kinds account for about 6 to 7 percent of our total caloric intake, and most of those polyunsaturates are of the Omega-6 type. When polyunsaturated Omega-6 fatty acids are substituted for saturated fatty acids, total blood cholesterol and LDL-cholesterol levels fall. The evidence that Omega-3 fatty acids will do this is limited.

Monounsaturated Fatty Acids

Monounsaturates are found primarily in olive oil, rapeseed (canola) oil and in high-monounsaturated forms of sunflower seed oil and safflower oil. For many years, monounsaturates were thought to be neutral, neither raising nor lowering blood cholesterol. Recent research suggests that monounsaturates do in fact lower LDL-cholesterol as much as polyunsaturates when used in place of saturated fatty acids in the diet.

Carbohydrates

Dietary carbohydrates occur in three types: simple sugars known as monosaccharides and disaccharides; digestible complex carbohydrates, otherwise known as starches; and indigestible complex carbohydrates called fiber. Some types of fiber, particularly the soluble type, may lower blood cholesterol. Examples of these are pectins, psyllium and certain gums. One such gum is beta-glucon, present in oat products and beans. A high intake (15 to 25 grams per day) of soluble fiber has been reported to slightly lower blood cholesterol levels. High intakes can produce gastrointestinal side effects, but improved tolerance usually is achieved after prolonged usage. The major sources of digestible complex carbohydrates and fiber are plant foods such as vegetables, fruits, legumes and grains, along with their products—breads and pastas.

APPENDIX C.

THE AMERICAN HEART ASSOCIATION/ NATIONAL HEART, LUNG, AND BLOOD INSTITUTE DIETS

These eating plans are designed to help you lower your blood cholesterol. The recommended dietary change is presented in two stages—the Step-One and Step-Two Diets. These eating patterns are low in saturated fatty acids and cholesterol.

Since weight reduction will be necessary for many individuals, sample eating plans are included for both reducing and maintaining weight. The weight-maintenance calorie eating plans are 2000 and 2500 calories for men and 1600 and 2000 calories for women. The 1600-calorie eating plan will achieve weight reduction for many men. The 1200-calorie eating plan is intended for weight reduction for women.

THE STEP-ONE DIET

The Step-One Diet will put you on the road to lowering your blood cholesterol.

FOOD GROUPS
In this eating plan, foods are categorized in seven groups according to fat, carbohydrate, protein and calories. The food groups are:

1. Meat, Poultry and Seafood
2. Eggs

365

3. Dairy Products
4. Fats and Oils
5. Breads, Cereal, Pasta and Starchy Vegetables
6. Vegetables and Fruits
7. Optional Foods—Desserts, Sweets and Alcohol

Within a food group, the foods contain similar amounts of nutrients. Initially, a food scale, measuring cups and measuring spoons may help determine portion sizes.

SAMPLE EATING PLANS FOR STEP-ONE DIETS*

	DAILY PORTIONS			
FOOD GROUP	2500 Calories	2000 Calories	1600 Calories	1200 Calories
Meat, Poultry and Seafood	6 ounces	6 ounces	6 ounces	6 ounces
Eggs, Whole	3/week	3/week	3/week	3/week
Dairy Products	4	3	3	2
Fats and Oils	8	6	4	3
Bread, Cereal, Pasta and Starchy Vegetables	10	7	4	3
Vegetables	4	4	4	4
Fruits	5	3	3	3
Optional Foods	2	2	2	0

* Your physician or dietitian should recommend the appropriate calorie plan for you.

Meat, Poultry and Seafood

This food group averages about 60 calories, 3 grams of fat, 1 of which is saturated, and 25 milligrams of cholesterol per ounce. These foods provide protein, phosphorus, vitamins B_6 and B_{12}, and other vitamins and minerals. Red meats are also good souces of iron and zinc.

Eat no more than 6 ounces of cooked meat, fish or poultry each day. An easy way to divide this is into two 3-ounce servings. Or, divide it into one 2-ounce serving and one 4-ounce serving. The following general guidelines for portion sizes are based on 3-ounce servings. The size of a 3-ounce portion of cooked meat (such as a roast) is comparable to a deck of cards or the palm of your hand.

APPROPRIATE FOOD	PORTION SIZE*
BEEF (trimmed of visible fat)	
I small hamburger patty	3 ounces
I piece cooked meat about the size of a deck of cards	3 ounces
¾ cup diced meat	3 ounces
VEAL (trimmed of visible fat)	
I medium chop	3 ounces
PORK (trimmed of visible fat)	
I medium chop	3 ounces
LAMB (trimmed of visible fat)	
2 small chops	3 ounces
POULTRY (without skin)	
½ chicken breast	3 ounces
I chicken leg and thigh	3 ounces
½ Cornish hen	3 ounces
SEAFOOD	
¾ cup flaked fish	3 ounces
¼ pound fish fillet	3 ounces
Approximately 12 medium shrimp	3 ounces
Approximately 10 medium scallops	3 ounces
Approximately 10 medium oysters	3 ounces

* Meat loses about 25 percent of its weight during cooking (e.g., 4 ounces raw will be about 3 ounces cooked).

FAT AND CHOLESTEROL INFORMATION
- Many processed meats (luncheon meat, wieners and sausage) are high in saturated fatty acids.
- "Prime" grade, heavily marbled and fatty meats are high in saturated fatty acids.
- Liver, brains, heart, kidney and sweetbreads are high in cholesterol and should be limited.
- Shellfish contains less fat than does meat or poultry. Al-

though shrimp and crayfish are relatively high in cholesterol, they can be eaten occasionally.

Eggs

Eggs are good sources of protein, phosphorus, vitamins A, D, B_6, B_{12} and other vitamins and minerals. Egg yolks are high in cholesterol, while egg whites contain no cholesterol. Three egg yolks per week are allowed in the Step-One Diet. One large egg has about 79 calories, 6 grams of fat, 2 of which are saturated, and 274 milligrams of cholesterol. Cholesterol-free egg substitutes can be used to further reduce dietary cholesterol.

HOW EGGS ADD UP

EGG-CONTAINING FOODS	APPROXIMATE PORTION OF WHOLE EGG
BEVERAGES	
Eggnog (½ cup)	¼
BREADS	
Cornbread (1/19 of 9 × 9-inch pan)	¼
Muffin (1)	1/10
Pancakes, 4-inch (2)	¼
DESSERTS	
Baked custard or crème brûlée (6-ounce custard cup)	½
Chocolate, lemon meringue or pumpkin pie (⅛ of 9-inch pie)	⅓
Pound cake (1/12 of loaf)	¼
Sponge cake (1/12 of 9 × 9-inch cake)	½
Tapioca pudding (½ cup)	⅓
Yellow or chocolate 2-layer cake (1/16 of 9-inch cake)	⅛
MAIN DISHES	
Cheese soufflé (1 cup)	½
Chicken salad (½ cup)	⅓

EGG-CONTAINING FOODS	APPROXIMATE PORTION OF WHOLE EGG
Corn pudding (½ cup)	½
Egg salad	1 to 2
Omelet (depends on size)	1 to 3
SALAD DRESSINGS	
Mayonnaise (¼ cup)	¼
Thousand Island (¼ cup)	⅓

Dairy Products

These dairy products average about 90 calories, 3 grams of fat, 2 of which are saturated, and 11 milligrams of cholesterol per portion. Milk and most milk products provide calcium (they are the major source of calcium in the American diet), riboflavin, protein and vitamins A, B_6 and B_{12}. Fortified (with vitamins A and D) lowfat or skim milk products have essentially the same nutrients (except fat) as whole-milk products. However, they have less fat and fewer calories.

APPROPRIATE FOOD	PORTION SIZE
MILK AND YOGURT	
Skim or 1-percent milk	1 cup
Nonfat or lowfat plain yogurt	1 cup
CHEESE	
Dry, grated cheese, e.g., Parmesan or Sap Sago (1 tablespoon)	¼ ounce
Lowfat cheese, 5 grams fat or less per ounce (¼ cup diced)	1 ounce
Lowfat or dry-curd cottage cheese	½ cup
Mozzarella, part-skim	1 ounce
Ricotta cheese from whole milk	1 ounce
FROZEN DESSERTS	
Frozen lowfat yogurt	½ cup
Ice milk	½ cup
Sherbet (see "Optional Foods")	

FAT AND CHOLESTEROL INFORMATION

- Cream substitutes—nondairy coffee creamers, sour-cream substitutes and whipped toppings often contain coconut, palm or palm kernel oil and are therefore high in saturated fatty acids. Read labels carefully.

Fats and Oils

Some of these foods are high in vitamins A or E; all are high in fat and calories. One portion from the "Fats and Oils" food group averages about 5 grams of fat, 1 of which is saturated, 45 calories and negligible cholesterol.

APPROPRIATE FOOD	PORTION SIZE
MARGARINES	
Margarine with liquid oil listed as the first ingredient	I teaspoon
Diet margarine	2 teaspoons
NUTS AND SEEDS	
Chopped nuts, except coconut	I tablespoon
Seeds, any variety (without shells)	I tablespoon
SALAD DRESSINGS	
French, Italian, Thousand Island or mayonnaise-type salad dressing	I tablespoon
Mayonnaise	2 teaspoons
SHORTENING	
Soybean oil	I teaspoon
OTHER FATS	
Olives	10 small or 5 large
Peanut butter	2 teaspoons
Avocado	⅛ medium
VEGETABLE OILS	
Safflower, corn, sunflower, soybean, olive, canola	I teaspoon

FAT AND CHOLESTEROL INFORMATION

- Chocolate, coconut, coconut oil, palm kernel oil and palm oil contain more saturated than unsaturated fat. When selecting commercial food items containing these ingredients, choose only those that provide fatty acid information on the label. The foods you buy should contain more polyunsaturated than saturated fatty acids. Currently, information about monounsaturated fatty acids is not listed on the nutrition label.

Bread, Cereal, Pasta and Starchy Vegetables

The foods in this group contain an average of 80 calories, 1 gram of fat with negligible saturated fatty acids and cholesterol per portion. Lowfat soups are included in this group. Whole-grain or enriched foods provide B vitamins and iron. They also provide protein and, in vegetarian diets, are a major source of this nutrient. Whole-grain products also contribute magnesium, folacin and fiber.

APPROPRIATE FOOD	PORTION SIZE
BREADS	
Bagel	½
Bread sticks, 4 inches long × ½-inch diameter	2
Bread, white, whole wheat, rye, oatmeal, pumpernickel	1 slice
Croutons, plain bread cubes	1 cup
English muffin	½
Hamburger or hot dog bun	½
Pita, 6-inch diameter	½
Roll, plain (1 ounce)	1
Tortilla, corn, 6-inch diameter	1
QUICK BREAD (1 serving = 1 Bread + 1 Fat)	
Banana bread (16 slices/loaf)*	1 slice
Biscuit (2 inches across)*	1
Cornbread (muffin)*	1
Pancake (4-inch diameter)*	1
Waffle (9-inch diameter)*	¼

* Prepared with skim milk, unsaturated oil, egg substitute or egg white. If whole egg is used, count as part of egg allowance.

APPROPRIATE FOOD	PORTION SIZE
CRACKERS	
Animal crackers	8
Graham crackers, 2½-inch square	3
Matzoth, 4 × 6-inch	¾ ounce
Melba toast	5 slices
Oyster crackers	24
Popcorn (popped, no fat added)	3 cups
Pretzels	¾ ounce
Saltine crackers	6
CEREAL, PASTA AND RICE	
Bran cereals	⅓ cup
Cooked cereal, bulgur, grits	½ cup
Flake-type cereal, ready-to-eat, unsweetened	1 cup
Pasta	½ cup
Rice	⅓ cup
STARCHY VEGETABLES	
Baked beans	¼ cup
Corn	½ cup
Corn on cob, 6 inches long	1
Dry beans, peas, lentils	⅓ cup
Green peas	½ cup
Lima beans	½ cup
Potato, baked (3 ounces)	1
Potato, mashed	½ cup
Squash, acorn or butternut	¾ cup
Sweet potato or yam	⅓ cup
COMMERCIAL SOUP, Prepared with Water**	
Bouillon, broth, consomme	As desired
Chicken noodle, gazpacho, minestrone, onion, tomato, vegetarian	1 cup
Beef noodle, chicken rice, chunky-style, turkey noodle, oyster stew, split pea	¾ cup

** Homemade soups made low in fat (made with skim milk, removing fat from meat, etc.) may be counted as the same portions as commercial soups of a similar type. If milk is used in the preparation, count as part of dairy allowance.

FAT AND CHOLESTEROL INFORMATION
- Canned or dehydrated varieties of soup should have no more than 2 grams of fat per cup.
- If skim or 1-percent milk is used in preparing soup, count ½ cup milk per 1 cup soup as part of dairy group.
- Cream soup is usually prepared with whole milk or cream in restaurants.

Vegetables and Fruits

An average portion of vegetables has about 25 calories. An average portion of fruit has about 60 calories. Nearly all vegetables and fruits are low in fat, and none contains cholesterol. Vegetables and fruits are important sources of vitamins A and C, and fiber. Dark green and deep yellow vegetables are good sources of vitamin A. Most dark green vegetables, if not overcooked, are important sources of vitamin C, as are citrus fruits (oranges, grapefruit, tangerines and lemons), melons, berries and tomatoes. Dark green vegetables are also valued for riboflavin, folacin, iron and magnesium. Certain greens—collards, kale, mustard, turnip and dandelion—provide calcium.

APPROPRIATE FOOD

VEGETABLES

1 portion = ½ cup raw or cooked

Many vegetables have negligible fat and few calories and can be used as desired. Some suggestions include: cabbage, celery, Chinese cabbage, cucumbers, green onion, peppers, mushrooms, radishes, zucchini and salad greens such as endive, escarole, lettuce, romaine and spinach.

FRUIT AND JUICE

1 portion = ½ cup or 1 medium-size piece of fresh fruit

Optional Foods (Desserts, Sweets and Alcohol)

Any one of the homemade desserts (cakes, cookies and pies) made with acceptable ingredients listed below has about

285 calories and 6 to 10 grams of fat. The amounts listed count as *two portions* of optional foods.

Any one of the sweets on the list contains about 75 calories and 0 to 1 gram of fat. Each counts as *one portion* of optional foods.

Any one portion of the listed alcoholic beverages contains ½ ounce ethanol and 90 to 150 calories. Count each as *one portion* of optional foods.

APPROPRIATE FOOD	PORTION SIZE
DESSERTS*	
2-layer cake, frosted (¹/₁₂ of cake)	1 slice
Sheet cake, frosted (2¼ × 2½ × 1½-inch piece or ¹/₂₀ of 9 × 13-inch cake)	1 slice
Cupcake, frosted (average size)	1
Oatmeal raisin cookies	4
Double-crust fruit pie (⅛ of 9-inch pie)	1 slice
SWEETS	
Angel food cake (¹/₂₄ of cake)	1 slice
Candy made primarily with sugar (e.g., candy corn, gumdrops, mints and hard candy)	¾ ounce
Carbonated beverage (sweetened)	6 fluid ounces
Fruit-flavored gelatin (sweetened)	½ cup
Fruit ice	⅓ cup
Gingersnaps	2
Lemonade (sweetened)	6 fluid ounces
Newton-type cookie	1
Sherbet	⅓ cup
Sugar, syrup, honey, jam, preserves or marmalade	1½ tablespoons
ALCOHOLIC BEVERAGES	
Beer	12 fluid ounces
80-proof spirits (bourbon, gin, rum, Scotch, tequila, vodka and whiskey)	1½ fluid ounces
Wine, red or white	4 fluid ounces

* Prepared with egg whites, egg substitute, skim or 1-percent milk, and vegetable oil or margarine. Each "dessert" serving counts as two optional food portions.

Free Foods

These foods and drinks contain fewer than 20 calories and no fat per portion. Items that have no portion size specified need not be limited. The others should be eaten in moderation—the portion sizes will guide you.

APPROPRIATE FOOD	PORTION SIZE
DRINKS	
Bouillon or broth without fat*	
Carbonated drinks, sugar-free*	
Carbonated water	
Club soda*	
Cocoa powder, unsweetened	1 tablespoon
Coffee or tea	
Drink mixes, sugar-free**	
Tonic water, sugar-free**	
SWEET SUBSTITUTES**	
Candy, hard, sugar-free	
Gelatin, sugar-free	
Gum, sugar-free	
Jam or jelly, sugar-free	2 teaspoons
Pancake syrup, sugar-free	
Sugar substitutes (saccharin or aspartame)	
FRUITS	
Cranberries, unsweetened	½ cup
Rhubarb, unsweetened	½ cup
CONDIMENTS	
Horseradish	
Ketchup	1 tablespoon
Mustard	
Pickles, dill, unsweetened*	
Salad dressing, oil-free	
Taco sauce	
Vinegar	

* High in sodium. Look for seltzers or soda with no salt added.
** Sweet substitutes are listed for the benefit of those following diabetic diets.

SAMPLE MENU—STEP-ONE DIET

2500 CALORIES PER DAY

	FOOD GROUP PORTIONS
BREAKFAST	
Pineapple juice (1 cup)	2 Fruits
Oatmeal (1 cup) with	2 Breads
Banana (½) and	1 Fruit
Milk, 1-percent (1 cup)	1 Dairy
Whole wheat toast (2 slices) with	2 Breads
Margarine (2 teaspoons)	2 Fats
Coffee or tea	
LUNCH	
Hamburger sandwich:	
Lean ground beef, broiled (3 ounces)	3 Meats
Mozzarella cheese, part-skim (1 ounce)	1 Dairy
Hamburger bun (1)	2 Breads
Lettuce (1 leaf)	Free
Tomato (1 slice)	Free
Relishes:	
Carrot curls (½ carrot)	1 Vegetable
Broccoli florets (1 cup)	1 Vegetable
Fresh Bartlett pear (1)	1 Fruit
Milk, 1-percent (1 cup)	1 Dairy
DINNER	
Broiled salmon (3 ounces) with dill and	3 Meats
Margarine (2 teaspoons)	2 Fats
Rice (1 cup) with	3 Breads
Margarine (2 teaspoons)	2 Fats
Steamed snow peas with onion slices (1 cup)	2 Vegetables
Cantaloupe cubes (⅓ melon)	1 Fruit
Roll (1) with	1 Bread
Margarine (2 teaspoons)	2 Fats
Devil's food cake with frosting (1 slice)	2 Optional
Milk, 1-percent (1 cup)	1 Dairy

NUTRIENT ANALYSIS   2509 Calories (distributed as follows):

18% Protein	8% Saturated fatty acids
52% Carbohydrate	160 mg Cholesterol*
30% Fat	2073 mg Sodium

* Cholesterol is less than 300 mg because an egg is not included.

SAMPLE MENU—STEP-ONE DIET

2000 CALORIES PER DAY

BREAKFAST	FOOD GROUP PORTIONS
Orange juice (1 cup)	2 Fruits
Poached egg (1)	1 Egg
Whole wheat toast (2 slices) with	2 Breads
Margarine (2 teaspoons)	2 Fats
Milk, 1-percent (1 cup)	1 Dairy
Coffee or tea	

LUNCH	
Roast beef sandwich:	
Lean roast beef (3 ounces)	3 Meats
Whole wheat bread (2 slices)	2 Breads
Mayonnaise (2 teaspoons)	1 Fat
Lettuce (1 leaf)	Free
Cottage cheese, lowfat (½ cup) with	1 Dairy
Zucchini sticks (4)	1 Vegetable
Grapes (15)	1 Fruit
Graham crackers (3 squares)	1 Bread
Milk, 1-percent (1 cup)	1 Dairy

DINNER	
Baked chicken breast (3 ounces) with	3 Meats
Onions and mushrooms (½ cup)	1 Vegetable
Steamed green peas (½ cup)	1 Bread
Steamed carrot strips (½ cup)	1 Vegetable
Tossed salad:	
Lettuce (1 cup)	Free
Tomato wedges (1 tomato)	1 Vegetable
Cucumber slices (¼ cucumber)	Free
Italian salad dressing (2 tablespoons)	2 Fats
Roll (1) with	1 Bread
Margarine (1 teaspoon)	1 Fat
Orange sherbet (⅓ cup)	1 Optional
White wine (4 fluid ounces)	1 Optional

NUTRIENT ANALYSIS   2024 Calories (distributed as follows):

23% Protein	8% Saturated fatty acids
43% Carbohydrates	473 mg Cholesterol*
4% Alcohol	2853 mg Sodium
30% Fat	

* Cholesterol is greater than 300 mg because an egg is included as breakfast.

SAMPLE MENU—STEP-ONE DIET

1600 CALORIES PER DAY

	FOOD GROUP PORTIONS
BREAKFAST	
Grapefruit (½)	1 Fruit
Bagel (1) with	2 Breads
Margarine (1 teaspoon)	1 Fat
Milk, 1-percent (1 cup)	1 Dairy
Coffee or tea	
LUNCH	
Broiled chicken thigh (2 ounces)	2 Meats
Tossed salad:	
Lettuce (1 cup)	Free
Cauliflower (4) with radishes (2)	1 Vegetable
Mushroom slices (4 mushrooms)	Free
Oil and vinegar dressing	
Olive oil (1 teaspoon)	1 Fat
Vinegar (2 teaspoons)	Free
Saltine crackers (6)	1 Bread
Nectarine (1)	1 Fruit
Milk, 1-percent (1 cup)	1 Dairy
DINNER	
Braised pot roast (4 ounces) with	4 Meats
Tomatoes, canned (½ cup)	1 Vegetable
Green bell pepper strips (½ cup)	Free
Diced onion (2 tablespoons)	Free
Steamed broccoli spears (½ cup)	1 Vegetable
Carrot-raisin salad:	
Shredded carrot (½ cup)	1 Vegetable
Raisins (2 tablespoons)	1 Fruit
Mayonnaise (2 teaspoons)	1 Fat
Roll (1) with	1 Bread
Margarine (1 teaspoon)	1 Fat
Gingersnap cookies (4)	2 Optional
Milk, 1-percent (1 cup)	1 Dairy

NUTRIENT ANALYSIS   1615 Calories (distributed as follows):

24% Protein	9% Saturated fatty acids
46% Carbohydrate	207 mg Cholesterol*
30% Fat	1775 mg Sodium

* Cholesterol is less than 300 mg because an egg is not included.

SAMPLE MENU—STEP-ONE DIET

1200 CALORIES PER DAY

BREAKFAST	**FOOD GROUP PORTIONS**
Fresh strawberries (1 cup)	1 Fruit
Plain lowfat yogurt (1 cup)	1 Dairy
Whole wheat toast (1 slice) with	1 Bread
Margarine (1 teaspoon)	1 Fat
Coffee or tea	

LUNCH

Open-face sandwich:

Lowfat cheese (1 ounce)	1 Dairy
Lean ham (2 ounces)	2 Meats
Tomato (1 slice)	Free
Whole wheat bread (1 slice)	1 Bread

Relishes

Carrot sticks (4) with green bell pepper rings (2)	1 Vegetable
Apple (1)	1 Fruit

DINNER

Broiled sirloin steak (4 ounces)	4 Meats
Pasta (½ cup) with herbs and	1 Bread
Margarine (1 teaspoon)	1 Fat
Steamed green beans (½ cup)	1 Vegetable
Steamed beets (½ cup)	1 Vegetable

Tossed salad:

Assorted greens (1 cup)	Free
French salad dressing (1 tablespoon)	1 Fat
Fresh Bartlett pear (1)	1 Fruit

NUTRIENT ANALYSIS   1224 Calories (distributed as follows):

25% Protein	9% Saturated fatty acids
45% Carbohydrate	163 mg Cholesterol*
30% Fat	1993 mg Sodium

---

* Cholesterol is less than 300 mg because an egg is not included.

THE STEP-TWO DIET

The Step-Two Diet is usually recommended for people whose blood cholesterol level did not decrease sufficiently on the Step-One Diet. These individuals need to make additional changes in their eating plans to reach the blood cholesterol goal recommended by their physicians. The Step-Two Diet will help them do that.

FOOD GROUPS

In this eating plan, as in the Step-One Diet, foods are categorized in seven groups according to fat, carbohydrate, protein and calories.

SAMPLE EATING PLANS FOR STEP-TWO DIETS*

FOOD GROUP	DAILY PORTIONS			
	2500 Calories	2000 Calories	1600 Calories	1200 Calories
Meat, Poultry and Seafood	6 ounces	6 ounces	6 ounces	6 ounces
Eggs, Whole	1/week	1/week	1/week	1/week
Dairy Products	3	2	2	2
Fats and Oils	8	7	5	3
Bread, Cereal, Pasta and Starchy Vegetables	10	8	5	4
Vegetables	5	4	4	4
Fruits	7	4	3	3
Optional Foods	2	2	2	0

* Your physician or dietitian should recommend the appropriate calorie plan for you.

Changes in food choices are needed for four food groups. The general changes are as follows:

1. Meat, Poultry and Seafood—Choose the very leanest.
2. Eggs—Limit egg yolks to one per week.

3. Dairy Products—Select nonfat products, skim milk and cheese with 2 grams of fat or less per ounce.
4. Fats and Oils—Use margarine or oils, but no shortening.

No changes are needed for the other three food groups. Accordingly, the information for these categories is the same as for the Step-One Diet and will be found on the preceding pages.

Meat, Poultry and Seafood

This group averages 55 calories, 2 grams of fat, of which 0.8 grams are saturated, and 25 milligrams of cholesterol per ounce. To reduce the amount of saturated fatty acids and cholesterol in the meat group, only the leanest cuts are allowed. Shrimp and organ meats should be limited because of their cholesterol content.

Eat no more than 6 ounces of cooked meat, fish or poultry each day. An easy way to divide this is into two 3-ounce servings. Or, divide it into one 2-ounce serving and one 4-ounce serving. The following general guidelines for portion sizes are based on 3-ounce servings. The size of a 3-ounce

APPROPRIATE FOOD	PORTION SIZE*
BEEF (trimmed of visible fat)	
1 small hamburger patty**	3 ounces
1 piece cooked meat about the size of a deck of cards	3 ounces
¾ cup diced meat	3 ounces
VEAL (trimmed of visible fat)	
1 medium chop	3 ounces
PORK (trimmed of visible fat)	
1 medium chop	3 ounces
LAMB (trimmed of visible fat)	
2 small chops	3 ounces

* Meat loses about 25 percent of its weight during cooking (e.g., 4 ounces raw will be about 3 ounces cooked).
** Note: To assure the leanest ground meat, select a lean cut, such as a round steak, and have it ground.

APPROPRIATE FOOD	PORTION SIZE*
POULTRY (without skin)	
½ chicken breast	3 ounces
1 chicken leg and thigh	3 ounces
½ Cornish hen	3 ounces
SEAFOOD	
¾ cup flaked fish	3 ounces
¼ pound fish fillet	3 ounces
Approximately 10 medium scallops	3 ounces
Approximately 10 medium oysters	3 ounces

* Meat loses about 25 percent of its weight during cooking (e.g., 4 ounces raw will be about 3 ounces cooked).

portion of cooked meat (such as a roast) is comparable to a deck of cards or the palm of your hand.

FAT AND CHOLESTEROL INFORMATION

- Regular "ground" meat (even extra lean) has more fat than is allowed in the Step-Two Diet. Select a lean meat cut, such as round steak, and have it trimmed and ground.
- Avoid liver and other organ meats since they are high in cholesterol.
- Shrimp and crayfish have about twice as much cholesterol as beef and chicken and should be limited in the Step-Two Diet.
- Combine large portions of pasta, rice, legumes and vegetables with small amounts of lean meat, poultry or seafood to get a complete protein source with less fat and fewer calories.

Eggs

To achieve the necessary reduction in cholesterol and saturated fatty acids, *limit egg yolks to one per week.* One large, whole egg contains 6 grams of fat, 2 grams of which are saturated, and 274 milligrams of cholesterol. Cholesterol-free egg substitutes can be used to further reduce dietary cholesterol.

Dairy Products

This group of dairy products differs from the group in the Step-One Diet because the types of dairy products are limited here. An average portion of this group has 80 calories, 2 grams of fat, of which 1 gram is saturated, and 9 milligrams of cholesterol. To achieve the necessary reduction in saturated fatty acids in this food group, choose only skim milk, nonfat dairy products and cheese with 2 grams of fat or less per ounce.

APPROPRIATE FOOD	PORTION SIZE
MILK AND YOGURT	
Skim milk*	1 cup
Nonfat or lowfat plain yogurt	1 cup
CHEESE	
Lowfat or dry-curd cottage cheese	½ cup
Lowfat cheese, 2 grams fat or less per ounce	1 ounce
FROZEN DESSERTS	
Frozen lowfat yogurt	½ cup
Sherbet (see Optional Foods)	

* 1-percent milk has 2.2 grams fat per cup more than skim milk. If skim milk is unacceptable to you, adjust the eating plan to allow 1-percent milk. One way to do this is by eliminating 1 serving of fats and oils from your eating plan.

FAT AND CHOLESTEROL INFORMATION

• Cream substitutes—nondairy coffee creamers, sour-cream substitutes and whipped toppings often contain coconut, palm or palm kernel oil and are therefore high in saturated fatty acids. Read labels carefully.

Fats and Oils

An average portion from this group contains 45 calories, 5 grams of fat, with less than 1 gram of saturated fatty acids. To reduce saturated fatty acids, margarine (stick or tub) is substituted for shortening.

APPROPRIATE FOOD	PORTION SIZE
MARGARINES	
Margarine with liquid oil listed as the first ingredient	1 teaspoon
Diet margarine	2 teaspoons
NUTS AND SEEDS	
Chopped nuts, except coconut	1 tablespoon
Seeds, any variety (without shells)	1 tablespoon
SALAD DRESSINGS	
French, Italian, Thousand Island or mayonnaise-type salad dressing	1 tablespoon
Mayonnaise	2 teaspoons
OTHER FATS	
Olives	10 small or 5 large
Peanut butter	2 teaspoons
Avocado	⅛ medium
VEGETABLE OILS	
Safflower, corn, sunflower, soybean, olive, canola	1 teaspoon

FAT AND CHOLESTEROL INFORMATION

- Chocolate, coconut, coconut oil, palm kernel oil and palm oil contain more saturated than unsaturated fatty acids. Look for the listing of these fats when you read package labels. Select only those that contain less saturated fatty acids than polyunsaturated fatty acids. Currently, information about monounsaturated fatty acids is not listed on the nutrition label.

SAMPLE MENU—STEP-TWO DIET

2500 CALORIES PER DAY

BREAKFAST	**FOOD GROUP PORTIONS**
Apple juice (1 cup)	2 Fruits
Corn flakes (1 cup) with	1 Bread
Sliced banana (1) and	2 Fruits
Milk, skim (1 cup)	1 Dairy
Whole wheat toast (2 slices) with	2 Breads
Margarine (2 teaspoons)	2 Fats
Coffee or tea	

LUNCH

Turkey sandwich:	
Roast turkey breast (2 ounces)	2 Meats
Whole wheat bread (2 slices)	2 Breads
Mayonnaise (2 teaspoons)	1 Fat
Lettuce (1 leaf)	Free
Marinated raw vegetables:	
Tomato wedges (1 tomato)	1 Vegetable
Green bell pepper rings (½ pepper)	Free
French salad dressing (2 tablespoons)	2 Fats
Nectarine (1)	1 Fruit
Graham crackers (6 squares)	2 Breads
Milk, skim (1 cup)	1 Dairy

DINNER

Roast beef (4 ounces)	4 Meats
Pasta (1 cup) with herbs and	2 Breads
Margarine (1 teaspoon)	1 Fat
Steamed green beans (1 cup)	2 Vegetables
Steamed yellow squash (½ cup)	1 Vegetable
Onion slices (½ cup)	1 Vegetable
Margarine (1 teaspoon) on vegetables	1 Fat
Orange slices (1 orange) with	1 Fruit
Raisins (2 tablespoons)	1 Fruit
Whole wheat bread (1 slice) with	1 Bread
Margarine (1 teaspoon)	1 Fat
Apple pie (1 slice)	2 Optional
Milk, skim (1 cup)	1 Dairy

NUTRIENT ANALYSIS   2526 Calories (distributed as follows):

17% Protein	6% Saturated fatty acids
57% Carbohydrate	173 mg Cholesterol*
26% Fat	2948 mg Sodium

* Cholesterol is less than 200 mg because an egg is not included.

SAMPLE MENU—STEP-TWO DIET

2000 CALORIES PER DAY

BREAKFAST	**FOOD GROUP PORTIONS**
Orange juice (1 cup)	2 Fruits
Cheese Omelet:	
Egg substitute (½ cup) with	Free
Lowfat cheese (1 ounce)	1 Dairy
Margarine (1 teaspoon)	1 Fat
Corn grits (½ cup)	1 Bread
Bagel (1) with	2 Breads
Margarine (1 teaspoon)	1 Fat
Coffee or tea	

LUNCH	
Barbecued beef sandwich:	
Lean beef (3 ounces)	3 Meats
Barbecue sauce (1 tablespoon)	Free
Hamburger bun (1)	2 Breads
Tossed salad:	
Lettuce (1 cup)	Free
Tomato wedges (1 tomato)	1 Vegetable
Shredded carrot (½ cup)	1 Vegetable
Green bell pepper strips (½ pepper)	Free
Italian salad dressing (2 tablespoons)	2 Fats
Grapes (15)	1 Fruit
Milk, skim (1 cup)	1 Dairy

DINNER	
Broiled filet of sole (3 ounces) with lemon and	3 Meats
Margarine (1 teaspoon)	1 Fat
Rice (⅔ cup) with	2 Breads
Margarine (1 teaspoon)	1 Fat
Steamed broccoli (½ cup) and	1 Vegetable
Cauliflower (½ cup)	1 Vegetable
Fresh strawberries (1 cup)	1 Fruit
Roll (1) with	1 Bread
Margarine (1 teaspoon)	1 Fat
White cake with frosting (1 slice)	2 Optional

NUTRIENT ANALYSIS   1996 Calories (distributed as follows):

21% Protein	6% Saturated fatty acids
52% Carbohydrate	153 mg Cholesterol*
27% Fat	2510 mg Sodium

* Cholesterol is less than 200 mg because an egg is not included.

SAMPLE MENU—STEP-TWO DIET

1600 CALORIES PER DAY

BREAKFAST	**FOOD GROUP PORTIONS**
Grapefruit juice (½ cup)	1 Fruit
Oatmeal (½ cup) with	1 Bread
Milk, skim (1 cup)	1 Dairy
Whole wheat toast (1 slice) with	1 Bread
Margarine (1 teaspoon)	1 Fat
Coffee or tea	

LUNCH

Tuna salad on lettuce:	
Tuna, canned in water (½ cup)	2 Meats
Diced celery (¼ cup)	Free
Mayonnaise (4 teaspoons)	2 Fats
Lettuce (1 leaf)	Free
Relishes:	
Broccoli florets (1 cup)	1 Vegetable
Tomato wedges (1 tomato)	1 Vegetable
Saltine crackers (6)	1 Bread
Apple (1)	1 Fruit

DINNER

Broiled sirloin steak (4 ounces)	4 Meats
New potatoes (½ cup) with parsley and	1 Bread
Margarine (1 teaspoon)	1 Fat
Steamed green beans (½ cup)	1 Vegetable
Steamed carrot strips (½ cup)	1 Vegetable
Watermelon chunks (1¼ cups)	1 Fruit
French bread (1 slice) with	1 Bread
Margarine (1 teaspoon)	1 Fat
Gingersnap cookies (4)	2 Optional
Milk, skim (1 cup)	1 Dairy

NUTRIENT ANALYSIS   1603 Calories (distributed as follows):

22% Protein	7% Saturated fatty acids
49% Carbohydrate	135 mg Cholesterol*
29% Fat	1684 mg Sodium

* Cholesterol is less than 200 mg because an egg is not included.

SAMPLE MENU—STEP-TWO DIET

1200 CALORIES PER DAY

	FOOD GROUP PORTIONS
BREAKFAST	
Fresh blueberries (1 cup)	1 Fruit
Plain nonfat yogurt (1 cup)	1 Dairy
English muffin (1) with	2 Breads
Margarine (1 teaspoon)	1 Fat
Coffee or tea	
LUNCH	
Chef's salad:	
Lettuce (2 cups)	Free
Tomato wedges (1 tomato)	1 Vegetable
Shredded carrot (½ cup)	1 Vegetable
Turkey (1 ounce)	1 Meat
Lean ham (2 ounces)	2 Meats
Lowfat cheese (1 ounce)	1 Dairy
French salad dressing (1 tablespoon)	1 Fat
Saltine crackers (6)	1 Bread
Fresh plums (2)	1 Fruit
DINNER	
Roast chicken breast (3 ounces)	3 Meats
Steamed asparagus spears (½ cup)	1 Vegetable
Steamed yellow squash (½ cup)	1 Vegetable
Roll (1) with	1 Bread
Margarine (1 teaspoon)	1 Fat
Fresh peach (1)	1 Fruit

NUTRIENT ANALYSIS   1191 Calories (distributed as follows):

28% Protein	6% Saturated fatty acids
50% Carbohydrate	150 mg Cholesterol*
22% Fat	2636 mg Sodium

* Cholesterol is less than 200 mg because an egg is not included.

APPENDIX D.

A SIMPLE WAY
TO CONTROL TOTAL FAT

When you modify your diet, instead of using the Step-One and Step-Two Diet exchange method described in Appendix C, you may want more precise information about individual foods. The "Grams of Fat Method" offered here provides this added precision. After using it for a while, you will become familiar with the foods that are highest in fat, saturated fatty acids and cholesterol. It will become easier for you to balance your intake of higher fat foods with those lower in fat. This is an important skill that will be helpful to you when eating away from home.

The method involves counting the grams of fat and saturated fatty acids consumed each day. Food selections should be made so that the grams of fat and saturated fatty acids are within your set goal. The table below shows fat and saturated fatty acids limits based on calorie levels for the Step-One and Step-Two Diets. The desired calorie level is based on whether you need to lose, gain or maintain weight, and your level of physical activity. As a guideline, typical calorie levels for men are 2000 to 2500 calories for weight maintenance, 1600 to 2000 for weight loss. For women, typical calorie levels are 1600 to 2000 for weight maintenance, 1200 to 1600 for weight loss.

The Food Table on the following pages shows the amount of fat and saturated fatty acids in foods. You can easily see which foods are low in fat and may be eaten often and which ones are high in fat and need to be avoided or eaten infrequently. When you eat a high-fat food, you can compensate by selecting other very low-fat foods that day.

389

FAT LIMITS BASED ON CALORIE LEVELS

Calorie Level	Total Fat (Grams)	Step-One: Saturated Fatty Acids (Grams)	Step-Two: Saturated Fatty Acids (Grams)
1200	40	13	9
1500	50	17	12
1800	60	20	14
2000	67	22	16
2200	73	24	17
2500	83	28	19
3000	100	33	23

A food scale, measuring cups and measuring spoons will help you accurately determine portion sizes.

Numerous commercial products are available, many of which have nutrition information on the label. That information can be used along with the information offered here to help you reach your fat intake goals. (Where discrepancies between the two occur, accept the information listed on the label.) For example, the label below shows 5 grams of fat in each 4-ounce portion of spaghetti sauce.

SPAGHETTI SAUCE LABEL

Nutrition information per serving

Serving size	4 ounces (113 grams)
Servings per container	7⅞
Calories	130
Protein (grams)	2
Total carbohydrates (grams)	18
Fat (grams)	5

FOOD TABLE

Foods listed in the table are grouped under major headings that are similar to the ones on pages 365–366. Foods listed under the subheading make it easy to compare values for similar foods.

ABOUT THE FOOD TABLE

A dash (—) means that a value could not be found although there is reason to believe that a measurable amount of the nutrient may be present.

ABBREVIATIONS USED IN THE TABLE

cal.	calories	poly. fatty acid	polyunsaturated fatty acid
chol.	cholesterol	sat. fatty acid	saturated fatty acid
gm	gram	tbsp.	tablespoon
mg	milligram	tr	trace
Na	sodium	pkg	package
oz.	ounce		

Note: Values have been rounded off; 0.5 or greater is rounded up; 0.4 or less is rounded down.

Food Description/Portion	Weight (gm)	Fat (gm)	Sat. Fatty Acid (gm)	Energy (cal.)	Chol. (mg)	Na (mg)
MEAT, POULTRY AND SEAFOOD						
Beef						
Lean only, average all grades, cooked (1 oz.)	28	2.9	1.1	63	25	18
Lean only, "Select" grade, cooked (1 oz.)	28	2.6	1.0	60	25	18
Lean only, "Choice" grade, cooked (1 oz.)	28	3.0	1.2	64	25	18
Lean only, "Prime" grade, cooked (1 oz.)	28	3.8	1.5	71	25	18
Flank steak, lean only, broiled (1 oz.)	28	4.2	1.8	69	20	19
Round steak, lean only, broiled (1 oz.)	28	2.3	0.8	55	23	18
Top loin steak, lean only, broiled (1 oz.)	28	2.7	1.1	59	22	19
Rib eye steak, lean only, broiled (1 oz.)	28	3.3	1.4	64	23	19
Chuck roast or steak, lean only, braised (1 oz.)	28	2.9	1.1	66	28	19
Tenderloin, lean only, broiled (1 oz.)	28	2.7	1.1	59	24	18
Arm roast or steak, lean only, braised (1 oz.)	28	2.9	1.1	66	28	19
Brain, simmered (1 oz.)	28	3.6	0.8	45	582	34
Ground beef, extra lean, broiled (1 oz.)	28	4.5	1.8	75	28	23
lean, broiled (1 oz.)	28	5.0	2.0	79	29	25
regular, broiled (1 oz.)	28	5.5	2.2	83	29	26
Heart, simmered (1 oz.)	28	1.6	0.5	49	55	18
Kidney, simmered (1 oz.)	28	1.0	0.3	41	110	38
Liver, braised (1 oz.)	28	1.4	0.5	46	110	30
Shortribs, lean only, braised (1 oz.)	28	5.1	2.2	84	26	17
Tongue, simmered (1 oz.)	28	5.9	2.5	80	30	17
Tripe (1 oz.)	28	1.1	0.6	28	27	13
Lamb						
Fore shank, braised (1 oz.)	28	1.7	0.4	53	29	21

Food Description/Portion	Weight (gm)	Fat (gm)	Sat. Fatty Acid (gm)	Energy (cal.)	Chol. (mg)	Na (mg)
Lamb (cont'd)						
Leg, shank portion, roasted (1 oz.)	28	1.9	0.5	51	25	19
Loin chops, broiled (1 oz.)	28	2.7	1.0	61	27	24
Rack, rib, roasted (1 oz.)	28	3.8	1.2	66	25	23
Pork						
Bacon, pan-fried, 4½ slices (1 oz.)	28	14.0	5.0	163	24	452
Canadian bacon, grilled (1 oz.)	28	2.4	0.8	52	16	438
Chitterlings, simmered (1 oz.)	28	8.2	2.9	86	41	11
Fresh pork, lean only						
center loin, fresh, broiled (1 oz.)	28	3.0	1.0	65	28	22
shoulder, arm picnic, roasted (1 oz.)	28	3.6	1.2	65	27	23
shoulder, Boston blade, roasted (1 oz.)	28	4.8	1.6	73	28	21
sirloin, fresh, broiled (1 oz.)	28	3.9	1.3	69	28	17
tenderloin, roasted (1 oz.)	28	1.4	0.5	47	26	19
whole leg, roasted (1 oz.)	28	3.1	1.1	62	27	18
Ham, boneless						
extra lean, roasted (1 oz.)	28	1.6	0.5	41	15	341
canned, extra lean, roasted (1 oz.)	28	1.4	0.5	39	8	322
canned, regular, roasted (1 oz.)	28	4.3	1.4	64	17	267
Liver, braised (1 oz.)	28	1.3	0.4	47	101	14
Spareribs, lean and fat, braised (1 oz.)	28	8.6	3.3	113	34	26
Veal						
Arm steak, braised (1 oz.)	28	1.4	0.3	55	45	27
Blade steak, braised (1 oz.)	28	1.6	0.4	56	46	30
Loin chop, braised (1 oz.)	28	2.4	0.7	64	46	25
Rib roast, cooked (1 oz.)	28	1.8	0.6	48	36	29
Luncheon Meat and Sausage						
Bologna, beef and pork (1 oz.)	28	8.0	3.0	89	16	289
Braunschweiger pork (1 oz.)	28	9.1	3.1	102	44	324
Chicken spread, canned (2 tablespoons)	26	3.3	—	55	—	—

Food Description/Portion	Weight (gm)	Fat (gm)	Sat. Fatty Acid (gm)	Energy (cal.)	Chol. (mg)	Na (mg)
Luncheon Meat and Sausage (cont'd)						
Frankfurter						
beef and pork (1 oz.)	28	8.3	3.1	91	14	318
chicken (1 oz.)	28	5.5	1.6	73	28	388
Pepperoni, pork, beef (1 oz.)	28	12.5	4.6	141	—	578
Salad spread, ham, cured						
(2 tablespoons)	30	4.7	1.5	64	12	274
Salami, dry, pork, beef (1 oz.)	28	9.8	3.5	119	22	527
Sausage						
Italian, pork, cooked (1 oz.)	28	7.3	2.6	92	22	261
knockwurst, pork, beef (1 oz.)	28	7.9	2.9	87	16	286
pork, fresh, cooked (1 oz.)	28	8.8	3.1	105	24	366
liverwurst, pork (1 oz.)	28	8.1	3.0	93	45	244
Polish, pork (1 oz.)	28	8.1	2.9	92	20	248
Vienna, beef and pork, canned (1½ links)	28	7.1	2.6	79	15	270
Mixed Dishes with Meat, Poultry and Seafood						
Chicken à la king (1 cup)	245	34.3	12.9	468	220	760
Chicken and noodle casserole (1 cup)	240	18.5	5.9	367	—	600
Chili con carne, with beans, canned (1 cup)	255	15.6	7.5	339	—	1354
Chop suey, beef and pork, without noodles (1 cup)	250	17.0	8.5	300	—	1053
Chow mein, chicken, without noodles (1 cup)	250	10.0	2.4	255	—	718
Macaroni and cheese, homemade (1 cup)	200	22.2	11.9	430	—	1086
canned (1 cup)	240	9.6	4.2	228	—	730
Pâté, chicken liver (2 tablespoons)	26	3.4	—	52	—	—
Pizza, cheese (1 slice)	120	8.6	4.2	290	56	698
pepperoni (1 slice)	120	11.5	—	306	—	817
Pot pie, chicken (⅓ of 9-inch diameter)	232	31.3	10.3	545	56	594
beef (⅓ of 9-inch diameter)	210	30.5	7.9	517	42	596

Food Description/Portion	Weight (gm)	Fat (gm)	Sat. Fatty Acid (gm)	Energy (cal.)	Chol. (mg)	Na (mg)
Mixed Dishes with Meat, Poultry and Seafood (cont'd)						
Spaghetti with meatballs and tomato						
sauce, canned (1 cup)	250	10.8	2.2	258	—	1220
Stew, beef and vegetable (1 cup)	245	10.5	4.4	218	72	292
Chicken						
Light meat, without skin, stewed						
(1 oz.)	28	1.1	0.3	45	22	18
with skin, stewed (1 oz.)	28	2.8	0.8	57	21	18
Dark meat, without skin, stewed						
(1 oz.)	28	2.5	0.7	54	25	21
with skin, stewed (1 oz.)	28	4.2	1.6	66	23	20
Breast, meat only, stewed (3 oz.)	95	2.9	0.8	144	73	59
meat and skin, stewed (4 oz.)	110	8.2	2.3	202	83	68
fried with batter, meat and skin						
(5 oz.)	140	18.5	4.9	364	119	385
Drumstick, meat only, stewed						
(1½ oz.)	46	2.6	0.7	78	40	37
meat and skin, stewed (2 oz.)	57	6.1	1.7	116	48	43
fried with batter, meat and skin						
(2½ oz.)	72	11.3	3.0	193	62	194
Thigh, meat only, stewed (2 oz.)	55	5.4	1.5	107	49	41
meat and skin, stewed (2½ oz.)	68	10.0	2.8	158	57	49
fried with batter, meat and skin						
(3 oz.)	86	14.2	3.8	238	80	248
Wing, meat only, stewed (1 oz.)	24	1.7	0.5	43	18	18
meat and skin, stewed (1½ oz.)	40	6.7	1.9	100	28	27
fried with batter, meat and skin						
(1¾ oz.)	49	10.7	2.9	159	39	157
Boneless, canned in broth (1 oz.)	28	2.2	0.6	47	62	143
Frankfurter, chicken (1 oz.)	28	5.5	1.6	73	28	388
Giblets—gizzard, heart, liver						
(1 each)						
(2½ oz.)	68	3.6	1.1	112	243	40
(1 oz.)	28	1.5	0.5	47	101	17
Liver pâté, canned (2 tablespoons)	28	3.7	—	57	—	—

Food Description/Portion	Weight (gm)	Fat (gm)	Sat. Fatty Acid (gm)	Energy (cal.)	Chol. (mg)	Na (mg)
Chicken (cont'd)						
Roll, chicken, light (1 oz.)	28	2.1	0.6	45	14	166
Spread, chicken, canned (1 oz.)	28	3.3	—	55	—	—
Turkey						
Light meat						
meat only, roasted (1 oz.)	28	0.3	0.1	40	24	16
meat with skin, roasted (1 oz.)	28	2.4	0.7	46	22	18
Dark meat						
meat only, roasted (1 oz.)	28	1.2	0.4	46	32	22
meat with skin, roasted (1 oz.)	28	3.3	1.0	63	25	22
Turkey						
Ham, cured thigh meat (1 oz.)	28	1.4	0.5	37	—	283
Pastrami (1 oz.)	28	1.8	0.5	40	—	297
Roll, light and dark meat (1 oz.)	28	2.0	0.6	42	16	166
Frozen with gravy, 1 pkg.						
(5 oz.)	142	3.7	1.2	95	—	786
(1 oz.)	28	0.8	0.2	19	—	157
Giblets—gizzard, heart, liver						
(1 each)						
(5½ oz.)	158	8.0	2.4	264	660	92
(1 oz.)	28	1.4	0.4	47	119	17
Game						
Goose, domesticated						
meat only, roasted (1 oz.)	28	3.6	1.3	67	26	20
meat with skin, roasted (1 oz.)	28	6.2	2.0	86	26	20
Finfish						
Catfish, breaded and fried (1 oz.)	28	3.8	0.9	65	23	79
Cod, Atlantic, cooked, dry heat						
(1 oz.)	28	0.2	0.1	30	16	22
Eel, cooked, dry heat (1 oz.)	28	4.2	0.9	67	46	18
Fish sticks and portions, frozen and						
reheated (1 oz.)	28	3.4	0.9	76	31	163
Flounder, cooked, dry heat (1 oz.)	28	0.4	0.1	33	19	30
Grouper, cooked, dry heat (1 oz.)	28	0.4	0.1	33	13	15
Haddock, cooked, dry heat (1 oz.)	28	0.3	0.1	32	21	25

Food Description/Portion	Weight (gm)	Fat (gm)	Sat. Fatty Acid (gm)	Energy (cal.)	Chol. (mg)	Na (mg)
Finfish (cont'd)						
Halibut, cooked, dry heat (1 oz.)	28	0.8	0.1	40	12	20
Herring, pickled (1 oz.)	28	5.1	0.7	74	4	247
Mackerel, canned, drained solids (1 oz.)	28	1.8	0.5	44	22	107
Mackerel, cooked, dry heat (1 oz.)	28	5.0	1.2	74	21	24
Ocean Perch, cooked, dry heat (1 oz.)	28	0.6	0.1	34	15	27
Perch, cooked, dry heat (1 oz.)	28	0.3	0.1	33	33	22
Pike, Northern, cooked, dry heat (1 oz.)	28	0.3	tr	32	14	14
Pollack, Walleye, cooked, dry heat (1 oz.)	28	0.3	0.1	32	27	33
Pompano, cooked, dry heat (1 oz.)	28	3.4	1.3	60	18	22
Redfish (see Ocean Perch)						
Rockfish, cooked, dry heat (1 oz.)	28	0.6	0.1	34	13	22
Salmon, Chinook, smoked (1 oz.)	28	1.2	0.3	33	7	220*
Salmon, Chum, canned, drained solids with bone (1 oz.)	28	1.6	0.4	40	11	138**
Salmon, Coho, cooked, moist heat (1 oz.)	28	2.1	0.4	52	14	17
Salmon, Sockeye, canned, drained solids with bone (1 oz.)	28	2.1	0.5	43	12	153**
Sardine, Atlantic, canned in oil, drained solids with bone (1 oz.)	28	3.2	tr	59	40	143
Sardine, Pacific, canned in tomato sauce, drained solids with bone (1 oz.)	28	3.4	0.9	50	17	117
Sea Bass, cooked, dry heat (1 oz.)	28	0.7	0.2	35	15	25
Scrod (see Cod, Atlantic)						
Snapper, cooked, dry heat (1 oz.)	28	0.5	0.1	36	13	16
Sole (see Flounder)						
Swordfish, cooked, dry heat (1 oz.)	28	1.5	0.4	44	14	33

* Regular lox has approximately 567 mg sodium per ounce.

** Value based on product with salt added.

Food Description/Portion	Weight (gm)	Fat (gm)	Sat. Fatty Acid (gm)	Energy (cal.)	Chol. (mg)	Na (mg)
Finfish (cont'd)						
Trout, rainbow, cooked, dry heat (1 oz.)	28	1.2	0.2	43	21	10
Tuna, light, canned in oil, drained solids (1 oz.)	28	2.3	0.4	56	5	100
Tuna, light, canned in water, drained solids (1 oz.)	28	0.1	0.1	37	—	101
Tuna, white, canned in oil, drained solids (1 oz.)	28	2.3	—	53	9	112
Tuna, white, canned in water, drained solids (1 oz.)	28	0.7	0.2	39	12	111
Tuna salad, prepared with light tuna in oil, pickle relish, salad dressing, onion, celery (½ cup)	103	9.5	1.6	192	14	412
Shellfish						
Clam, cooked, moist heat (1 oz.)	28	0.6	0.1	42	19	32
Crab, Alaskan king, cooked, moist heat (1 oz.)	28	0.4	tr	27	15	304
Crab, Alaskan king, imitation, made from surimi (1 oz.)	28	0.4	—	29	6	238
Crab, blue, cooked, moist heat (1 oz.)	28	0.5	0.1	29	28	79
Crab cakes, prepared with egg, fried in margarine (1 cake)	60	4.5	0.9	93	90	198
Crayfish, cooked, moist heat (1 oz.)	28	0.4	0.1	32	50	19
Lobster, northern, cooked, moist heat (1 oz.)	28	0.2	tr	28	20	108
Oyster, eastern, cooked, breaded and fried (1 oz.)	28	3.6	0.9	56	23	118
Shrimp, cooked (1 oz.)	28	0.3	0.1	28	55	63
Shrimp, breaded and fried (4 large)	30	3.7	0.6	73	53	103
Shrimp, imitation, made from surimi (1 oz.)	28	0.4	—	29	10	200
Scallop, breaded and fried (2 large)	31	3.4	0.8	67	19	144

Food Description/Portion	Weight (gm)	Fat (gm)	Sat. Fatty Acid (gm)	Energy (cal.)	Chol. (mg)	Na (mg)
Fast Food						
Bacon cheeseburger (1)	150	27.3	—	464	68	660
Burrito (1)	174	13.6	—	392	56	1030
Cheeseburger: regular (1)	112	15.1	—	299	45	672
4-oz. patty (1)	194	31.4	—	524	105	1224
Eggs, scrambled (2)	95	14.7	—	175	346	226
Enchilada (1)	230	20.9	—	396	—	1332
English muffin sandwich with egg, cheese, bacon (1)	138	18.1	—	359	214	832
Fish sandwich, regular with cheese (1)	140	22.7	—	421	56	668
large (1)	170	26.7	—	469	90	621
French-fried potatoes (3 oz.)	85	14.2	—	274	14	152
Ham and cheese sandwich (1)	155	16.0	—	372	70	1118
Hamburger: regular (1)	98	11.1	4.0	245	32	463
double meat and double-decker roll (1)	190	29.6	10.0	524	78	893
4-oz. patty, regular roll (1)	174	21.1	7.0	444	71	762
4-oz. patty, large roll (1)	264	37.2	13.0	668	114	1019
Hot dog (1)	82	13.7	5.0	214	37	636
Hot fudge sundae (1)	165	10.9	—	312	18	177
Hushpuppy (3 pieces)	45	5.5	—	153	—	—
Onion rings (3 oz.)	85	15.6	—	285	16	485
Pancake, butter, syrup (3)	200	10.4	—	468	46	1020
Roast beef on bun (5 oz.)	150	13.4	4.0	347	56	756
Taco (1)	81	15.0	4.0	187	21	456
Tuna sub (1)	255	27.8	—	566	—	1288
Turnover, apple (1)	85	14.1	—	255	4	326
EGGS						
Whole, raw (1)	50	5.6	1.7	79	274	69
Yolk, raw (1)	17	5.6	1.7	63	272	8
White, raw (1)	33	tr	0.0	16	0	50
Fried in butter (1)	46	6.4	2.4	83	246	144
scrambled with butter and milk (1)	64	7.1	2.8	95	248	155

Food Description/Portion	Weight (gm)	Fat (gm)	Sat. Fatty Acid (gm)	Energy (cal.)	Chol. (mg)	Na (mg)
EGGS (cont'd)						
Egg substitute,* liquid (¼ cup)	60	2.0	0.4	50	1	106
frozen (¼ cup)	60	6.7	1.2	96	1	120
Omelet with butter and milk (1 egg)	64	7.1	2.8	95	248	155
DAIRY PRODUCTS						
Milk						
Buttermilk, cultured (1 cup)	245	2.2	1.3	99	9	257
Condensed, sweetened, canned (1 cup)	306	26.6	16.8	982	104	389
Evaporated, skim, canned (½ cup)	128	0.3	0.2	99	5	147
Evaporated, whole, canned (½ cup)	126	9.5	5.8	169	37	133
Hot cocoa, with whole milk (1 cup)	250	9.1	5.6	218	33	123
Malted milk beverage (1 cup whole milk + 2 to 3 heaping teaspoons malted milk powder)	265	9.9	6.0	236	37	215
Milk						
skim or nonfat (1 cup)	245	0.4	0.3	86	4	126
1-percent fat (1 cup)	244	2.6	1.6	102	10	123
2-percent fat (1 cup)	244	4.7	2.9	121	18	122
whole (1 cup)	244	8.2	5.1	150	33	120
whole, chocolate (1 cup)	250	8.5	5.3	208	30	149
Milkshake, vanilla, thick (11 oz.)	313	9.5	5.9	350	37	299
Yogurt						
Nonfat or skim, plain (1 cup)	227	0.4	0.3	127	4	174
Lowfat, plain (1 cup)	227	3.5	2.3	144	14	159
Whole, plain (1 cup)	227	7.4	4.8	139	29	105
Frozen Desserts						
Frozen yogurt (½ cup)	113	2.3	1.5	123	9	60
Ice cream, rich, 16% fat (½ cup)	74	11.8	7.4	175	44	54
Ice cream, regular, 10% fat (½ cup)	67	7.1	4.5	135	30	58
Ice milk, regular (½ cup)	66	2.8	1.8	92	9	53

* Check label—several brands are fat-free.

Food Description/Portion	Weight (gm)	Fat (gm)	Sat. Fatty Acid (gm)	Energy (cal.)	Chol. (mg)	Na (mg)
Frozen Desserts (cont'd)						
Ice milk, soft serve (½ cup)	88	2.3	1.4	112	7	82
Sherbet, orange (½ cup)	97	1.9	1.2	135	7	44
Cream, Nondairy Creamers and Toppings						
Half & half cream (1 tablespoon)	15	1.7	1.1	20	6	6
Sour cream, real (1 tablespoon)	12	2.5	1.6	26	5	6
Whipped cream, pressurized (1 tablespoon)	3	0.7	0.4	8	2	4
Whipping cream, heavy, fluid (1 tablespoon)	15	5.6	3.5	52	21	6
Creamer, nondairy, liquid (1 tablespoon)	15	1.5	0.3	20	0	12
Creamer, nondairy, powder (1 teaspoon)	2	0.7	0.7	11	0	4
Dessert topping, nondairy, frozen (1 tablespoon)	4	1.0	0.9	13	0	1
Cheese*						
American (1 oz.)	28	8.9	5.6	106	27	406
Blue, Brie, Cheddar, Colby, Edam, Gouda, Gruyère, Monterey, Parmesan, Roquefort, Swiss (1 oz.)	28	9.4	6.0	114	30	176
Cheese spread, processed, American (1 oz.)	28	6.0	3.8	82	16	381
Cottage cheese, dry curd (½ cup)	73	0.3	0.2	62	5	10
lowfat, 1-percent fat (½ cup)	113	1.2	0.7	82	5	459
lowfat, 2-percent fat (½ cup)	113	2.2	1.4	101	9	459
creamed (½ cup)	105	4.7	3.0	109	16	425
Cream cheese, regular (1 oz.)	28	9.9	6.2	99	31	84
Cream cheese, Neufchâtel (1 oz.)	28	6.6	4.2	74	22	113
Mozzarella, part skim (1 oz.)	28	4.5	2.9	72	16	132
Ricotta, part skim milk (1 oz.)	28	2.2	1.4	39	9	35
Ricotta, whole milk (1 oz.)	28	3.7	2.4	49	14	24

* Many lowfat varieties are in grocery stores—check label.

Food Description/ Portion	Weight (gm)	Fat (gm)	Sat. Fatty Acid (gm)	Poly. Fatty Acid (gm)	Energy (cal.)	Chol. (mg)	Na (mg)
FATS AND OILS							
Margarine							
Corn oil, stick (1 teaspoon)	5	3.8	0.6	0.8	34	0	44
Corn oil, tub (1 teaspoon)	5	3.8	0.7	1.5	34	0	51
Diet (2 teaspoons)	10	3.8	0.6	1.6	33	0	92
Safflower oil, tub (1 teaspoon)	5	3.8	0.4	2.1	34	0	51
Soybean, hydrogenated, tub (1 teaspoon)	5	3.8	0.6	1.3	34	0	51
Soybean, hydrogenated, whipped, tub (1 teaspoon)	5	2.9	0.6	0.3	26	0	48
Nuts (Approximately 3 Tablespoons)							
Almonds, dried	28	14.8	1.4	3.1	167	0	3
Brazil nuts, dried	28	18.8	4.6	6.9	186	0	0
Cashews, dry roasted	28	13.2	2.6	2.2	163	0	4
Chestnuts, roasted	28	0.3	0.1	0.1	68	0	1
Coconut, flaked, sweetened	28	9.0	8.0	0.1	126	0	76
Filberts/hazelnuts, dried	28	17.8	1.3	1.7	179	0	1
Macadamia nuts, oil roasted	28	21.7	3.3	0.4	204	0	2
Mixed nuts, dry roasted	28	14.6	2.0	3.1	169	0	3
Peanuts, oil roasted	28	14.0	1.9	4.4	165	0	4
Pecans, dried	28	19.2	1.5	4.8	190	0	0
Pistachio, dry roasted	28	15.0	1.9	2.3	172	0	2
Walnuts, Black	28	16.1	1.0	10.6	172	0	0
Walnuts, English, dried	28	17.6	1.6	11.1	182	0	3
Seeds (Approximately 3 Tablespoons)							
Pumpkin, squash, dried	28	13.0	2.5	5.9	154	0	5

Food Description/ Portion	Weight (gm)	Fat (gm)	Sat. Fatty Acid (gm)	Poly. Fatty Acid (gm)	Energy (cal.)	Chol. (mg)	Na (mg)
Seeds (Approximately 3 Tablespoons) (cont'd)							
Sesame, roasted and toasted	28	13.6	1.9	6.0	161	0	3
Sunflower, dried	28	14.1	1.5	9.3	162	0	1
Salad Dressing							
Blue cheese (1 tablespoon)	15	8.0	1.5	4.3	77	—	—
French (1 tablespoon)	16	6.4	1.5	3.4	67	—	214
Italian (1 tablespoon)	15	7.1	1.0	4.1	69	0	116
Mayonnaise (1 tablespoon)	14	11.0	1.6	5.7	99	8	78
Mayonnaise-type (1 tablespoon)	15	4.9	0.7	2.6	57	4	104
Sandwich spread, commercial (1 tablespoon)	15	5.2	0.8	3.1	60	12	—
Thousand Island (1 tablespoon)	16	5.6	0.9	3.1	59	5	109
Vinegar and oil (1 tablespoon)	16	8.0	1.5	3.9	72	0	0
Other Fats							
Bacon (see page 393)							
Butter (1 teaspoon)	5	4.1	2.5	0.2	36	11	41
Olives, green (10 small)	34	3.6	0.4	0.3	33	0	686
Olives, ripe (5 extra large)	28	3.3	0.4	0.3	30	0	193
Peanut butter, smooth (2 teaspoons)	11	5.5	0.9	1.6	63	0	52
Shortening, hydrogenated soybean and cottonseed (1 teaspoon)	4	4.3	1.1	1.1	38	0	—

Food Description/Portion	Weight (gm)	Fat (gm)	Sat. Fatty Acid (gm)	Poly. Fatty Acid (gm)	Energy (cal.)	Chol. (mg)	Na (mg)
Oil							
Canola (1 teaspoon)	5	4.5	0.3	1.5	40	0	0
Corn (1 teaspoon)	5	4.5	0.6	2.7	40	0	0
Olive (1 teaspoon)	5	4.5	0.6	0.4	40	0	0
Peanut (1 teaspoon)	5	4.5	0.8	1.4	40	0	0
Safflower (1 teaspoon)	5	4.5	0.4	3.4	40	0	0
Sesame (1 teaspoon)	5	4.5	0.6	1.9	40	0	0
Soybean (1 teaspoon)	5	4.5	0.7	2.6	40	0	0
Soybean/cottonseed (1 teaspoon)	5	4.5	0.8	2.2	40	0	0
Soybean, hydrogenated (1 teaspoon)	5	4.5	0.7	1.7	40	0	0
Sunflower (1 teaspoon)	5	4.5	0.5	3.0	40	0	0

Food Description/Portion	Weight (gm)	Fat (gm)	Sat. Fatty Acid (gm)	Energy (cal.)	Chol. (mg)	Na (mg)
BREADS, CEREALS, PASTA AND STARCHY VEGETABLES						
Breads, Pancakes and Waffles						
Bagel, 3-inch diameter (1)	100	2.6	—	296	—	360
Biscuit, made with milk, 2-inch diameter (1)	28	2.6	0.6	91	—	272
Bread, white (1 slice)	23	0.9	0.2	63	—	114
Bun, hamburger, 3½-inch diameter, or hot dog, 6 inches long (1)	40	2.2	0.5	119	—	202
English muffin, plain (half)	29	0.6	—	69	—	185
French toast (1 slice)	65	6.7	—	153	—	257
Muffin, bran, 2-inch bottom diameter (1)	40	3.9	1.2	104	—	179
Pancake, with egg, milk, 6-inch diameter × ½-inch thick (1)	73	5.3	1.9	164	—	412
Popover, 2¾-inch top, 2-inch bottom, 4 inches high in center (1)	40	3.7	1.3	90	—	88

Food Description/Portion	Weight (gm)	Fat (gm)	Sat. Fatty Acid (gm)	Energy (cal.)	Chol. (mg)	Na (mg)
Breads, Pancakes and Waffles (cont'd)						
Roll, hard, 3¾-inch diameter × 2 inches high (1)	50	1.6	0.4	156	—	313
Waffle, 9 × 9 × ⅝-inch square (1)	200	19.6	6.3	558	—	290
Crackers						
Bread sticks, 7¾ inches × ¾-inch diameter (5)	25	0.8	0.2	96	0	175
Cheese crackers (10)	31	6.7	2.6	150	—	325
Graham crackers, 2½-inch square (4 squares)	28	2.6	0.6	110	—	190
Saltine crackers (10)	28	3.4	0.8	123	—	312
Sandwich-type, cheese-peanut butter (4 sandwiches)	28	6.8	1.8	139	—	281
Zwieback crackers (4 pieces)	28	2.8	1.1	121	6	66
Cereal, Ready-to-Eat						
40% bran flakes (1 oz.)	28	0.5	0.0	93	0	264
Corn flakes (1 oz.)	28	0.1	0.0	110	0	351
Granola, homemade (1 oz.)	28	7.7	1.4	138	—	3
Grape-nuts (1 oz.)	28	0.1	0.0	101	0	197
Puffed wheat, plain (1 oz.)	28	0.4	0.0	104	0	2
Shredded wheat (1 large biscuit)	24	0.3	0.0	83	0	0
Wheat germ, plain, toasted (1 oz.)	28	3.0	0.5	108	0	1
Cereal, Cooked						
Corn grits, regular and quick (1 cup)	242	0.5	0.0	146	0	0*
Cream of wheat, regular (1 cup)	251	0.5	0.0	134	0	2*
Oatmeal, regular, quick and instant (1 cup)	234	2.4	0.4	145	0	1*
Pasta and Rice, Cooked						
Noodles, chow mein, canned (1 cup)	45	10.6	2.0	220	5	450
Noodles, egg (1 cup)	160	2.4	—	200	50	3*
Rice, white, brown or wild (1 cup)	205	0.2	0.0	223	0	4*
Spaghetti (1 cup)	140	0.6	0.0	155	—	1*

* Product cooked in unsalted water.

Food Description/Portion	Weight (gm)	Fat (gm)	Sat. Fatty Acid (gm)	Energy (cal.)	Chol. (mg)	Na (mg)
Starchy Vegetables						
Corn, lima beans, green peas, plantain, white potato, winter or acorn squash, yam or sweet potato (½ cup)		0.0	0.0	80	0	**
Prepared Vegetables						
Coleslaw/dressing with table cream (½ cup)	60	1.6	0.2	42	5	14
Corn pudding, whole milk, egg, butter (½ cup)	125	6.6	3.2	136	115	69
French fries						
oven-heated, cottage-cut (10)	50	4.1	1.9	109	0	23
fried in animal and vegetable fat (10)	50	8.3	3.4	158	6	108
Onion rings, frozen, oven-heated (7)	70	18.7	6.0	285	0	263
Potato chips (1 oz.)	28	10.1	2.6	148	0	133
Potato						
au gratin with whole milk, butter and cheese (½ cup)	122	9.3	5.8	160	29	528
candied sweet potatoes, brown sugar, butter, 2½ × 2-inch piece (1)	105	3.4	1.4	144	8	73
hashed brown, oil (½ cup)	78	10.9	4.2	163	—	19
mashed, whole milk, margarine (½ cup)	105	4.4	1.1	111	2	309
O'Brien, whole milk, butter (½ cup)	97	1.3	0.8	79	4	211
pancake, eggs, margarine (1)	76	12.6	3.4	495	93	388
potato sticks (1 oz.)	28	9.8	2.5	148	0	71
potato puff, vegetable oil (½ cup)	62	6.7	3.2	138	0	462
scalloped, whole milk, butter (½ cup)	122	4.5	2.8	105	14	409
salad, egg, mayonnaise (½ cup)	125	10.3	1.8	179	86	661

** Canned vegetables are high in sodium unless label states canned without salt.

Food Description/Portion	Weight (gm)	Fat (gm)	Sat. Fatty Acid (gm)	Energy (cal.)	Chol. (mg)	Na (mg)
Soup, Canned						
Bean with bacon, prepared with water (1 cup)	253	5.9	1.5	173	3	952
Beef broth or bouillon, ready-to-serve (1 cup)	240	0.5	0.3	16	tr	782
Beef, chunky-style, ready-to-serve (1 cup)	240	5.1	2.6	171	14	867
Chicken broth, prepared with water (1 cup)	244	1.4	0.4	39	1	776
Chicken, chunky-style, ready-to-serve (1 cup)	251	6.6	2.0	178	30	887
Chicken noodle, prepared with water (1 cup)	241	2.5	0.7	75	7	1107
Chicken rice, prepared with water (1 cup)	241	1.9	0.5	60	7	814
Chili beef, prepared with water (1 cup)	250	6.6	3.3	169	12	1035
Cream of chicken, prepared with water (1 cup)	244	7.4	2.1	116	10	986
Cream of mushroom, prepared with water (1 cup)	244	9.0	2.4	129	2	1031
Gazpacho, ready-to-serve (1 cup)	244	2.2	0.3	57	0	1183
Minestrone, prepared with water (1 cup)	241	2.5	0.5	83	2	911
Oyster stew, prepared with water (1 cup)	241	3.8	2.5	59	14	980
Split pea with ham, prepared with water (1 cup)	253	4.4	1.8	189	8	1008
Tomato, prepared with water (1 cup)	244	1.9	0.4	86	0	872
Tomato rice, prepared with water (1 cup)	247	2.7	0.5	120	2	815
Vegetarian vegetable, prepared with water (1 cup)	241	1.9	0.3	72	0	823

Food Description/Portion	Weight (gm)	Fat (gm)	Sat. Fatty Acid (gm)	Energy (cal.)	Chol. (mg)	Na (mg)
Baking Ingredients						
Cornmeal, dry (1 cup)	138	1.7	—	502	—	1
Cornstarch, not packed						
(1 tablespoon)	8	tr	0.0	29	—	tr
Flour, white (1 cup)	115	1.2	—	419	—	2
VEGETABLES AND FRUITS						
Vegetables						
All vegetables are low in fat and						
saturated fat (½ to 1 cup)		0.2	0.0	25	0	*
Fruits						
Apple, raw, 2¾-inch diameter (1)	138	0.5	0.1	81	0	1
Applesauce, canned, unsweetened						
(½ cup)	122	0.1	0.0	53	0	2
Apricots, medium, raw (4)	141	0.6	0.0	68	0	1
Banana, 9 inches long (half)	57	0.3	0.1	53	0	1
Blackberries, raw (¾ cup)	108	0.4	0.0	56	0	0
Cantaloupe (1 cup, cubes)	160	0.4	0.0	57	0	14
Cherries, sweet, raw (12)	82	0.8	0.2	59	0	0
Figs, medium, raw (2)	100	0.3	0.0	74	0	2
Fruit cocktail, canned, juice packed						
(½ cup)	124	0.1	0.0	56	0	4
Grapefruit (half)	123	0.1	0.0	37	0	0
Grapes, raw (15)	36	0.1	0.0	23	0	0
Honeydew melon (1 cup, cubes)	170	0.2	0.0	60	0	17
Kiwifruit (1 large)	91	0.4	0.0	55	0	4
Mango, raw (half)	104	0.3	0.0	68	0	2
Nectarine, 2½-inch diameter (1)	136	0.6	0.0	67	0	0
Orange, 2½-inch diameter (1)	131	0.2	0.0	62	0	0
Papaya (1 cup, cubes)	140	0.2	0.1	54	0	4
Peach, 2½-inch diameter (1)	87	0.1	0.0	37	0	0
Peaches, canned, water packed						
(2 halves)	154	0.1	0.0	36	0	6

* Sodium values vary from 2 to 63 mg per ½ cup cooked.
  Canned vegetables are higher in sodium than fresh or frozen.

Food Description/Portion	Weight (gm)	Fat (gm)	Sat. Fatty Acid (gm)	Energy (cal.)	Chol. (mg)	Na (mg)
Fruits (cont'd)						
Pear, raw (1)	166	0.7	0.0	98	0	1
Pineapple, raw (¾ cup)	116	0.5	0.0	58	0	2
Pineapple, canned, juice pack (⅓ cup)	83	0.1	0.0	50	0	1
Plum, raw, 2⅛-inch diameter (2)	132	0.8	0.1	72	0	0
Pomegranate (half)	77	0.2	0.0	52	0	3
Raspberries, raw (1 cup)	123	0.7	0.0	61	0	0
Strawberries, raw, whole (1¼ cup)	186	0.7	0.0	56	0	3
Tangerine, 2½-inch diameter (2)	168	0.3	0.0	74	0	2
Watermelon (1¼ cup, cubes)	200	0.9	0.0	63	0	4
Dried Fruits						
Apples, uncooked (4 rings)	26	0.1	0.0	62	0	22
Apricots, uncooked (7 halves)	25	0.1	0.0	58	0	2
Dates (2½)	21	0.1	0.0	57	0	1
Figs, uncooked (1½)	28	0.3	0.1	72	0	3
Prunes, uncooked (3)	25	0.1	0.0	60	0	1
Raisins (2 tablespoons)	21	0.1	0.0	62	0	2
Fruit Juices						
Apple juice (½ cup)	124	0.1	0.0	58	0	4
Cranberry juice cocktail (⅓ cup)	84	0.0	0.0	49	0	3
Grapefruit juice, unsweetened (½ cup)	124	0.1	0.0	47	0	2
Grape juice (⅓ cup)	84	0.1	0.0	52	0	2
Orange juice (½ cup)	125	0.3	0.0	55	0	1
Pineapple juice (½ cup)	125	0.1	0.0	70	0	1
Prune juice (⅓ cup)	85	0.0	0.0	60	0	4
DESSERTS AND SNACKS						
***AHA Cookbook* Quick Breads**	**Portion**					
Banana bread (1/16 of loaf)	1 slice	4.0	0.6	132	0	172
Biscuit, oil and skim milk (2-inch)	1 biscuit	4.7	0.6	116	0	174
Cornbread muffin, oil and skim milk (2¼-inch)	1 muffin	4.8	0.6	125	0	171

Food Description/Portion	Weight (gm)	Fat (gm)	Sat. Fatty Acid (gm)	Energy (cal.)	Chol. (mg)	Na (mg)
AHA Cookbook Quick Breads (cont'd)	**Portion**					
French toast, 1 slice	1 serving	4.3	0.7	113	0	176
Muffin, egg white, oil (2¼-inch)	1 muffin	6.2	0.8	143	0	270
Waffle, whole wheat, oil and skim milk, approximately 4 inches square	1 waffle	5.6	0.9	127	55	101
AHA Cookbook Desserts						
Cake, sheet, devil's food (½₀ of cake)	1 serving	7.7	1.1	179	1	137
minute fudge frosting	1 serving	2.4	0.5	61	0	35
Cake, white, 2-layer, made with oil, skim milk, egg white (⅟₁₆ of cake)	1 slice	6.0	1.2	197	1	143
seven-minute frosting	2 tbsp.	0.0	0.0	73	0	7
Cookies, raisin-oatmeal, made with oil, egg white	4 cookies	9.1	1.2	317	0	74
Pie, apple, double crust						
crust made with oil, skim milk	⅛ of pie	8.5	1.1	179	0	309
apple filling	⅛ of pie	1.6	0.3	135	0	19
Cakes, Cookies, Pies and Other Baked Goods	**Weight Gm.**					
Brownies, with nuts and icing (⅟₆ of 7½ × 5¼ × ⅞-inch pan)	60	12.6	4.3	257	—	123
Cake, without frosting angel food (½ of 10-inch diameter)	60	0.1	0.0	161	0	170
devil's food, sheet cake (3 × 3 × 2-inch piece)	88	15.1	—	322	41	259
white, 2-layer (⅟₁₆ of 9-inch diameter)	53	8.5	2.2	198	3	171

Food Description/Portion	Weight (gm)	Fat (gm)	Sat. Fatty Acid (gm)	Energy (cal.)	Chol. (mg)	Na (mg)
Cakes, Cookies, Pies and Other Baked Goods (cont'd)	**Weight Gm.**					
Boston cream pie, 2-layer (½ of 8-inch diameter)	69	6.5	2.0	208	—	128
fruitcake (¹/₃₂ of 7-inch diameter)	43	7.1	1.6	167	60	83
pound cake (¹/₁₂ of 8½-inch loaf)	42	7.8	2.0	171	32	74
sponge cake (¹/₁₂ of 9¾-inch diameter)	66	3.8	1.2	196	7	110
yellow, 2-layer (¹/₁₆ of 9-inch diameter)	54	6.9	1.9	197	36	140
Cake frosting						
chocolate, prepared with milk and fat (1 tablespoon)	17	2.4	1.3	65	—	11
coconut with boiled frosting (1 tablespoon)	10	0.8	0.7	38	—	12
fudge made with water, from mix (1 tablespoon)	15	1.0	0.3	52	—	36
white boiled (1 tablespoon)	6	0.0	0.0	19	0	8
Cheesecake (1 portion)	100	19.2	—	302	170	222
Cookies, sandwich, 1¾-inch diameter (4)	40	9.0	2.4	198	—	193
chocolate chip, 2⅓-inch diameter (4)	40	12.0	3.4	206	—	139
fig bars (4)	56	3.1	0.9	200	—	141
gingersnaps, 2-inch diameter (4)	28	2.5	0.6	118	—	160
Cupcake, plain, no icing, 2½-inch diameter (1)	25	3.5	1.0	91	—	75
plain, with white uncooked icing, 2½-inch diameter (1)	35	4.1	1.1	128	—	79
Doughnut, cake type, 3⅝-inch diameter (1)	58	10.8	2.7	227	—	291
yeast type, 3¾-inch diameter (1)	42	11.3	2.8	176	—	99
Pastry, Danish, plain, 4¼-inch diameter × 1-inch thick (1)	65	15.3	4.5	274	—	238
Pastry, toaster, commercial (1)	52	6.0	—	203	—	239

Food Description/Portion	Weight (gm)	Fat (gm)	Sat. Fatty Acid (gm)	Energy (cal.)	Chol. (mg)	Na (mg)
Cakes, Cookies, Pies and Other Baked Goods (cont'd)	**Weight Gm.**					
Pie, apple, 2 crust (⅛ of 9-inch diameter)	118	13.1	3.4	302	—	355
custard (⅛ of 9-inch diameter)	114	12.7	4.3	249	—	327
pumpkin (⅛ of 9-inch diameter)	114	12.8	4.5	241	—	244
pecan (⅛ of 9-inch diameter)	103	23.6	3.3	431	—	228
cherry, 2 crust (⅛ of 9-inch diameter)	118	13.3	3.5	308	—	359
Pie crust, baked (⅛ of 9-inch diameter)	23	7.5	1.8	113	—	138
Candy						
Candy corn (approximately 20 pieces)	28	0.6	0.1	103	—	60
Caramels, plain or chocolate (1 oz.)	28	2.9	1.6	113	—	64
Chocolate coated peanuts (8 to 16)	28	11.7	3.0	159	—	17
Fudge, plain (1 oz.)	28	3.5	1.2	113	—	54
Gumdrops (1 oz.)	28	0.2	0.0	98	0	10
Hard candy (1 oz.)	28	0.3	0.0	109	0	9
Marshmallow (1 oz.)	28	tr	0.0	90	0	11
Milk chocolate, plain (1 oz.)	28	9.2	5.1	147	—	27
Milk chocolate, almond (1 oz.)	28	10.1	4.5	151	—	23
Mints, uncoated (1 oz.)	28	0.6	0.1	103	0	60
SAUCES AND GRAVIES						
Dehydrated Sauces						
Béarnaise, prepared with milk and butter (¼ cup)	64	17.1	10.4	175	47	316
Cheese, prepared with milk (¼ cup)	70	4.3	2.3	77	13	92
Hollandaise, prepared with milk and butter (¼ cup)	64	17.1	10.5	176	47	284
Mushroom, prepared with milk (¼ cup)	67	2.6	1.4	57	9	383

Food Description/Portion	Weight (gm)	Fat (gm)	Sat. Fatty Acid (gm)	Energy (cal.)	Chol. (mg)	Na (mg)
Dehydrated Sauces (cont'd)						
Sour cream, prepared with milk (¼ cup)	79	7.6	4.0	127	23	252
Stroganoff, prepared with milk and water (¼ cup)	74	2.7	1.7	68	10	457
Sweet and sour, prepared with water and vinegar (¼ cup)	78	0.0	0.0	74	0	195
White, prepared with milk (¼ cup)	66	3.4	1.6	60	9	199
Ready-to-Serve Sauces						
Barbecue (¼ cup)	63	1.1	0.0	47	0	510
Soy (1 tablespoon)	18	0.0	0.0	11	0	1029
Teriyaki (1 tablespoon)	18	0.0	0.0	15	0	690
Canned Gravy						
Au jus (¼ cup)	60	0.1	0.1	10	0	—
Beef (¼ cup)	58	1.4	0.7	31	2	29
Chicken (¼ cup)	60	3.4	0.8	47	1	344
Mushroom (¼ cup)	60	1.6	0.2	30	0	340
Turkey (¼ cup)	60	1.3	0.4	31	1	—
Dehydrated Gravy						
Au jus, prepared with water (¼ cup)	62	0.2	0.1	5	0	145
Brown, prepared with water (¼ cup)	65	0.1	0.0	22	tr	31
Chicken, prepared with water (¼ cup)	65	0.5	0.1	21	1	283
Mushroom, prepared with water (¼ cup)	64	0.2	0.1	18	0	351
Onion, prepared with water (¼ cup)	65	0.2	0.1	20	0	259
Pork, prepared with water (¼ cup)	64	0.5	0.2	19	1	309
Turkey, prepared with water (¼ cup)	65	0.5	0.1	22	1	375

REFERENCES FOR FOOD TABLE

USDA AGRICULTURE HANDBOOK NO. 8 SERIES

Series No.	Food Group Issued	Year
8-1	Dairy and Egg Products	1976
8-3	Baby Foods	1978
8-4	Fats and Oils	1979
8-5	Poultry Products	1979
8-6	Soups, Sauces and Gravies	1980
8-7	Sausages and Luncheon Meats	1980
8-8	Breakfast Cereals	1982
8-9	Fruits and Fruit Juices	1982
8-10	Pork Products	1983
8-11	Vegetables and Vegetable Products	1984
8-12	Nut and Seed Products	1984
8-13	Beef Products	1986
8-15	Finfish and Shellfish Products	1987

American Heart Association Cookbook. David McKay, Fourth Edition, 1984.

Breidenstein, Burdette C.: Nutrient Value of Meat. Food & Nutrition News, Vol. 59, No. 2, 1987.

Communication with USDA, 1987.

USDA Nutritive Value of American Foods in Common Units. Agricultural Handbook No. 456, 1975.

USDA Provisional Table on the Fatty Acids and Cholesterol Content of Selected Foods, 1984.

USDA Provisional Table on the Nutrient Content of Fast Foods, 1984.

APPENDIX E.

HINTS FOR
STAYING WITH YOUR DIET

The tips presented here can help you achieve your dietary goal. The methods work well for success in a cholesterol-lowering diet as well as a weight reduction diet. Because human beings are creatures of habit, it's difficult to alter eating patterns overnight. In fact, people who make instantaneous changes usually revert to their old ways just as quickly. That's why we suggest that you ease into your new routine gradually. For example, if you never eat breakfast, don't start forcing yourself to do so right away. If you like having lunch in the cafeteria, you needn't force yourself to bring lunch from home; just start making more careful selections. By taking your time, you allow yourself to form new, positive habits that will eventually become just as firmly established as your old ones.

As you embark on your diet, it's also important to examine your old eating habits and understand your behaviors, attitudes and motivations. This will require reflection and discussion with other family members; for some, consultation with a Registered Dietitian is desirable. It may be helpful to keep a written record of your eating habits for a few days. As you reflect on those habits, look for signs of unconscious behaviors. Ask yourself the following questions:

- Do I eat compulsively?
- Do I use food to relieve anxiety or depression?
- Do I give in to social pressure from family or friends to eat foods that are wrong for me?

• Are there times when I overeat excessively or go on eating binges?

What you learn from your answers may help you as you change your eating behaviors. Your family is an important component in adopting a new diet. Unfortunately, your family and social environment may not provide easy access to the right foods. Nor is moral support from family members always available. You may find it necessary to have frank discussions with members of your family about the importance to you of your dietary changes. It you consult a Registered Dietitian, take your spouse or other family members along, so they'll understand your dietary requirements. Ideally, the whole family should be educated about the dangers of high blood cholesterol and should adopt a cholesterol-lowering diet. But whether or not you enlist their participation in your diet, do try to enlist their support.

HOW TO WIN AT LOSING

The biggest obstacles to losing weight and maintaining your normal weight are your own thoughts and habits. The following suggestions may help you. If you really want to lose weight, nothing can stop you—unless you let it.

Tips for Living at Your Best Weight

• Be your own cheerleader. It's okay to be proud of yourself when you succeed at new habits and make good choices. Argue with yourself when temptation appears. Know that your weight has nothing to do with whether you are loved or whether you are a good person.

• Analyze your environment and eliminate those things that stimulate you to choose the overweight way of life.

• Store food out of sight. Candy dishes and snack food on tables and countertops are big temptations.

• Get rid of tempting foods until you can handle having them around.

• Portion food onto plates in the kitchen rather than putting serving dishes on the table.

• Eat in a designated place and sit down. Eating while standing in front of the refrigerator or pantry contributes to overeating.

• Don't do other things when you eat. Just enjoy your food. Chew slowly. TV or reading are pleasant distractions that lead to nibbling snack foods.

• Find friends and neighbors who support and encourage your new lifestyle changes.

• Concentrate on maintaining a gradual weight loss. It's natural to reach a temporary plateau, but commit yourself to moving on—not gaining weight back.

• Plan your meals ahead of time. Don't leave important details to chance. Social engagements, holidays and business luncheons will always happen. There will always be depressing or upsetting episodes in life. You can always find an excuse for not getting more exercise. Plan out the kind of life you really want, and live it, every day.

• While you want lifelong changes, appreciate the smaller goals along the way. If you can't lose 5 pounds, you won't be able to lose 30. So, don't worry about losing 30 pounds; just work on each 5-pound segment.

• Set realistic goals. Remember that people lose weight at varying rates. Generally, 4 to 6 pounds per month is a safe, average weight loss. Cutting 500 calories a day or using up 500 calories by increasing physical activity will result in losing one pound a week. These figures are approximate. No two people respond exactly alike.

• Depriving yourself of special treats only makes you crave them. Plan to enjoy a small treat once or twice a week. Yes, treats are possible on a cholesterol-lowering diet.

• Recording the food eaten daily helps most people lose weight—especially in the beginning. It's easy to forget small snack samples eaten while meals are being prepared. Stay aware by writing them down.

• The scale is a problem for many dieters. Some people

want a reward if their weight is down. If their weight is up, they think, "What's the use, I might as well eat." Actually, the scale is a limited measurement. It can't distinguish between gaining muscle weight (while exercising) and losing fat weight. The scale weighs the natural fluctuations in body water and waste products the same as it weighs fat. Because of this, weigh yourself no more than once a week, preferably in the morning, without clothing and after going to the bathroom. Some find that keeping a weight grid is helpful in tracking progress. A calender can also be useful for recording weight, entering goals and jotting down progress notes.

• If you need support for your dieting efforts, find it. Consider individual consultations by a Registered Dietitian.

Eating Habits

If you want to win at losing weight, make these four minor changes in your eating habits:

• Learn to eat certain foods differently. Eat high-calorie foods in smaller portions and less often.

• Eat food for nourishment—not as a release for anger or for comfort.

• When you exercise more or less than usual, adjust the amount of food you eat to maintain your best weight. To lose weight you don't have to eat *diet* foods. That's a misconception. Just eat normal foods in smaller portions.

• To feel your best and control hunger, eat regularly. Divide your daily calorie allotment into three regular meals or six small meals.

Keep Moving

Before beginning an exercise program, check with your doctor. If he or she tells you there is no reason why you can't engage in moderate exercise, here are some ideas.

• Try to add a daily walk to your schedule. Start slowly and gradually build to 45 minutes or an hour. Use the time to relax, make plans and enjoy life. If you would rather swim or ride a bicycle, by all means do so. It's important to choose activities you enjoy.

• Look for ways to put more activity back into your life. Walk to the store or post office, or park farther away from your office or home. Take the stairs instead of the elevator. Turn off the TV and work outside or go dancing.

• To make your outdoor exercise safer and more enjoyable, wear good exercise shoes, comfortable clothing and a hat in hot weather. Be sure to drink plenty of water. Avoid exercising outdoors in very cold or very hot or humid weather. During hot weather, walk in the early morning or after the temperature drops in the evening.

Losing weight is not easy. It requires commitment and hard work. But once you reach your goal and learn to adopt a lifestyle that will keep you at your best weight, you'll forget you ever had to fight with being overweight.

WINNING FOR LIFE

After you lose the weight, you face the most important challenge to your weight-loss efforts—keeping it off. You'll be around food several times each day and at most social events, so you will be tempted by high-calorie foods and old habits. Sticking with your daily exercise also takes commitment.

You have to learn how to handle life's lapses, relapses and collapses. A *lapse* is a slight error or return to your overweight habits, the first instance of backsliding. For example, you may have a bad day and overeat, or skip a week of exercise. A *relapse,* on the other hand, is if you return to your former habits for several days or weeks. A *collapse* occurs if you are unable to reverse the negative trend, and you go back to old ways of eating and not exercising.

The critical thing to realize is that a lapse or even relapse *should not be seen as a failure,* but, instead, as a challenge to overcome. Use the following easy behaviors to help handle these times.

Identify Urges and High-Risk Situations

It is important to tell the difference between hunger (gnawing in your stomach and light-headedness) and urges (mental cravings for food). Hunger or low blood sugar tells you it is time to eat, either a meal or a small piece of fruit or glass of lowfat milk. Urges are another matter. They include situations like eating a large meal after you have several glasses of wine or eating candy to reward yourself after a stressful incident. You can handle these urges with some of the following techniques:

• Delayed gratification.

Delayed gratification is a behavioral tool that many people use successfully to stop their impulsive grabbing for food. It is a lesson in tolerance. When you feel the urge to eat, set a timer for 15 minutes and wait, or find something else to do, before eating. This will teach you to postpone your desire for food.

• ABC Theory.

Use behavior other than eating to help you find ways to respond to life's stresses. The theory works like this: if A happens (you have an argument with your spouse, for example), you always do B (you leave the argument with hard feelings) and this always causes C (you respond by gorging). How can you change this? Change A or B so that you don't have a reason to do C, or find a release for your frustrations other than eating, such as jogging, going for a walk or meditating.

Eat Like a Normal Person

By now you know that eating healthy to stay slim is not an exercise in starvation or self-deprivation, like crash dieting. It's a way of life in which you can look forward to enjoying mealtimes, not just enduring them.

When you reach your best weight, add about 200 calories of healthy food each day. Select some nutritious foods you have been eating during your weight loss period—fruits and vegetables, whole-grain products and lowfat dairy items. Save your rich favorites for special occasions. After four or five days, if you are still losing weight add several hundred more calories. By adding calories slowly, you will eventually be able to maintain your weight at your present exercise level. If you alter the amount of exercise, adjust your eating accordingly. Again, keeping a record of your food intake and exercise can make this process much easier.

Hints for Staying at Your Best Weight Forever

• Accept the idea that wise eating doesn't mean eating diet foods—it just means eating usual foods in smaller amounts.

• Stock up on good, fresh foods that make you look forward to meals. Make a shopping list, and always shop after a meal instead of on an empty stomach.

• Plan your meals, and don't leave your eating habits to chance. Before meals, parties and potlucks, decide what you can do to make it easier on yourself. Offer to bring a fresh fruit, a vegetable appetizer or a fruit dessert. If the meal will be later than usual, eat something before you go, such as a slice of lowfat cheese, lean meat or a piece of fruit, or drink a glass of lowfat milk.

• When confronted with a delicious banquet or dinner at a friend's house, use your head. There will always be special occasions. And it's okay to splurge occasionally, but don't eat everything in sight. Choose between the options. If the dinner is lasagna, green beans, tossed salad, garlic bread, wine and a special cherry dessert, don't panic. You can pick and choose what to eat. Most people face this situation often. One way to handle it might be to eat a medium serving of lasagna and salad and an extra serving of green beans. Then choose one from the bread, wine or dessert. Another way might be to eat a little of everything. Try to see if you can handle it. You'll find it works best to have your host or hostess serve only the small portion you want to eat. It is often too difficult to resist the urge to clean your plate when it is filled to the brim with large portions.

• When you feel hungry between meals, drink a glass of water, skim milk, iced tea, hot tea or coffee, or eat a piece of fruit. Then get out of the kitchen. Keep your mind and body busy.

• It is usually better to eat a little bit of a high-calorie food you crave than to avoid it for so long that you gorge on it when you finally decide to eat it. Eat a small amount, and leave it at that. If you don't trust yourself with just a small amount, don't eat any at all.

Staying Active as a Way of Life

Physical fitness and strength are abilities you have to learn, and you have to work at keeping them. Normally, your body slowly adjusts to the level of fitness needed to handle the lifestyle you choose. If you regularly exercise and stretch your muscles, they will become slightly larger, more flexible and stronger. Your body will carry oxygen, nutrients and blood more efficiently. It will also use more calories each day, so you can afford to eat more food. Unfortunately, however, these changes are reversible if your activity level slows down.

To keep up your enthusiasm for exercise, consider finding a partner or a class to exercise with so the session will be fun and the time will pass quickly. It is easy to talk yourself out of taking a walk when the weather isn't just right or when something else comes up. But if a friend knocks on your door and says, "Come on, let's go," it's hard to refuse.

Another tactic to help you continue lifelong exercise habits is to choose activities that fit easily into your present lifestyle. Why join a health club across town if you hate driving that far? Why buy a stationary bicycle to use in the basement when you know you haven't been near that room since you bought your house? Look for sports, activities, exercise partners and programs that you will enjoy and stick with.

Remember that you can increase your physical activity

level without taking up organized sports or exercise programs. Try parking your car farther from the office to build walking into your day. Take the stairs instead of the elevator. Instead of spending an hour at a "sit down" lunch, bring a light lunch from home and go for a walk.

The Best You Can Be

When you learn and accomplish these techniques, your days of being overweight will be finished. You can enjoy shopping for clothes, the swimsuit season and dinner with friends without guilt or fear. These techniques will help you keep your weight off and are the tools you need to stay your best weight forever. This new lifestyle will always work for you. Why? Because you're in control.

APPENDIX F.

TIPS FOR DINING OUT

Americans are eating out more than ever before. In fact, more than half of all our meals take place in restaurants.

If you're a member of the group that enjoys letting someone else do the cooking, don't despair. A low-cholesterol, lowfat diet doesn't have to mean a lifetime of housebound meals. It just means taking the time to learn a few tips to heart-healthy restaurant dining.

- It takes a little more time to plan your selection when you're on a restricted diet. Start studying the menu before the waiter appears to avoid making split-second—and often regrettable—decisions.
- If your companions don't mind, have the waiter remove unnecessary temptations like butter.
- Don't be reluctant to ask the waiter about ingredients or preparation methods for the dishes you're not familiar with.
- Feel free to ask the waiter to make substitutions like green vegetables in place of french fries or a dry salad in place of mayonnaise-laden cole slaw.
- If you find it impossible to order from the menu without ruining your diet, ask the waiter if the chef could prepare a fruit or vegetable platter for you. Most are eager to please.
- Order all dressings and sauces on the side, so you can control your portions.
- Stay away from fried appetizers or creamy soups and begin your meal with broth-based soups such as minestrone or gazpacho instead.
- Salad bars can be your friend or foe depending on what you choose. Stay away from high-fat items such as grated cheese, cream dressings, chopped eggs and croutons.

- Try a squeeze of lemon on your salad instead of dressing.
- Stick to the basic guidelines of your diet as you choose an entree. Pick fish or chicken in place of fatty meats.
- Choose an entree that's broiled, baked, grilled, steamed or poached instead of fried.
- Ask to have your food prepared without butter or cream sauces.
- If you choose chicken, remove the skin before eating.
- If you choose meat, remove all visible fat.
- Order plenty of vegetable side dishes whenever possible. And be sure to ask the waiter to leave off any sauces or butter.
- If you order potatoes, choose baked, boiled or roasted instead of fried. And ask the waiter to skip the butter and sour cream.
- Order fresh fruit instead of cake or pie for dessert. Or pick a fruit sorbet in place of ice cream.
- If you go to an Oriental restaurant, try a stir-fried chicken or fish and vegetable dish. Better still, choose a steamed main dish. And be sure to ask for steamed instead of fried rice.
- If you go to an Italian restaurant, steer clear of white creamy sauces and opt for red marinara sauce instead. Try a fish selection or meatless pasta in place of an entree with sausage or meatballs. Ask for plain Italian bread instead of buttery garlic bread. And be sure to go easy on the grated Parmesan.

APPENDIX G.

DRUGS:
WHEN DIET ALONE WON'T WORK

For some people, diet alone won't lower blood cholesterol sufficiently. For example, one in five hundred people has a genetic condition called familial hypercholesterolemia, which typically causes blood cholesterol levels to be over 300 mg/dl and often as high as 500. If you have this or a related condition, your doctor may prescribe drug therapy immediately.

In most cases, however, your physician will want you to try to lower your cholesterol through diet before considering drug treatment. If, after changing your diet, you're still unable to lower your LDL-cholesterol level to below 190, drugs may be an appropriate alternative. The same holds true if you have an LDL-cholesterol level between 160 and 190 in combination with coronary heart disease or other serious risk factors. But whatever the reason for resorting to medication, a change in diet should always go along with the drug treatment to maximize the effect.

The types of drugs used to lower cholesterol are varied and work in a number of different ways.

Bile acid binding drugs. There are two drugs in this category: colestipol, known by the trade name Colestid, and cholestyramine, known by the trade name Questran. Cholestyramine was the drug used in the Coronary Primary Prevention Trial to prove the connection between lowering blood cholesterol and preventing heart attack.

Bile acid binding drugs stay within the intestinal tract and are not absorbed into the body. They act by binding the bile acids, which are breakdown products of cholesterol. This binding action leads to more excretion of bile acids and hence to a more rapid breakdown of cholesterol in the liver; this in turn causes the liver to make more LDL receptors, thus allowing it to remove more cholesterol. At a dose of two packets twice daily, these drugs typically lower blood cholesterol by 15 to 25 percent. A lower dose, one packet twice daily, usually reduces blood cholesterol by 10 to 20 percent.

Both colestipol and cholestyramine exist in powder form and must be mixed with water or fruit juice. Colestipol comes in packages of 5 grams each or in bottles. Cholestyramine is currently available in packets, each containing 4 grams, or in large cans of bulk powder. Both are relatively expensive, but are less so when bought in bulk.

It may be easier to take the usual dosage for colestipol or cholestyramine if you start out with one package twice daily. In fact, some patients get sufficient results at this dosage. If your cholesterol is very high, you may be asked to take two packets three times a day. The packets are equivalent to measured scoops of the bulk powder.

The bile acid binding drugs sometimes cause gastrointestinal side effects, such as constipation, bloating, intestinal gas, feelings of stomach fullness and nausea. Constipation is a consequence of the bile acid's binding process, because, left in their natural state, bile acids are natural laxatives. A good way to control the constipation is to add more fiber to your diet with bran cereals, or fiber laxatives containing psyllium. Also, your physician may recommend a stool softener. Regular laxatives should not be used because prolonged use may produce side effects.

Many patients have some trouble taking bile acid binding drugs at first. If you're one of them, don't give up. Eventually, you'll adjust. Start at very low doses and work up the dose slowly. While these drugs are somewhat inconvenient to take, they've proven both safe and effective for preventing heart attacks.

Nicotinic acid. This is an inexpensive drug that's been used for many years to treat high blood cholesterol. Nicotinic acid was used in a major clinical trial, the Coronary Drug Project, with patients who had suffered previous heart attacks. Throughout the trial, half took nicotinic acid and half took a placebo. Nicotinic acid was found to significantly reduce the recurrence rate of heart attack. Moreover, after 15 years, there were fewer deaths among the nicotinic-acid group.

Nicotinic acid works by reducing the formation of lipo-proteins in the liver. In doing so, it lowers blood triglycer-ides, VLDL-cholesterol and LDL-cholesterol; by lowering triglycerides it also raises the HDL-cholesterol.

The major problem with nicotinic acid is its troublesome side effects. One is a flushing of the skin, especially the face, which occurs several minutes after taking the drug. Itching and skin rash can also result. Gastrointestinal problems can make the drug a poor choice for people who are prone to peptic ulcers. At the very least, this drug necessitates peri-odic monitoring through certain types of blood tests. There can be other side effects, too. For some persons, the drug proves mildly toxic to the liver and has to be discontinued. It may also raise the blood uric acid level and possibly lead to gout; if you have gout, you probably should not take nicotinic acid. Additionally, nicotinic acid can make a dia-betic condition worse.

If your doctor has prescribed nicotinic acid, be sure to avoid confusing it with the vitamin nicotinamide, which is not effective for lowering cholesterol. Nicotinic acid comes in tablets of 50, 100 and 500 milligrams. It also comes in sustained-release pills that will reduce flushing but are also more expensive. Choose only one method, because switch-ing back and forth between tablets and sustained release increases the likelihood of side effects.

Nicotinic acid is best started in very low doses that are easily tolerated. Commonly, one starts by taking one 50-milligram tablet three times a day. Another way is to take 100 milligrams after dinner to avoid the initial flushing during working hours. Flushing can sometimes be controlled by taking an aspirin 30 minutes before taking the drug. But with or without aspirin, the flushing usually goes away or can be easily tolerated after several weeks.

After starting with a low dose, it is best to build the dosage slowly. For example, if you start with 50 milligrams three times daily, you could increase to 100 milligrams three times daily within a couple of days. By raising each dose in 50-milligram increments, you can reach a dosage of 1,000 to 1,500 milligrams three times daily over a period of three to four weeks. This is the dosage range you should aim for. There's little evidence that taking less than 1,000 milligrams a day is effective in lowering blood cholesterol. It's a good idea to take the drug after meals, never on an empty stomach.

Statins. Statins are a relatively new type of drug used to lower blood cholesterol. They include lovastatin, pravastatin, simvastatin and fluvastatin. They work by interfering with the formation of cholesterol in the liver, forcing the liver to produce more LDL receptors to take LDL-cholesterol out of the bloodstream. The result is a major reduction in blood cholesterol, often by 25 to 35 percent. This is a much greater reduction than other drugs and requires only relatively small doses. Because of their high effectiveness and low dose requirement, statins are extremely attractive drugs for treating high blood cholesterol.

There remains, however, the important question of side effects. So far serious effects have been very rare. Only a few people have some problem with the drugs. Some have gastrointestinal complaints shortly after starting the drug. Others get a high blood level of certain liver enzymes because the enzymes leak out of the liver cells. This change may reflect mild toxicity to the liver but can be reversed rapidly when the drug is stopped. In still others, enzymes from muscle cells escape into the bloodstream, resulting from mild muscle damage. Patients may have occasional complaints of muscle soreness. This too is reversed when the drugs are stopped. If you take these drugs and develop sore muscles, report it immediately to your physician. Failure to stop the medication may result in muscle and kidney damage.

There was an early concern that statins might cause cataracts. There are certain theoretical reasons why this might occur, but careful research has shown that cataracts do not develop as a result of taking statins.

Statins should not be viewed as an easy answer to high blood cholesterol. After all, the possibility exists that these drugs could have serious long-term, not-yet-detected side effects. Standard drugs, such as the bile acid binding medications, may be a preferable way for many people to lower blood cholesterol when the level is not extremely high but diet alone is not enough. Nonetheless, for some patients with very high cholesterol or several risk factors, a statin drug may prove beneficial.

Gemfibrozil. Sold under the trade name of Lopid, gemfibrozil lowers blood triglycerides. In some people gemfibrozil also may raise HDL and lower LDL; these effects, however, are generally relatively small. How gemfibrozil lowers the blood lipids is not well understood. In the Helsinki Heart Study, a large clinical trial, it reduced the risk of heart attacks among patients with high blood cholesterol. It was useful in treating patients with moderately elevated blood cholesterol who couldn't tolerate more potent drugs. However, in a post-trial follow-up, there was a suggestion of increased total mortality. Nonetheless, no definite side effects leading to fatalities have been identified for this class of drugs.

The typical dose of gemfibrozil is 600 milligrams twice a day. Patients taking this drug should be aware of certain dangers and side effects. The drug increases the risk of developing gallstones. It sometimes causes gastrointestinal discomfort or diarrhea. In some patients, gemfibrozil causes muscle pain similar to the statins. Others report a variety of other minor problems.

Clofibrate. Sold under the name Atromid-S, clofibrate's

actions are similar to gemfibrozil's. The two drugs are chemically related. Clofibrate, like gemfibrozil, proved effective in a clinical trial (the World Health Organization's Clofibrate Trial). Unfortunately, the trial also uncovered some possible side effects that may offset its benefit for coronary risk reduction. In the group treated with the drug, the number of non-heart-related deaths appeared to be somewhat greater than in the placebo group, which raises the possibility that clofibrate has occasional serious side effects. However, there remains some skepticism about the validity of this finding, and the actual occurrence of serious side effects has not been proven. Nonetheless, since the publication of the trial's results, the use of the drug for treating high blood cholesterol has declined dramatically.

Probucol. Also known as Lorelco, probucol has been used for many years in the treatment of high blood cholesterol. The standard dose is 500 milligrams twice a day. It's generally well tolerated, and the side effects are few. Gastrointestinal discomfort and diarrhea occur in a few patients taking the drug.

Probucol can reduce total blood cholesterol by 10 to 15 percent. Unfortunately, it causes some reduction of the HDL-cholesterol as well as the LDL-cholesterol. This has led some investigators to question whether probucol provides any benefit for prevention of heart attack. To date, there have been no clinical trials carried out with probucol to determine whether it will actually prevent heart attack, but results of such trials should be available in a few years. Probucol usually is reserved for patients who cannot tolerate other cholesterol-lowering drugs.

Estrogens. In postmenopausal women who have high blood cholesterol, consideration can be given to using estrogen replacement for the express purpose of protecting against development of coronary heart disease. Several large studies provide strong suggestive evidence that estrogens may be protective. In addition, they have been shown to lower the LDL-cholesterol level and to raise the HDL-cholesterol level. Both of these changes may be protective. In spite of potential benefits of estrogen replacement, several points need to be made. An action to protect against heart disease has not been proven with certainty. In addition, estrogens may have side effects. In some women, estrogens cause breast tenderness, vaginal bleeding and lower abdominal discomfort. Moreover, their use in women with a uterus increases the risk of endometrial cancer. This danger can be reduced by concomitant progestin administration, but this approach is not satisfactory to all women. When estrogen replacement is employed, regular gynecological checkups are required. Further, the question of whether estrogen replacement leads to a slight increase in risk for breast cancer is not completely settled. Even if there is a possibility of that, many women would prefer not to use estrogens. Nonetheless, available evidence suggests that the apparent benefit in reduction of heart disease in women with high cholesterol levels may outweigh chances for increases in breast cancer.

OTHER CORONARY RISK FACTORS

High blood cholesterol is one of many factors that can increase your coronary risk. If other risk factors are also present, the danger of heart attack may be significantly greater. That's why it's even more important for people with high blood cholesterol to eliminate or minimize other risks whenever possible.

Cigarette smoking. Heavy smoking is probably the worst of all risk factors for first heart attacks. Smoking doubles or triples your chance of heart attack. If you smoke two packs a day, your risk is twice as high as if you smoke one pack. As soon as you quit, that risk begins to drop. And within ten years after quitting, your chances of having a heart attack drop back to near normal.

High blood pressure. High blood pressure is dangerous because it has no symptoms. It's important to have your blood pressure checked regularly. If it's 140/90 or above, your doctor can help you control it through diet or medication.

A family history of heart attack. If your parent or sibling has had a heart attack, there's an increased chance that you will have one, too. High blood cholesterol tends to run in families. Consequently, if you find that your blood cholesterol is high, it's a good idea to urge your family members to be tested as well.

A previous heart attack. You are at greater risk of a second heart attack, regardless of whether other risk factors are present, if you've already had one.

Overweight or obesity. Excess body weight causes a reduction in HDL-cholesterol and may increase LDL-cholesterol. It also predisposes people to high blood pressure and adult diabetes. If you're one of the millions of Americans who are overweight, be aware that it is possible to lose weight and to maintain a desirable weight for life through exercise and diet. (See Appendix E, pages 415–423.) The table at right shows the proper weight range for your sex and height.

Diabetes. The 3 million Americans who have adult diabetes are major candidates for heart attack. In fact, heart attack is the number one killer of diabetic patients. Since the two risk factors of diabetes and overweight often go hand in hand, it's particularly important for diabetic patients to watch their diets and maintain their proper weights.

DESIRABLE BODY WEIGHT RANGES

HEIGHT WITHOUT SHOES	WEIGHT WITHOUT CLOTHES	
	MEN (LBS)	WOMEN (LBS)
4'10"	—	92–121
4'11"	—	95–124
5'0"	—	98–127
5'1"	105–134	101–130
5'2"	108–137	104–134
5'3"	111–141	107–138
5'4"	114–145	110–142
5'5"	117–149	114–146
5'6"	121–154	118–150
5'7"	125–159	122–154
5'8"	129–163	126–159
5'9"	133–167	130–164
5'10"	137–172	134–169
5'11"	141–177	—
6'0"	145–182	—
6'1"	149–187	—
6'2"	153–192	—
6'3"	157–197	—

Note: For women 18–25 years, subtract one pound for each year under 25.
Source: Adapted from the 1959 Metropolitan Desirable Weight Table.

Lack of exercise. There is growing evidence that regular, vigorous physical activity protects against heart disease. It raises HDL-cholesterol and, in some individuals, reduces LDL-cholesterol as well as blood pressure. Exercise also reduces the danger of dying suddenly if you do have a heart attack. If you decide to begin an exercise program, remember to consult your physician first, especially if you're middle aged or older and haven't exercised for a long time.

Stress. Social and professional stress may provoke other risk factors (for example, a rise in blood pressure or blood cholesterol), lead to excessive smoking or eating or, perhaps, induce coronary thrombosis. However, stress levels are difficult to measure, and responses to stress vary markedly. It has been suggested that persons with an overdeveloped sense of time urgency, drive or competitiveness are more prone to heart attack than those who are more complacent and do not respond excessively to social stresses. This is an issue that requires further investigation.

The male sex. Men are more prone to heart attack than women. While the reasons for this are not entirely clear, men tend to have higher levels of LDL-cholesterol and lower levels of HDL-cholesterol than women. Because of the higher coronary risk, men should pay particular attention to other risk factors. Nonetheless, heart disease is the number one killer of American women as well, particularly those past menopause.

APPENDIX I.

AMERICAN HEART ASSOCIATION AFFILIATES

**American Heart Association
National Center
Dallas, TX**

American Heart Association
Alabama Affiliate, Inc.
Birmingham, AL

American Heart Association
Alaska Affiliate, Inc.
Anchorage, AK

American Heart Association
Arizona Affiliate, Inc.
Phoenix, AZ

American Heart Association
Arkansas Affiliate, Inc.
Little Rock, AR

American Heart Association
California Affiliate, Inc.
Burlingame, CA

American Heart Association
Metropolitan Chicago, Inc.
Chicago, IL

American Heart Association
Colorado/Wyoming, Inc.
Denver, CO

American Heart Association
Connecticut Affiliate, Inc.
Wallingford, CT

American Heart Association
Dakota Affiliate, Inc.
Jamestown, ND

American Heart Association
Delaware Affiliate, Inc.
Newark, DE

American Heart Association
Florida Affiliate, Inc.
St. Petersburg, FL

American Heart Association
Georgia Affiliate, Inc.
Marietta, GA

American Heart Association
Hawaii Affiliate, Inc.
Honolulu, HI

American Heart Association
Idaho/Montana, Inc.
Boise, ID

American Heart Association
Illinois Affiliate, Inc.
Springfield, IL

American Heart Association
Indiana Affiliate, Inc.
Indianapolis, IN

American Heart Association
Iowa Affiliate, Inc.
Des Moines, IA

American Heart Association
Kansas Affiliate, Inc.
Topeka, KS

American Heart Association
Kentucky Affiliate, Inc.
Louisville, KY

American Heart Association
Greater Los Angeles Affiliate, Inc.
Los Angeles, CA

American Heart Association
Louisiana, Inc.
Destrehan, LA

436

American Heart Association
Maine Affiliate, Inc.
Augusta, ME

American Heart Association
Maryland Affiliate, Inc.
Baltimore, MD

American Heart Association
Massachusetts Affiliate, Inc.
Framingham, MA

American Heart Association
Michigan, Inc.
Lathrup Village, MI

American Heart Association
Minnesota Affiliate, Inc.
Minneapolis, MN

American Heart Association
Mississippi Affiliate, Inc.
Jackson, MS

American Heart Association
Missouri Affiliate, Inc.
St. Louis, MO

American Heart Association
Nation's Capital Affiliate, Inc.
Washington, D.C.

American Heart Association
Nebraska Affiliate, Inc.
Omaha, NE

American Heart Association
Nevada Affiliate, Inc.
Las Vegas, NV

American Heart Association
New Hampshire Affiliate, Inc.
Manchester, NH

American Heart Association
New Jersey Affiliate, Inc.
North Brunswick, NJ

American Heart Association
New Mexico Affiliate, Inc.
Albuquerque, NM

American Heart Association
New York City Affiliate, Inc.
New York City, NY

American Heart Association
New York State Affiliate, Inc.
North Syracuse, NY

American Heart Association
North Carolina Affiliate, Inc.
Chapel Hill, NC

American Heart Association
Northeast Ohio Affiliate, Inc.
Cleveland, OH

American Heart Association
Ohio Affiliate, Inc.
Columbus, OH

American Heart Association
Oklahoma Affiliate, Inc.
Oklahoma City, OK

American Heart Association
Oregon Affiliate, Inc.
Portland, OR

American Heart Association
Pennsylvania Affiliate, Inc
Camp Hill, PA

Puerto Rico Heart Association,
    Inc.
Hato Rey, Puerto Rico

American Heart Association
Rhode Island Affiliate, Inc.
Pawtucket, RI

American Heart Association
South Carolina Affiliate, Inc.
Columbia, SC

American Heart Association
Southeastern Pennsylvania
    Affiliate, Inc.
Conshohocken, PA

American Heart Association
Tennessee Affiliate, Inc.
Nashville, TN

American Heart Association
Texas Affiliate, Inc.
Austin, TX

American Heart Association
Utah Affiliate, Inc.
Salt Lake City, UT

American Heart Association
Vermont Affiliate, Inc.
Williston, VT

American Heart Association
Virginia Affiliate, Inc.
Glen Allen, VA

American Heart Association
Washington Affiliate, Inc.
Seattle, WA

American Heart Association
West Virginia Affiliate, Inc.
Charleston, WV

American Heart Association
Wisconsin Affiliate, Inc.
Milwaukee, WI

Index

American Heart AssociationSM

*Fighting Heart Disease
and Stroke*

More indispensable guides from the American Heart Association for your home health library

American Heart Association Cookbook, 5th Edition
Hardcover: 656 pages; $25.00; ISBN: 0-8129-1895-9
Trade paperback: 656 pages; $14.00; ISBN: 0-8129-2282-4

American Heart Association Low-Fat, Low-Cholesterol Cookbook
Hardcover: 352 pages; $21.00; ISBN: 0-8129-1783-9
Trade paperback: 352 pages; $13.00; ISBN: 0-8129-1982-3

American Heart Association Low-Salt Cookbook
Hardcover: 368 pages; $20.00; ISBN: 0-8129-1852-5
Trade paperback: 368 pages; $13.00; ISBN: 0-8129-2045-7
Mass market paperback: 400 pages; $5.99; ISBN: 0-8129-2476-2

American Heart Association Kids' Cookbook
Hardcover: 128 pages; $15.00; ISBN: 0-8129-1930-0

American Heart Association Family Guide to Stroke
Hardcover: 336 pages; $23.00; ISBN: 0-8129-2011-2

American Heart Association Brand Name Fat and Cholesterol Counter
Mass market paperback: 352 pages; $4.99; ISBN: 0-8129-2366-9

American Heart Association Quick and Easy Cookbook
Hardcover: 352 pages; $25.00; ISBN: 0-8129-2251-4

AVAILABLE IN BOOKSTORES EVERYWHERE

OR CALL

1-800-733-3000

TO ORDER DIRECT